Lesse

from the

Mountaintop

Ten Modern Mystics and Their Extraordinary Lives

Lessons from the Mountaintop

Ten Modern Mystics and Their Extraordinary Lives

Lawrence Pintak

Author of America & Islam
Finalist, Religion News Association
2020 Award for Religion Reporting Excellence

SENTIENT PUBLICATIONS

ADVANCE PRAISE FOR *LESSONS FROM THE MOUNTAINTOP*

"A magnificent tapestry of wisdom and love that can inspire us all."
Joseph Goldstein, author of *Mindfulness: A Practical Guide to Awakening*

"*Lessons from the Mountaintop* is a rare jewel. As a guide, Lawrence Pintak is at once skeptical and sincere, neither dismissive nor credulous. And his subjects are the real deal: not wellness influencers, but legit mystics who share their wisdom with Pintak—so he can share it with you."
Rabbi Dr. Jay Michaelson, winner of the 2022 National Jewish Book award and author of *The Secret That Is Not a Secret: Ten Heretical Tales*

"In this remarkably accessible book, Lawrence Pintak offers rich portraits of the spiritual journeys of unheralded mystics of our time. Written for the layperson yet useful for the scholar and the college classroom, *Lessons from the Mountaintop* is an existentially illuminating experience."
William Parsons, Professor of Religion, Rice University and author of *Teaching Mysticism*

"These compelling portraits remind us that no religion has a monopoly on intuitive truth. The mountaintop lies within us all. If we connect with our hidden self, as these extraordinary individuals have done, we can all hear the Divine voice and touch the Light."
Fr. Richard Rohr, OFM. Author of *The Universal Christ* and *The Tears of Things*

"Inspirational."
Sharon Salzberg, author of *Real Change*

"We forget sometimes that spiritual and religious giants live amongst us. This book is a beautiful reminder of these stories—and of our own human capacity for goodness and joy."
Simran Jeet Singh, author of *The Light We Give*

"The real story of religion may not be found in those high-profile clergy and institutional leaders that capture public attention, but instead in the lives of those faithful souls who seek for realization within the familiar conditions of everyday life, as Lawrence Pintak has so beautifully reminded us."
Kabir Helminski, Sufi Shaikh and author of *The Knowing Heart* and *The Mysterion: Rumi and the Secret of Becoming Fully Human*

"Lawrence Pintak has rendered a great service to his readers by showing that spiritual paths are not only ascetic feats which may be deemed out of reach today, but also humble daily steps ever available to spiritual seekers amid the confusion of our disoriented world. One may hold reservations or serious disagreements with a few of their premises or conclusions, as this reader does, but such intriguing or inspiring lives suggest that the 'mountain top' is also, from another point of view, the heart of it all."
Patrick Laude, Georgetown University. Author of *Shimmering Mirrors: Reality and Appearance in Contemplative Metaphysics East and West*

PRAISE FOR OTHER BOOKS BY THE AUTHOR

AMERICA & ISLAM: SOUNDBITES, SUICIDE BOMBS, AND THE ROAD TO DONALD TRUMP

"Insightful, well-written, challenging. Pintak is both a globe-trotting journalist and a distinguished scholar. He's not afraid to challenge assumptions, group-think, and the powerful."

Dan Rather, former anchor, The CBS Evening News

TARGET HOLLYWOOD (A NOVEL)

"A captivating, big-stakes thriller that deserves to be turned into a blockbuster movie."

Goodreads

THE NEW ARAB JOURNALIST: MISSION & IDENTITY IN A TIME OF TURMOIL

"Lawrence Pintak remains the foremost chronicler of the interaction between the Arab and Western media worlds."

Rami Khouri, The Daily Star (Beirut)

REFLECTIONS IN A BLOODSHOT LENS: AMERICA, ISLAM & THE WAR OF IDEAS

"… an example of the best of contemporary journalism … an intriguing mix of journalism and scholarship."

Middle East Journal

SEEDS OF HATE: HOW AMERICA'S FLAWED MIDDLE EAST POLICY IGNITED THE JIHAD

"A tour de force…"

Anthony Lewis, The New York Times

BEIRUT OUTTAKES: A TELEVISION CORRESPONDENT'S PORTRAIT OF AMERICA'S ENCOUNTER WITH TERROR

"Reminiscent of early Hemingway."

John Cooley, Middle East Journal

ISLAM FOR JOURNALISTS (CO-EDITED WITH STEPHEN FRANKLIN)

"This book is an invaluable starting point for journalists who want to understand one of America's fastest-growing religions."

Doyle McManus, Washington, DC, columnist, The Los Angeles Times

First Sentient Publications edition 2025

A paperback original

Book Design by Laura Johanna Waltje
Cover Art by Bijay Shresta
Cover Typography by Najla Hafez

Library of Congress Control Number: 2024949392
Publisher's Cataloging-in-Publication Data

Names: Pintak, Lawrence, author.

Title: Lessons from the mountaintop : ten modern mystics and their
extraordinary lives / Lawrence Pintak.

Description: Boulder, CO: Sentient Publications, 2025.

Identifiers: LCCN: 2024949392 | ISBN: 978-1-59181-332-3
(paperback) | 978-1-59181-333-0
Subjects: LCSH Mystics--Biography. | Mysticism. | Spiritual life.
| BISAC BIOGRAPHY & AUTOBIOGRAPHY / Religious |
BODY, MIND & SPIRIT / Mysticism | BODY, MIND & SPIRIT /
Inspiration & Personal Growth | RELIGION / Mysticism
Classification: LCC BL72 .P56 2025 | DDC 200.92/2--dc23

SENTIENT PUBLICATIONS
A Limited Liability Company
PO Box 1851
Boulder, CO 80306
www.sentientpublications.com

Photo Credits

Shems Friedlander; the estate of Shems Friedlander
Michael Holleran; Michael Holleran
Ram Alexander; Parvati Alexander
Atmananda; Shree Ma Anandamayee Archive
Jetsunma Tenzin Palmo; Dongyu Gatsal Ling Nunnery
Nick Ribush; Lama Yeshe Wisdom Archive
Jill Hammer; Veronique Zork
Swami Atmarupananda; Centre Vedantique Ramakrishna Paris
Emma Restall Orr; David Orr
Sister Clear Grace; Stacey Van Berkel

Contents

For my dakini, Indira; loving companion on this endless adventure.

About the Author

Lawrence Pintak has spent his life grounded in facts while fascinated by the ethereal. An award-winning former CBS News Middle East correspondent with a PhD in Islamic Studies, Pintak has been a practitioner of Tibetan Buddhism for three decades and is an avid student of the perennial truths at the core of the world's religions.

The author of seven books at the intersection of religion, media, and policy, his reporting and analysis on religion and international affairs has been published by *The New York Times*, *Foreign Policy*, *The Washington Post*, and many of the world's leading media organizations. He also wrote about Buddhism and Eastern traditions for *Shambhala Sun/Lion's Roar*, *Buddhadharma*, Beliefnet.com and others before 9/11 drew his focus back to the Middle East. Pintak's most recent nonfiction book, *America & Islam*, was a finalist for the 2020 Religion News Association award for Religion Reporting Excellence.

Pintak served as founding dean of The Edward R. Murrow College of Communication at Washington State University, dean of the Graduate School of Media and Communications at The Aga Khan University in East Africa, director of the Arab world's leading media training center in the years leading up to the Arab Spring, and helped establish Pakistan's Centre for Excellence in Journalism. He was named a Fellow of the Society of Professional Journalists in 2017 for "extraordinary service to the profession of journalism" around the world.

Introduction

*"I want to know more about the yogis," said Isabel. "Did you get
to know any of them intimately?"
Larry smiled. "As intimately as you can know persons who pass
the best part of their time in the Infinite."*
W. Somerset Maugham, *The Razor's Edge*

I am a journalist, which means I'm a professional skeptic.
I've spent large chunks of my life covering war. This has left
me with a deep cynicism about the nature of man. Tear away the
thin veneer of civilization and we descend into *Lord of the Flies*. I
saw it in Africa, in the Middle East, in Southeast Asia, and in the
Caucasus. But you only needed to visit the toilet tissue aisle during
the Covid crisis to get a glimpse of our potential to turn on each
other.

I have also seen the carnage wrought by religious doctrine. Catholics and Protestants. Muslims and Christians. Sunnis and Shi'ites.
Hindus and Muslims. Buddhists and Muslims. The list is endless.

"Maybe there is a beast," said Simon, in William Golding's classic exploration of the savagery that underlies even the most civilized human beings, "maybe it's only us."

But my life—and my reporting—has not been all about war and
humankind's trials; what the Buddhists call *samsara*, the cycle of
suffering. My travels have also led to encounters with grace and
glory. Bathed in a sense of peace as I held hands with Pope John
Paul II. Enveloped in joy as I chatted with Mother Theresa. Transported beyond self as I meditated with an incarnate Tibetan lama on
the steps of an ancient Buddhist stupa in Java.

My encounters with believers of many traditions—Christians, Muslims, Jains, Sikhs, Jews, Hindus, Buddhists, and others I cannot recall—have inevitably shaped my worldview and my curiosity.

Which brings us to this book. I was (marginally) raised Catholic, going through the motions of confirmation and attending the obligatory Christmas and Easter masses. My PhD is in Islamic Studies, but the formal doctrine of religion has never touched my heart. What fascinates me are the truths that lie beyond dogma and ritual. Few of us will ever retreat to a mountaintop or spend years in monastic silence. Some of the individuals profiled in these pages have done exactly that; others have spent decades studying with spiritual masters.

A New York record company art director, a medical doctor from Australia, the daughter of a London fishmonger, and other once "ordinary" folk who have carved out their own unique paths. You will not find them on the best seller lists or the Spiritual 100 rankings. They quietly pursue their truths far from the media spotlight. What prompted them to walk away from it all? What do they see that the rest of us do not? What lessons do they bring "back" from their spiritual journeys? What can we learn from them?

"Take care that none of those foolish people who live by their senses hear of these matters," Dionysius the Areopagite, author of the *Theologia Mystica*, wrote to his fellow fifth century mystics about their encounters with the Divine. Luckily for us, the spiritual explorers we meet in these pages have ignored that advice. They agreed to share a bit about their journeys. From them, we catch a glimpse of the profound experiences and simple encounters that have shaped their beliefs and taken them one step closer to answering the big questions of life.

And, in the process, perhaps we "foolish people" will gain a few lessons we can apply in our far more prosaic lives.

A Rumi Life

The tale of Shems Friedlander, who danced with God

"The outward of a thing is its illusion and the inward of a thing its reality."

Rumi

The energy is primordial. The room is filled with the names of Allah as our bodies sway to the hypnotic beat of the bendir drums. At least sixty men crowd the floor around me, lost in contemplation of the Divine. I feel a breeze from the billowing skirts of eight Whirling Dervishes gliding in their moving meditation a few feet away.

The walls of this three-hundred-year-old Sufi *tekke* hidden in the old quarter of Istanbul are covered with calligraphy, quotations from the Qur'an, and portraits of the ancient men of wisdom who trace their spiritual authority to a seventeenth century sage whose body lies entombed in the lodge's oldest room.

A group of elders is arranged on a divan at the front of the room. In the seat beside the red embroidered chair of the lineage-holder is a Sufi with long white hair and a curling beard, looking every inch the spiritual master come down from the mountaintop. His face carries a look of deep contentment, borne of decades of contemplation, meditation, and prayer.

His name is Ira Friedlander.

I am a bird of the heavenly garden
I belong not to the earthly sphere,
They have made for two or three days
A cage of my body.

Those lines from the thirteenth century mystic, whom the West knows as Rumi, were the first words of Friedlander's 1975 book, *The Whirling Dervishes: Being an Account of the Sufi Order Known as the Mevlevis and Its Founder the Poet and Mystic Mevlana Jalalu'ddin Rumi.*[1] The dance, or "turn," of the dervishes is the physical manifestation of man's aspiration to escape this earthly "cage" and return to the embrace of the Creator.

"Before they begin to whirl, each [Dervish] lets fall the black cloak and, like a fledgling bird, unfolds and stretches out his arms as the long white tenure, the shroud of their future, engraves a circle in the air," Friedlander recounts in the book, which was the first nonacademic work on Rumi published in the U.S.

"The editor at Macmillan was skeptical, so I pulled off my jacket and began to whirl in his office and that convinced him," Friedlander recalled in several days of conversations at his home on the outskirts of Istanbul.[2] The book was illustrated with his own otherworldly photographs of the *sema*, as the Mevlevi meditation turn is called.

Like the movements of the Whirling Dervishes, Friedlander's own life was irrevocably shaped by the Sufi poet and saint.

Ira Friedlander was not always a Sufi mystic. In the 1960s and early '70s, he lived and worked at the heartbeat of his generation. As art director for Columbia Records, Friedlander designed some of the era's most iconic album covers. He was a central player on the New York scene. At dinner in his 57th Street carriage house that once belong to Garbo, "John [Lennon] broke into song, 'Goodnight Irene.'" As he recounted in his 2015 memoir, *Winter Harvest: Bob Dylan to Jalaluddin Rumi*:

> Lena Horne would come over with Geoffrey Holder to shoot her latest album cover. Flowers for Barbara Streisand, dancing with Janis Joplin, lamenting with Leonard Cohen.[3]

He was also at the nexus of his generation's search for meaning. Friedlander was part of the first circle of Gurdjieff acolytes in America. He took psychic "flying lessons" from Swami Muktananda, attended the local zendo, studied with Tibetan lamas, and meditated with Omraan Mikhaël Aïvanhov. Hinduism and Sufism came together when Baba Ram Dass, the Harvard psychologist turned spiritual icon, and Pir Vilayat Inayat Khan, head of the Sufi Order International, met in Friedlander's New York carriage house, where Pir Vilayat lived for a time.

> They carried treasure maps across the oceans of the world, and they taught us how to tune into the celestial sounds in our bodies that were temples of God.[4]

An encounter with the Whirling Dervishes of the Mevlevi order on their first visit to New York, when they performed at the Brooklyn Academy of Music in 1972, reoriented Ira Friedlander and set him firmly on the path that would define his life. As with many spiritual seekers, the allure of mysticism, what Muslims call *tariqa*, initially attracted him to Sufism; only later did he commit himself to the teachings of Islam.

> This was the gate for many in the West. We were first drawn to the spiritual, the esoteric, and later embraced the religion.[5]

It was on a visit to Turkey in the 1970s that Friedlander was first invited to join the circle of the Mevlevi Whirling Dervishes, an honor rarely given to those outside the order.

> Tears came to my eyes as I was carried in the whirling motion of the dervishes and the sound of the *zikr*. Men, whose names I did not know, embraced me and called me brother. Here in this small underground room was the key to inner peace. Here was the universal love that Mevlana [Rumi] lived.[6]

Pir Vilayat initiated him as *sheikh* in the Chishti Sufi Order, giving him the name Shems, after Rumi's spiritual confidant. Years later, in a converted firehouse in New York, Friedlander was made *khalifa*, deputy, to the leader of the three-hundred-year-old Halveti-Jerrahi Sufi Order, tasked with helping to bring Sufism to America.

> My heart is fluttering like that of a small bird in an invisible cage. … Concentric circles of a hundred dervishes from Istanbul and New York witness the ceremony. [The sheikh] places the golden *taj*, wrapped at the base with several layers of green cloth, on my head. A green tail of this cloth is left hanging over my heart, like a snake, to remind me to protect my heart from making idols of the world.[7]

In the years between that first meeting and his initiation, Fried-lander embraced Islam: "I realized that to be a Muslim doesn't mean you have to be a Sufi, but to be a Sufi meant you have to be a Muslim," he told me during our many hours of conversations. He recalled the moment that realization came to him. It took place in the bookshop run by the man who would become his sheikh, the late Muzaffer Ozak. "Every day, I'd go there and sit and sort of listen to him talk. He would tell stories, talk about Islam, the Prophet Muhammad, Mevlana Jalaluddin Rumi, and Sufi masters from the past. I would just absorb this. It was like a master class. Then it was time for prayer. He stood up, put his prayer mat down and I watched him pray, and something in me said, 'I want to do this.'" He was lost in thought for a moment. "It was, let's call it, the magic moment. I returned to Istanbul as much as I could to be with him, and he began traveling to the States. It's more than forty years later. Either I'm a bad learner or I'm terribly in need more than anyone else, because I'm still around."

> I knew this Sufi knowledge was permeating my being ... because I would say things that I did not know and do things that I did not know how to do.[8]

Friedlander sensed that his connection to Sufism—and Islam—came long before he ever met Sheikh Muzaffer. "When I was about ten or twelve years old, I remember reading just two lines of a poem. It said, 'I cried because I had no shoes and then I met a man who had no feet.'" It moved him deeply. Years later, he would learn that the lines were written by the Persian Sufi poet Hafez.

Friedlander would eventually leave behind New York and what he called its "mill of nonsense" for a low-key career as a professor at the American University of Cairo, where he taught photography, painting, and graphic design, while delving deep into the Sufi *dergahs* of Egypt and making frequent visits to Turkey, home of his primary teacher and the order in which he would play such a prominent role. While mystics of some religions retreat to a mountaintop or nun's cell, the Sufi way follows the Qur'an's call for engagement with the world. "There's a saying in Islam," Friedlander told me with a smile, "you should work as if you will never die and pray as if you will die tomorrow." In between, there was meditation—the slow, deliberate focus on the breath—and contemplation of Allah.

To those of us who knew him in Cairo, it was no secret that Shems was a Sufi. We also knew he was a scholar of Jalaluddin Rumi and the Whirling Dervishes. In addition to the books, he produced a breathtaking documentary series. But few of us were aware that he played such a prominent role in the religion and was recognized as far afield as Mecca and Sarajevo:

> They seat me in a place of honor after Mevludin introduces
> me as a khalifa of a Turkish sheikh of the Halveti Order.[9]

When we spoke, Friedlander was in his eightieth year. He had lived and breathed Rumi for the previous four decades. Remembrance of Allah, the Prophet Muhammad, and the poet and mystic Mevlana Jalaluddin Rumi had been woven into every fiber of his being. The Sufi's internal repetition of the names of Allah had been the soundtrack of his life. He saw God in everything around him. "The aim of the dervish is to open the eyes of the heart and see infinity in eternity," he wrote in *Mevlana Jalaluddin Rumi's Forgotten Message*. "The cure for our spiritual amnesia is the integration of Rumi's lessons into daily life."[10]

Sufis believe that we are all an aspect of God. Rumi channels the mystic voice of Allah: "If you find Me not within you, you will never find Me. For I have been with you, from the beginning of Me." Sitting in his studio on the shores of the Marmara Sea, I ask Friedlander his view of our relationship with God. "It is like a broken mirror lying on the floor in many shards. There is a reflection of a part of the whole in each section. Allah has placed a part of His beauty in each of us. When we recognize the beauty of Allah in another then we understand how to relate to people. Our relationship with Allah cannot exist if it is devoid of His creation."

He points to an unfinished painting he is working on. It depicts a man with one wing, representing our desire to break free of the earthly plane and fly back to Allah. Within the outlines of the body is a cornucopia of plants and animals. He quotes a line from his 1987 book, *When You Hear Hoofbeats Think of a Zebra*, a collection of Sufi parables. "Man is the macrocosm or greater world while the universe is the microcosm of the lesser world. For Allah has shown us what He has put *outside* us is also *inside* us; we are a universe unto ourselves."[11]

Upstairs in the guest apartment where we are staying hangs another painting. My wife, Indira, tells him that each time she looks at it, she sees a different image. The first day, it was the shape of a wing. The next day, the face of a man. The third day, some words.

"It's based on an old Chinese proverb," Friedlander tells us. "A man dreamed he was a butterfly and when he woke, he wasn't certain he was a butterfly who dreamed he was a man, or a man who dreamed he was a butterfly."

La illah il al 'Llah, meaning there is no god but God. This is the *tawhid*, the phrase of Divine unity. This essential teaching of Islam was a message to the polytheists of Mecca that their idols were imposters. There was only one *real* God with a capital "G." But to Sufis, the tawhid is just the first level of understanding. It is, Friedlander's sheikh taught, "the prayer for beginners." Beyond that, Muzaffer Ozak said in a 1981 talk in New York, are many progressive steps of understanding. "Finally, 'Nothing exists except Allah.' That is the highest level of realization."[12]

Even the Qur'an cannot be taken at face value. Sufis believe there are seven layers of meaning in the Muslim holy book. They believe that the Qur'an, as well as the Torah, Psalms, and Gospel are part of an inexhaustible celestial Font of Wisdom, which they call *Umm al-Kitab*, the Mother of the Book. Their quest is to find the keys to unlock the inner truths, as Friedlander wrote in *Mevlana Jalaluddin Rumi's Forgotten Message*:

> Rumi's words [are] a bridge to the heart of man, making it possible for truth to unfold in the heart of the seeker.[13]

When Friedlander published *The Whirling Dervishes* in 1975, there were no other books on Rumi and his teachings for the general audience. Even for academic specialists, there had only been a few previous works. It would be two decades before a major U.S. publisher would release another book about Rumi.

A search for "Rumi" on Amazon today produces more than one hundred pages of books, CDs, calendars, tarot cards, and "soul journals," some of which have made the best-seller lists. They include titles such as *Love Poems of Rumi: Falling in Love Again*, which features a bodice-ripping cover worthy of a romance paperback. Meanwhile, a plethora of websites transform the ancient mystic's divine longing into dating advice. "The Meaning of Rumi is All About Love, Beyonce's Mother Shares on Instagram," EliteDaily. com breathlessly reported when it was announced that the singer had named one of her twins after Mevlana.

Rumi's profound mystical insights have been reduced to clichés on Hallmark cards. Almost literally. Coleman Barks, who has written numerous best-selling books based on Rumi's poetry, told me that he was once asked by the greeting card company to produce a series of Valentine's Day cards with Rumi quotes. He explained that Mevlana Jalaluddin Rumi wrote about love, but not *that* kind of love. The Divine, not a physical lover, was the *bride* in the *spiritual wedding* for which Rumi yearned. "Enough of phrases, concept, and metaphors," Mevlana proclaimed. "I want burning, burning, burning."

"These words of Jalaluddin Rumi excite the very essence of our being, reflecting the man Moses, barefoot, his body vibrating with light from the Divine Light," Friedlander explained in *Rumi's Forgotten Message*:

> Moses experienced what the Sufis call *fana*, complete annihilation in the Truth of Certainty.
>
> Rumi said, 'When I came to the word love, my pen broke.' Mevlana was not a temporary teacher of the heart, but a sheikh whose message [revealed] the truth of humanity, instilled, perhaps buried within each of us like a distant muffled prayer attempting to break through the crust of the heart of man.

Friedlander had respect for those, like Coleman Barks, who focus primarily on Rumi as a poet, not religious sage, but he insisted that it was critical to keep things in context. "It's not Islam and it's not Sufism and it's not Mevlana. It's poetry. If it makes you feel good to put the sayings of Rumi on your shower curtain, great." But he told me, to extricate the Prophet Muhammad and the Qur'an and Allah from Rumi's teaching was the equivalent of changing the ingredients in a recipe.

Mevlana himself seemed to have anticipated such distortion. Eight hundred years ago, the Sufi master wrote:

> *I am the slave of the Qur'an While I still have life.*
> *I am dust on the path of Muhammad, The Chosen One*
> *If anyone interprets my words in any other way,*
> *I deplore that person, and I deplore his words.*

Still, Friedlander did not object to mass marketed Rumi. Buried in each collection of Rumi's poetry, he believed, was the key to deeper teachings. "But even if you have the key, it doesn't mean you get in," he told me of Rumi's poems. "If you open yourself to them, Mevlana's words will open themselves to you. But it's a commitment. We need time to read a book or read a passage. We need to keep going back to it. It's like looking at a painting." He motioned toward an easel in his studio. "There's a responsibility of the painter and there's a responsibility of the viewer. If you want to see a Picasso, you have to sit with it. We can't walk through a room and say, 'Ah. Nice Picasso.' What does that mean? Where does that hit you? How does that influence you?" The payoff, he said, was eternal, but we must have patience and perseverance.

"The Buddha didn't become the Buddha in one minute. He was the Buddha a long time before he discovered that he was the Buddha. Allah had to show him a sick person, a dead person, a lame person, a poor person, because he was a prince, guarded in his princely prison. Until he went out one day and saw. 'What is that?' He had never seen an old man before, walking with a stick. And he was told, 'That's an old man.' 'You mean we will all be like that?' the Buddha asked, understanding for the first time we all grow old. So, Allah sends sickness so we can learn that there's health. He sends death so we can appreciate life. People in our family die, they get sick. We learn about illness. By learning about illness, you learn about health."

Muslims recognize Christians and Jews as people of the book, since the Talmud and Bible are considered prophetic books in Islam. But Islamic jurists specifically condemn *idolaters*. Buddhism generally falls in that category. I told Friedlander that I was surprised to hear him speaking of Allah giving lessons to the Buddha. "I believe that God exists and created everyone, including the Buddha," he replied. "Allah said, 'There are various paths and people that I've created so that you can understand one another.' Which means that he brought the Buddha to a certain understanding to create an entity that others can mirror and balance and reflect on. Lots of roads lead to Rome. The Prophet Muhammad is the Seal of all the Prophets, meaning that no more prophets will come after the Prophet

Muhammad. But it doesn't mean that Allah doesn't give light to other people. He gives light to many people in various degrees, some a lot of light, some a little light. The light of Allah cannot be extinguished."

Friedlander shrugged and touched his chest. "*I'm* saying that, it's not in books or anything. It's just my feeling." Ultimately, he said it's all a mystery.

At the Sufi lodge in Istanbul, a crowd of acolytes parts like the sea to allow Friedlander to pass. Some try to kiss his hand and even the most senior figures bow to him with respect. He was among the few still alive who were old enough to have "taken hand" with renowned Sufi teacher Muzaffer Ozak al-Jerrahi, a reference to the Sufi initiation ceremony in which the *murid*, the Sufi term for student, sits knee-to-knee with his sheikh and they grasp hands. The initiate symbolically—and, Sufis believe, mystically—becomes part of the unbroken spiritual lineage reaching back to the Prophet Muhammad.

It was to Ali, his son-in-law and the fourth rightful caliph, according to Sufi teachings, that the Prophet Muhammad first transmitted what is now the audible *zikr Allah* of the Halveti-Jerrahi Sufis—the repetition of "*La illah il al 'Llah.*"

When Muzaffer Ozak made Friedlander a *khalifa*, or deputy, in New York in the 1970s, the American shocked, and pleased, him by saying he wanted to pray and study for at least a year before assuming the role. Forty years later, Friedlander was still not comfortable in the sheikh's cloak. "I don't acknowledge any kind of position or anything like that," he whispered to me back at the tekke after the last dervish had kissed his hand. "A position of being old, yes, I have to acknowledge that, because there are mirrors."

That modesty belied the fact that his influence stretched well beyond the walls of one Istanbul prayer lodge. "Shems Baba is very well recognized, known and respected among American dervishes and Sufis," Shaykh Yurdaer Doganata, head of the Jerrahi Order of America, told me, using the honorific for father. "His book *When You Hear Hoofbeats Think of a Zebra* is known as a classic in Sufi circles. It is one of the first books recommended to new dervishes for reading."

When I reminded him of that back at his apartment, Friedlander downplayed the deference he received. "Islam is a religion of respect, you respect your elders, and I'm one of the oldest people in the room now, so I'm shown a lot of respect from the young people in their thirties and forties." He referred to his teacher, Muzaffer Ozak: "He has become a kind of legend. And it's just your association with him. People want to talk to you." That was apparent as we lunched on the patio of a seafront restaurant the day after the visit to the tekke. The waiters noticed a copy of *Winter Harvest* on the table and immediately asked for selfies. Friedlander indulged them, but Indira and I could tell he was uncomfortable.

"I feel my job is finished when the book I am working on is finished. And then it's not necessary to know me. I put the material I understand in the book and I'm sharing that with you. You won't get any more by rubbing my elbow." He laughed. "It doesn't work that way." He told us about a student at the American University in Cairo who was interested in Sufism. "And one day he came in and says, 'Doctor Shems, I feel you're my sheikh.' And I said, 'Well you're wrong.' And he says, 'No, no, no, I really, I really feel that you're my sheikh.' And I said, 'Well, it's a misunderstanding, I'm not.' He kept insisting, and I said, 'Don't make me become something that you may have to look at in a certain way every day. Come and sit and have a coffee and tea and talk.' He kept insisting, and finally I said, 'Okay, look. Let's assume I'm your sheikh, okay? Now your sheikh is telling you, he is not your sheikh."

Friedlander had always preferred to sit in the background. "My grandfather was a quiet man, my father was a quiet man, and I, too, am a quiet man." And he had grown to realize that title and position were meaningless. "I can learn from the man of knowledge, the sheikh, the teacher, whatever. And I can learn from the one who goes against the precepts of what the other is saying. And maybe in some cases, even learn more."

How then, I asked, did he see his role? "I always felt that if people wanted to, they could come and talk to me. I always felt I was better one on one with people than I was one in front of a group. I wanted to be a Dervish, not a sheikh," he said, using the term for an ordinary member of a Sufi fraternity. "I just wanted to learn, I wanted to understand how to live my life and use the conditions of Islam and the precepts of Islam and Sufism within it, to live a life according to the way Allah prescribed. Which is still what I hope to be able to do."

Art and poetry were two of the vehicles Friedlander used in his search for answers. "My questions haven't changed that much. Because even when you get an answer to your question, it adds another ten questions. It opens a door to other possibilities. The answer to the question is usually in the question."

In his study *Sufism: A New History of Islamic Mysticism*, Alexander Knish of the University of Michigan argued that for scholars of Sufism "to maintain a modicum of objectivity, one should remain immune to Sufism's potent allure." Friedlander strenuously disagreed. "One must become educated by one's heart to the things that cannot be understood intellectually," he wrote in *Rumi's Forgotten Message*. "Some scholars ... have the intellectual prowess to translate but lack the hidden key to Sufism that can unlock its deep meaning. If you cannot 'sit like him,'" he said of Rumi, referring to the act of remembrance, "how will you fathom jewels from the ocean of his mind?"

Friedlander reminded me that Shams al-Tabrizi, who was both Rumi's spiritual equal and a mentor, threw all of Rumi's books in a well and told him that theoretical knowledge was meaningless. Rumi himself would later tell his followers, "The scholar's provision consists of marks of the pen. The provisions of the Sufi are the footprints of the saints."

Friedlander did have respect for a handful of today's non-Muslim Sufi scholars, but his deep dedication to Islam left him perplexed. "How can they have studied Islam and Sufism all these years and not converted?" he asked me rhetorically one evening in a taxi as we returned from the tekke, referring to those scholars. I reminded him that although I had written about Islam for much of my professional life and had a PhD in Islamic Studies, I was not a Muslim. He nodded in acknowledgement; I thought I detected a shadow of sadness cross his face.

In 1925, after the collapse of the Ottoman Empire, the founder of the modern, secular Turkish state, Mustapha Kemal Ataturk, shuttered the Sufi lodges, banned the use of terms like "sheikh" and "dervish," and ordered the Mevlevis to whirl no more.

"The Dervishes wept. Their once billowing skirts hung limp like the shrouds they represented," Friedlander wrote of the day the tekkes were padlocked. Ataturk had declared Turkey a modern country, "and a modern society has no time for Dervish magic."

Decades later, Sufi leaders convinced the government to allow the Mevlevi Dervishes to begin turning again, but only to perform for the tourists at the annual December 17 celebration of Rumi's "wedding night," referred to as *Shebi Arus*—the day he returned to unity with Allah—in the Turkish city of Konya. That prohibition on Sufi practice was still in force. The ancient Halveti-Jerrahi lodge where I accompanied Friedlander to the zikr officially operated as the Foundation for Research and Conservation of Turkish Sufi Music and Folklore. It was one of the few Sufi gathering places in Istanbul that had not deteriorated from disuse. Its official mission was the discovery and preservation of historic Sufi songs and culture, which its leaders took very seriously. But the living spiritual energy in the ancient prayer rooms, where Sufis gather each Monday and Thursday to sing praises of Allah, were a mystical testament to the devotion that still lives today.

It is early evening, after Maghreb prayers. Friedlander and I have just finished sharing communal bowls of stew with the elders of the lodge. We are sitting on a divan in the room where we will soon sing *illahis*, Sufi songs of praise, and recite the names of Allah. Friedlander is explaining the symbolism of the zikr circle. "Man continuously journeys around the circle of himself, repeating past actions and trapping himself in a net of his own creation. From the time the skull of Abel, the first man to die, was placed into the earth, man has buried the sacred; buried the maps to his freedom." Those maps, he tells me, are waiting to be discovered in the zikr. The music that guides the meditation, Friedlander continues, traces back to Mevlana himself. "This is not just for entertainment. If you allow yourself to be absorbed by the music, it can be a gate to a higher state of consciousness." From *Winter Harvest*:

> As my eyes grow accustomed to the darkness, the white robed men take on an ethereal look, the look of angels. For indeed, there is an angelic feeling here. Hearts and breath merge with the Name of Allah, the proclamation that there is no reality but Allah, and that the Blessed Prophet Muhammed is His Messenger. In this darkness I hear the weeping of spiritual warriors.[14]

Later, as we sit on the floor repeating the names of Allah in unison, *Ya Hayy, Ya Haay, Ya Haay*, accompanied by the haunting sounds of the *ney* flute and long necked *tambur* lute, and the pulsating rhythm of the drums, a half-dozen Whirling Dervishes turn as they seek spiritual annihilation though the moving meditation of the *sema*. Rumi put it this way:

> Sema is to fight with one's self, to flutter, struggle desper-
> ately like a half-slaughtered bird, bloodstained and covered
> with dust and dirt. ... Sema is a secret. ... Sema is to attain
> that place where even an angel cannot go.

Back in the early 2000s, I interviewed the Sufi elder Pir Vilayat Inayat Khan, who had initiated Friedlander into Sufism. Pir Vilayat told me that the mystic branches of all the world's great religions ultimately take the adept to the same place: union with the Divine. His Chishti branch of Sufism was later inherited by his U.S.-born son, who changed the name to The Inayat Order and took a decid-edly ecumenical approach to Sufism, jettisoning references to Allah in favor of the *Divine Spirit* or *the One*. The U.S. website explained the organization's evolving approach this way: "The descriptive term 'Sufi' being used less frequently, with the 'Sufi Message' be-coming more frequently referred to as simply 'the Message.'"

Friedlander shook his head sadly at what he saw as New Age repackaging that stripped Sufism of its Islamic soul. As his teacher Muzaffer Ozak put it, "Sufism without Islam is like a candle burn-ing in the open without a lantern."

"One of the problems regarding spirituality in general in the West," Friedlander told me, "is that we want to embrace a practice because we're seekers, but don't want to *give* ourselves to it. We want *it* to give itself to *us*. We would like Sufism, or Hinduism, or Buddhism to change so that it just comes into our lives, and then I can live my life the way I want, and do what I call Sufi practices, or yoga practices, or something, without any of the spirituality. By jumping from one path to another, you'll just obtain surface knowl-edge. The search for Truth is often more important than the Truth itself."

At a talk in Europe in the 2000s, Friedlander was challenged by a young member of the audience who argued that in an age of social media, Rumi and religion had become irrelevant and the internet was now our God.

"You worship Apple and I'll worship Allah," Friedlander responded. He believed with all his being that one cannot be a Sufi without being a Muslim; but he also believed the Sufi path and Islam contain many lessons for nonbelievers. "There are a lot of sad, lonely and depressed young people today. Apple is not going to get them where they want to go. And they end up pawns of psychologists who feed them drugs; and when one doesn't work, they give them another," he told me.

I mention the college-age daughter of a mutual friend who had committed suicide. "How can a young person commit suicide?" Friedlander asked sadly. "It's the world's fault. It's not their fault. It's horrible. That's why I'm saying that Mevlana is the answer to our spiritual amnesia."

"We can tell stories about the great saints and teachers, what they did, how they suffered or remembered Allah, but the real question each of us must ask and face is this: How do we live our lives?" Friedlander wrote in *When You Hear Hoofbeats*. "Are we always caught up doing what is urgent and not what is important in life? When we look at our lives, can we see what really matters? All life is a weaning process," he continued, advising, "Wean those things out of our life that are no longer useful."[15]

In the day's headlines, Friedlander found sadness, hope and lessons. "Every religion began with a refugee," he told me, exasperation in his voice. "And yet we're turning refugees away from our countries now with the idea that no, this is ours, and you can't come here. But Jesus's parents fled to Egypt. The Prophet Muhammad went from Mecca to Medina. The Buddha traveled out into the world. They were all refugees. They all had to leave the place that they were comfortable in to be able to establish something. And yet we look at refugees now and say, 'No, no, no. We're not gonna feed them.' 'Them?' What *them*? They're *us*."

During our many hours of conversations, he kept returning to this central theme: "The world is a learning field. It's not a place to accumulate money and accumulate power. It's a place to learn how to be. And we don't see that the secret is within us. Very few people, I think, will just sit quietly during the day and just breathe in and breathe out. Even for one minute, thirty seconds. We don't even close our eyes during the day for any period of time, just to breathe in and feel ourselves. We're just so taken by everything outside. It's like this huge magnet and we're an iron filing. We have no choice. We're just taken, but we *do* have a choice."

As we spoke, there was a real-time example of the ephemeral nature of money and power playing out 1,500 miles away in Saudi Arabia, where dozens of the world's richest men had been imprisoned by the country's crown prince, Muhammed bin Salman. "If we had one hundred lives, we'd never even dream of accruing as much wealth and power," he told me. "And they've been reduced to basically nothing. They were the richest, most powerful people in the world. They're all under house arrest. They're wearing a strap on their ankle."

Friedlander's essential advice, found in *Rumi's Forgotten Message*, sounded much like that of mystics of every religion.

> When you slow down, leave certain things in life that are not necessary, frivolous things that waste time, then you can sit quietly, breathe in and out, contemplate the beauty and magnitude of Allah and see yourself as a miracle instead of a tired, depressed, aging person whose entertainment and information comes from screens that are programmed, unfettered, by unknowns.[16]

For his eightieth birthday, Friedlander traveled to Konya, the Turkish town where Rumi spent much of his life. A few days after the quiet celebration with a few friends, he suffered a heart attack and underwent double bypass surgery. A year later, he was diagnosed with an aggressive form of cancer that would claim his life in a matter of months. He submitted to treatment but was sanguine about the inevitable outcome. He had long ago told his wife what he wanted written on his headstone:

Shems Friedlander
has completed his breathing practices.

Double Belonging

Michael Holleran. In the cosmic energy of God.

"In the future Christians will be mystics, or they will not be anything."
Karl Rahner, German Theologian

Father Michael Holleran sat gazing out at the dozen or so men and women who had gathered in the Church of St. Francis of Assisi in Manhattan.

"In tantra, you're weaving together these different dimensions of energy, which is all interconnected," he told the group, who were listening with rapt attention:

Just as you have to find the masculine-feminine balance in
yourself, and not be looking for it in another person, you
have to find the balance between absolute and relative in
yourself as well. So, you're the whole thing: You're Christ,
the universe, [the Primordial Buddhas] Samantabhadra and
Samantabhadri. You're the Ramakrishna and the dakinis. All
of you are One: everything at the same time.

They were unusual words coming from a man who had spent
twenty-two years contemplating the glories of Christ as a monk in
one of the Catholicism's most cloistered monastic orders. But this
was not a homily at Sunday mass; it was a Tuesday evening dharma
talk about tantric sex, and the man sitting at the front of the room
was both a parish priest and a sensei, or teacher, in the Zen tradition
of Buddhism.

The members of his Dragon's Eye Zendo saw nothing incongru-
ous in that. They knew their teacher was equally comfortable on the
zazen cushion and on his knees at the altar. As he taught them in
his weekly *teishos*, Japanese for "presentation of insight," Michael
Holleran's many decades spent in mystic contemplation had led him
to the firm conclusion that beyond doctrine, beyond labels, "it's all
part of the perfection of the Absolute."

Few outside the Church are likely to have heard of the Carthusian
monks, an order that traces its roots to an eleventh century German
cleric. Meditation and mysticism run deep and rich behind the walls
of its ancient "mother" monastery at Grande Chartreuse in France.
The anonymous author of *The Cloud of Unknowing*, the classic Medieval work of mysticism, is believed by some scholars to have been
a Carthusian.[1] So, too, was Guigo II, the twelfth century prior of
Grande Chartreuse, who formalized an approach to contemplation
used by Catholics to this day.

It was this tradition of single-minded devotion that drew Michael Holleran to the order in the early 1970s. The son of an Irish Catholic family from Long Island, he had joined the Jesuits right out of high school and was soon studying theology, Greek, and Latin under Jesuit scholars at Fordham University. There he discovered the interior life of contemplation and meditation. And in a class on Eastern religion, he met the Jesuit priest who would ordain him as a Zen sensei decades later.

"I always had a contemplative attitude to life, without even realizing it. Very religiously attuned, spiritually attuned," Holleran told me in one of our early conversations. During college, he began to practice a form of interior prayer that involved reading the Gospel and then having a silent dialogue with Christ. "That opened up the paths of the inner life." Meanwhile, he read Thomas Merton, an influential Trappist monk and mystic who was leading a revival of Christian contemplative practices. Contemplation, as Merton described it, is "to rise above thought and penetrate into the mystery of truth which is experienced intuitively as present and actual."[2] Mysticism, in the words of spiritual philosopher Beatrice Bruteau, "then grasps the reality directly as lived experience, without any mediating story or explanation."[3] A contemplative is not necessarily a mystic, but a mystic might be called an advanced contemplative.

After five years with the Jesuits, Holleran concluded that their focus on missionary work and education was not his path. "I realized I felt called to devote myself completely to this inner exploration of silence and solitude and union with God," he told me almost a half-century later. Looking back, he was grateful to the Jesuits for providing him with an important way station on his journey. "Modern culture is so different from monastic silence and the solitary life that you need a transition. You need a buffer. So, to go from the world to the Jesuits, and then from the Jesuits to the Carthusians—that made sense."

Holleran had considered other orders; he even did a retreat at Merton's Trappist monastery but decided that the Trappists' emphasis on community and manual labor was not for him. That led him to the Carthusians and, as he later wrote, their "solitary life in modest and austere hermitages around a cloister" and "the Mystery that both sustains and outstrips it."[4] He would spend twelve years at the Carthusian Order's only North American monastery, the Charterhouse of the Transfiguration, in Vermont. During that time, he became the first Carthusian priest ordained in the Western hemisphere.

Life in the Charterhouse involved a single-minded focus on prayer, meditation, and contemplation. Holleran and his fellow monks left their tiny cells, heated by a wood stove, just three times a day for mass and Gregorian chanting. The rest of the time they spent in silent prayer and contemplation. Even the single meatless meal was delivered through a slot in his cell door. Once a week, they were allowed to walk alone in the woods. Sleep was punctuated by prayer, reading, and chanting around the clock. "You never get a seven- or eight-hour rest. It is always broken. It's very hard if you don't have a call," Holleran said of the spiritual vocation. As the Statutes of the Carthusian Order explain:

> Our principal endeavor and our vocation is to devote ourselves to the silence and solitude of the cell. ... There, the faithful soul is often united to the Word of God, the bride with her Spouse, earth is joined to heaven and the human to the divine.

Those who mistakenly think they have been called to the Carthusian life "climb the walls right away," Holleran said. "If you *do* have a call, it's a totally, totally engrossing thing. You're completely given over to it, given over to God, to the experience of God. You live your whole life in that perspective of pure faith and union with God and community. You could call it a community of hermits, if that's not an oxymoron."

This extreme isolation was essential, Holleran later wrote in the preface to *The Wound of Love*, a book about the order that he edited:

> [S]lowly through the course of the years ... the corporeal
> and spiritual components of our being and our prayer are
> seamlessly integrated. ... allowing our "complications," our
> "resistances," and our narrow, twisted a priori to be burned
> away under the desert sun ... So that he who truly "laughs"
> with the serenity of God's Joy may be born again from the
> ashes of Holocaust.

There had been a handful of other American Carthusian priests, but they had been *formed* at the order's motherhouse in France. "I was the first one entirely formed in America. Eventually they said, 'This didn't work. We've got to send him over to France,'" Holleran told me with a wry grin.

He loved life at Grand Chartreus, the order's ancient headquarters high in the Grenoble Alps in France. When he arrived there in 1984, he felt like he had been "reborn"; the motherhouse took him "into a whole new depth of the Carthusian life."

He was put in charge of production of the euphoniously named liqueur, the recipe for which could be traced to a Medieval alchemical formula given to the order by Henry IV of France in 1605. He was also head cantor in the choir and taught philosophy and theology to novice monks. But most of his day was spent alone in his cell. "It was a very rich life, very full and very demanding, living in solitude and spending so many hours a day in prayer."

After seven years, he was transferred to the Carthusian monastery in Britain. He would last in the order just three more years: "A lightbulb went off. It was kind of a midlife crisis." Despite the meditative solitude and total commitment to a life in communion with Christ, Holleran realized the Carthusian life in which he had been immersed for twenty-two years was no longer enough. "I knew I wanted to explore more of the mystical depths of not only Catholicism, but of other traditions. I wanted to explore psychology more, also, to share in the world. I needed more of an outlet. I can't say they were particularly surprised," he added, arching his eyebrows.

Looking back, he saw his life behind the walls of the monastery as just a natural part of his spiritual evolution. "We can't just say, 'This is my vocation forever and ever and ever, from the time I'm thirteen to the time I'm eighty-three.' No. We change, we integrate new insights about ourselves and about the world and about God, and we have to keep going, theologically and spiritually as well as psychologically. Keep informed and see where the spirit leads."

To speak with Michael Holleran is to attend a master's class in twenty-first century Christian contemplative theology. Our conversations opened a door to a world of modern Christian mystics who have transcended traditional orthodoxy and touched a face of Christ in ways few sitting in the pews at Sunday mass could ever imagine.

"We are not just humans having a God experience," writes theologian Richard Rohr. "The Eucharist tells us that, in some mysterious way, we are God having a human experience."[5] That is a central theme in the inspired vision of Holleran and his Christian contemplative contemporaries, who are grounded in this alternative orthodoxy.

"Christ," argues Episcopal priest and acclaimed contemplative Cynthia Bourgeault, whom Holleran frequently quotes, is not the static figurehead of what she calls "the Jesus theme park" of organized religion, but rather "the evolutionary principle of a universe in movement," of which the Trinity is the "hidden driveshaft."[6] "Father-Son-Holy Spirit takes its place among many triads of God's expressiveness in a ternary metaphysical system—each revealing a different facet of the divine wholeness."[7]

Woven through the works of these inspired thinkers is a vision of what Jesuit paleontologist Pierre Teilhard de Chardin—Holleran's "Bible" as a young cleric—calls the "hominization" or spiritualization of mankind as we evolve from Alpha, the creation, to Omega, reunification with the Godhead.[8] "The new universe story is the intercommunion of life itself," writes another Holleran favorite, Ilia Delio, a Franciscan nun whose work sits at the intersection of religion and science. Ultimately, she believes, spiritual evolution will result in the emergence of "a new God consciousness ... steeped in love. This will be the second coming of Christ."[9]

It's not the stuff of Sunday schools.

"I think it's very useful to have all of these different approaches, because each one highlights a different element of the truth, whereas the traditional one had many dangers," Holleran says of Church doctrine. "For example, having Jesus' humanity completely swallowed up in the divinity, and that's what happened to spirituality and theology for hundreds of hundreds of years, so that we never appreciated the human Jesus, and that's just been recovered in the last fifty to sixty years, in Catholic theology."

But, yes, he agrees, "it's complicated stuff."

"You're much better off if you've experienced some of this" in a direct or mystic sense, he says patiently, "so you know what you're talking about more directly. But I would say that all of them would agree that the Trinity, the Christ, is God manifested in the world. So it's divinity, and not just humanity, divinity uncreated and created together that's Christ. And the spirit is the energy that penetrates from the Godhead, from the Father, if you will, the Trinity, and then back again, to the fullest."

Simply put, he continues, "God is an energy field." The Holy Spirit is "the dynamism between the unmanifest" energy of God and the energy that manifests "in the form of Christ."

Holleran then reaches beyond Christianity to elaborate on this all-encompassing vision of the cycle of existence as a shifting flow of divine, cosmic energy. "The Godhead is beyond the Trinity and more primordial than the Trinity. What is true is that it all returns, if you want to express it this way, more traditionally, into the bosom of the Father. It all goes back to the source. The Kabbalah is very strong on this. That it all goes back, and is absorbed, and substantiated, and disappears back into the original source. That's the dance of the Trinity, the dance of creation, the dance of the universe or universes, but then it all returns. It all came from the depths of silence and returns to the depths of silence."

He once more puts this Oneness in specifically Christian terms: "Christ is God Manifest in the world, from the Big Bang on, then becoming incarnate individualized in Jesus, and then in His own humanity in the resurrection, subsuming the whole universe in himself, not just in His divinity, but in His humanity. That's our goal and our destiny as well, our own resurrection in Him. It's just astounding, overwhelming, and an inspiring vision for the whole cosmos. I think that's what God had in mind when he created the universe to begin with," he continues, awe in his voice. "And maybe God's self is experiencing it in a way that God-self couldn't just in God-self. Of course," he adds, "it's even clearer with Buddhism. Everything is interconnected. We don't have a self. We're all energy, consciousness. That's all, it's even easier. It's part of the perfection of the Absolute. That's who we are, the vastness, the emptiness, including in every dimension of our life."

The soul, in Holleran's view, "is not something you start with, it's what you *finish* with. Whatever happened to Christ is going to happen to us, and that's wonderful!"

"Christ is just another word for *everything*," he told me in another conversation. "It's not just one Son of God. We are all, ultimately, Christ, which is what the fathers of the Church said. In the end, Christ is everything and everyone, it says in the letter to the Colossians. That sounds pretty inclusive."

But that's not what most priests teach at Sunday mass. "We haven't begun to assimilate that truth yet," Holleran acknowledged, sadly. "We're *not* these miserable, sinful, separate, beings that elementary and immature Christianity likes to present to the world. We are sparkling diamonds, which Buddhism says as well. We just have to wake up to that marvelous dignity and live it out."

And that, he said, should be our ultimate takeaway: "No matter what trials you have in your life, or what traumas and struggles, to realize that ultimately, and from the beginning, and for all eternity, you are radiant and precious. You can live with yourself when you know that. That's just so encouraging."

"But if we are all a manifestation of God," I asked him, "what makes Jesus different from Noah, Moses, Mohammad, Buddha or any of the other prophets and spiritual masters who achieved some level of realization?"

"What I think is the main difference, is that the humanity of Jesus was in the state of perfect union with God from the first instant of its existence. And Jesus lived from that all through his life, whereas everybody else woke up to it, which is the exact phrase the Buddha used. Whereas Jesus had it from the very first instant. From the very first instant it was God living the life of Jesus. But it's all on a continuum. We're all connected to the reality."

I raised the issue of Christ's so-called "lost years" between ages twelve and thirty, about which there is no historical record. Some scholars believe this was a period when he wandered the desert in search of spiritual enlightenment, much as Prince Shakyamuni did before his enlightenment as Buddha. Didn't that, I asked, argue against the idea that Jesus was different from the other prophets and sages?

Holleran cited a startling proposition suggested by Bernadette Roberts. "She seems to think that those years were God getting used to being human. Not the human getting used to being God, but the other way around. I think that's absolutely fascinating."

"What is this? What is this?" Holleran said, holding up his arms and imagining Christ looking confused and inspecting his body. "I mean look at all the stuff we've got to work through. All the evolutionary energies, the primitive millions of years of evolution. For the *no self* to actually take on a human self and all that, is quite a proposition—even for God."

"When you talk about the universe, the cosmos, it's not just the evolution of Planet Earth, which is exciting enough, but of the whole universe," he added, pushing the envelope of orthodoxy even further. Many of the mystics he admired, he said, talk about this evolution. "Ilia Delio specifically speaks about the possibility of alien life," he said, referring to an acclaimed Franciscan Sister who held the Endowed Chair in Theology at Villanova University. "How could other life in the universe not be? It would be incredible if it's not the case."

Many of his spiritual contemporaries speak of Holleran with awe. "It takes your breath away," Roshi Kennedy said of the scope and depth of Holleran's spiritual vision. "He is so insightful and brave." Sister Margaret Galliardi, a Dominican nun, was so taken by Holleran the first time she attended a Zen talk he gave that she then made it a point to watch his Catholic homilies online and was "delighted" to find them "equally profound."

"He's outside the box," she told me, explaining that she was drawn by "his openness, his probing, the depth of his internal silence, the depth of his own contemplative prayer. That reaches in and touches me." Galliardi, a former member of the International Commission of the Dominican Order, told of a New Year's greeting Holleran sent to her Zen sangha a few years before: "May 2016 expand our hearts and minds even more into the unknowable and ineffable where our lack of footing is what truly grounds us."

"That's what makes him different," she observed. "There's a profoundly mystical understanding of being comfortable in not knowing."

Others acquainted with his teachings are struck by his ability to connect with advanced spiritual practitioners and ordinary parishioners alike. "There are probably three levels of depth," Mahri Leonard-Fleckman, a professor of Religious Studies at Holy Cross University, said of the message in Holleran's homilies. "People catch it superficially, people catch it in the middle, and people catch it at depth. So, he's servicing all of them. He's not looking down at the people with superficial understanding, and saying, 'I'm not going to preach to you.' He's preaching to everybody and doing it masterfully."

For Leonard-Fleckman and her husband Judson Brewer, whose wedding Holleran officiated, the priest-sensei was a bridge between their spiritual paths. Brewer, who studies the brain as director of the Mindfulness Institute at Brown University, was a practitioner of Theravada Buddhism. Leonard-Fleckman, who was born Jewish, was a Catholic convert who also practiced Zen. "I'm someone who lives with a kind of a constant state of tension, being what I would call a border walker between traditions," she told me. Holleran, her spiritual counselor, "was the one person who was actually able to understand how all of these traditions connect. Not from a superficial place, which is the most dangerous way to view them, but as someone who is so deeply immersed, that it's like he's fallen out the bottom and into that place of transcendence. That's who he really is."

In the fourteenth century classic work of mysticism, *The Cloud of Unknowing*, the anonymous author imagines God praising the work of those who pursue *active* lives of mercy and charity, then admonishing them: "But don't interfere with my contemplatives. You don't know what is happening to them."[10]

"So, what *is* happening to them?" I asked Holleran of mystic experience. He reminded me that Teresa of Avila, the sixteenth century Spanish saint and monastic reformer, used the analogy of the caterpillar and the butterfly to describe to her nuns the spiritual metamorphosis of the soul through all-consuming prayer. "It's a total transformation," Holleran explained of the internal process of the mystic. "We know scientifically now that the body of the caterpillar basically disintegrates, dissolves. And the potential that was hidden there in the genes takes over and it becomes a whole new being. That's what happens in our mystical transformation." The passion in his voice removed any doubt he was speaking from experience. "I mean, you could never imagine beforehand who you really are and what you really look like, based on just your own superficial ego awareness of self and world and the judgments you make and the desires you have. All of that is totally reshuffled; totally transformed."

Bourgeault described her insight into the Trinity as arriving with a "Whoosh!" and providing "a breathtaking glimpse of the journey of divine love into time, through time, and out of time—from Alpha to Omega, from origin to final *Consummatum est*."[11] Such "glimpses" fundamentally change the meditator, and eventually, according to Holleran, "You're on a different level of consciousness habitually. It's not just a fleeting moment. At some point in the early stages of the spiritual life, it may just be a spark, a sudden illumination that quickly passes, but it becomes more and more habitual as you go on." Most of these visionaries make no pretense to experiencing anything more than a step on what de Chardin calls the "progressive planes of knowledge," he said, referring to the late French theologian and philosopher.[12] Bernadette Roberts, a former monastic who has been described as one of the most significant contemplatives of our time, cautions:

> To come to the fullness of Truth is not within the human dimension; whatever we know, even by way of our most mystical experiences, is still through a glass darkly. Self or consciousness precludes or hides final Truth in order to make the human dimension possible. ... An authentic unmediated glimpse of ultimate Truth and man would go out like a light.[13]

At root is the notion of shedding the ego, a concept central to the meditative practices of so many of the world's religions. The goal is that of achieving a "nondual" state; there is no God *there*, or "me" *here*. "In the end, every self, even the true self, is a false self because it's a *self*. That's the thing that finally gets washed away. That you're not separate, you're not even fully real. It's very Buddhist, in that sense," Holleran explained.

The process of shedding the ego means that ultimately the *self* cannot be differentiated from God. "That's a little scary for us," Holleran conceded. "'I'm going to lose my precious individuality.' But it's so much more than you could ever desire or wish, because the reality is so much bigger than that. What's real? Not a lot of our ego stuff, which we think is so real. It's not. It's the most rapturous and magnificent thing when we—and everything we thought we were—are Christ. It's not that we transform," he paused, struggling for the words. "It's hard to express exactly because it's not an ego. The self doesn't experience it. The self disappears. No self."

This has been called, the "crucifixion of the false self,"[14] during which the external self "*dies* and is cast aside like a soiled garment in the genuine awakening of the contemplative."[15] In her account of reaching what she called this "unitive or transcendent state," Roberts described the wrenching experience of reaching beyond self in a deep meditative trance. "The divine's breaking through the center of consciousness shatters the ego like a hole made in the center of ourselves." It was, she wrote, "a kind of resurrection."[16]

Holleran tried to explain her experience to me. "It's not self [that is being resurrected], it's the resurrection of Christ, which is a very bold way, and unique way, of saying it, but I think it's very true, because she's pointing beyond what all mystics, up to now, except maybe Meister Eckhart, have not dared to say, or could say, or would say."

Roberts continued:

> A few seconds into this phenomenon, of the body dissolving into divine air, there was instant recognition of the ascension experience. ... Having to leave this divine condition could only be described as hell. It was God awful. It was monstrous and unbearable."[17]

St. John of the Cross described it as "the dark night of the soul." Holleran says the anguish of the return to the physical is understandable. "We don't realize the amount of utter freedom, and vastness, and expansiveness that will be ours, once we're no longer in the body." Though the return journey is wrenching, the experience forever changes how the mystics who have reached this level of union see themselves and the world. "You do reach a habitual level of union—they call it the spiritual marriage—where you are living in constant conscious union with God. It's not transitory, it's not fleeting, it's not momentary. It's habitual," Holleran explains. "There's only Christ. And that's who we ultimately are. So, our self disappears. This is the kind of mystical language that the mystics always get in trouble for." He quotes St. Augustine: "In the end, there will just be one Christ loving himself."

But the modern Church, he argues, does nothing to encourage such a spiritual quest. "How many people actually get there? Or are even encouraged to get there? Or even know they *can* get there? That's kind of the tragedy, not only of civilization, but of religions. Religions themselves don't always encourage this, as Jesus found out. Or the Sufis found out," he says, referring to their persecution by other Muslims through history. So, it's ironic and tragic that religion itself doesn't always realize what its hidden treasure is. It stays hidden."

Holleran and this elite band of modern mystics have deep roots in the Church, but in their view those official doctrines are nothing more than a set of signposts for one—*but not the only*—possible path to higher truths. They do not buy into what has been called "the myth of the given," the idea that just because a religion has a set of written teachings, those hold all the answers.[18]

"Experience is to be taken seriously, along with Scripture and tradition," he said of meditative insights, whether those of Medieval saints or twenty-first century spiritual seekers. By ignoring the value of what he called "this contemplative eye," he wrote in the

National Catholic Reporter, the "blind dogmatism" and "spiritual schizophrenia" of the Church "has wrought inestimable damage on many levels, and only a narrow clericalism has any interest in maintaining it."[19]

After reading two of the modern mystics whom he admired, Cynthia Bourgeault and Bernadette Roberts, I told Holleran that I came away with the impression that they held a dim view of the structures of the Catholic Church. "Well, I don't want to say that too loudly, but I share that, as well." A few minutes later, after we switched topics, he returned to the point, adding that, despite their cynicism about the structures, he and the others did continue to work within the church, "because we see what's beautiful, and what's rich, and ancient, at the same time. It's worth it to wade through all the ..." he stopped himself, "put up with all of the nonsense."

That "nonsense," included the fact that, as asserted by former monk Thomas Moore, "We have replaced secret wisdom with information."[20] In Holleran's view, until the advent of the Christian contemplative movement in the 1970s, the rich contemplative traditions of the Church had been lost under the weight of centuries of bureaucratic orthodoxy. "Despite the centrality of prophecy and mysticism in the tradition, these themes are often downplayed or ignored," Holleran wrote in that *National Catholic Reporter* article. "Seminaries seem more liable to turn out defenders of the institution than spiritual leaders with any mystical depth."

Too often, he argued, the Church is satisfied to watch as spiritual insight is replaced by blind faith. "Empires, whether political or religious, are invested in the status quo," Holleran told his parishioners during a Sunday homily in 2016.

And he did not shirk from eviscerating sacred *shibboleth*. "God does not inscribe tablets with lightning bolts on Mt. Sinai; these are all metaphors for the presence and action of God in our lives," he wrote in an article on Biblical interpretation. "There was not a literal tree, with a literal talking snake, in a literal garden, with two naked humans, one male and one female. The truth of that wondrous tale is more on the archetypal, mythical, mystical level, and to take it as actual history, in the modern sense, is ludicrous, and extremely dangerous, giving the Bible a bad name."

"It is an enormous distance from the radiant revelation of God as love," Holleran wrote in the same article, "to the warlike desert sheikh in the sky who commanded the Israelites to take over alien territory and slaughter all the inhabitants, including the animals! Does anyone really think the latter was a transparent revelation of God's innermost heart and will? A huge amount of projection was going on, in the midst of a literally infinite divine patience. That was perhaps the only way the Chosen People could believe themselves chosen in that epoch, and that he was really *on our side!*"[21]

Even Heaven is not off-limits. Holleran's homilies and funeral talks are peppered with a very different interpretation of the afterlife than we hear from the pulpit of most churches. "People say, 'I'm here and I'm going to live a good life and be good. And then if I die in God's grace, I'll get my body back and I'll live happily ever after up in Heaven with all my relatives and friends and with Jesus. I'll be looking at him and saying hello to Jesus.' And that's sheer nonsense," he said firmly. "I tell them, "We are transformed *into* Christ and share his Life and Vision of all space and time!"

Holleran recognized that to some, his words were blasphemy. "It is not the least bit blasphemous or presumptuous to examine and question the Bible. On the contrary, we run the risk of blasphemy if we do *not* seriously question our hermeneutics," he told me, referring to Biblical interpretation. "Otherwise, we will ascribe to God the most heinous and primitive of sentiments, simply because we have, willfully or not, failed to understand that the Word is always filtered through our own human words, cultures, and psychologies." The Bible is "a mythical and mystical treatise whose depth of truth is vastly more challenging and astonishing as a metaphor of our spiritual journey than just as an account, however glorious and poetic, of the origins of our material universe," Holleran wrote elsewhere.[22] This "wisdom document" contains "a dazzling number of inner correspondences and levels of meaning," and "the fact that these traditional levels of meaning are unknown to nearly everyone is shattering proof that the majority of Christians have lost touch with their own 1500-year tradition."[23]

Holleran was equally direct in his dim view of the politization of religion in America and the "nonsense" of fundamentalist revival meeting preachers. "Religion is not about moral rules or dogmatic proclamations, and it's certainly not about politics. [It's about] the personal encounter with Jesus," he said in a January 2021 homily to his parishioners. "And I'm not taking about the noisy frothing at the mouth, 'Jesus is our Savior!'"—he waved his arms about, mimicking a revival meeting—"the music and the manipulation and all that, no, no, no, no. Jesus FLED politics," the priest continued, shouting the word. "He wanted NOTHING TO DO with worldly power. Ideologies are so much more comfortable and flattering to our ego. But we'll never be happy—we'll be violent, but we'll never be happy—and we'll never make anybody else happy the way Jesus does [by substituting] hateful websites and ideologies, even in the Catholic Church, for true spirituality and true religion."

The antidote, Holleran told the congregation, was, "Meekness, mercy, forgiveness, healing, love patience, an openness and closeness to those who are rejected and despised by church and state."

Holleran had been walking that walk since almost the moment he left the monastery. Arriving back in the U.S. in 1994, he soon found himself at the forefront of gay rights activism as assistant to the pastor at St. Joseph's Church in Greenwich Village, one of the most welcoming parishes in the city for what is now known as the LGBTQ+ community. "A number of people have asked, 'Wasn't that a big shock, to come from solitude back to Greenwich Village in New York?'" Holleran recalled. "I said, 'Well, no, because both of those places push the boundaries of the human spirit. Each in their own way.' So, I was ready for a new way. People appreciated my preaching, and I enjoyed the work. So, to my relief and maybe a little bit my surprise, it did prove to be what I was called to."

Holleran was part of a group of eight individuals, including two priests and two bishops, who formed what came to be called the LGBTQ Interparish Collaborative, which seeks to build greater acceptance of the gay community in the New York metropolitan area. "It's not very flashy and it's not confrontational," said Holleran, who was still involved two decades later. "It simply tries to work within the structure [of the Church] to encourage Catholics to treat the gay community with compassion, respect, and sensitivity, which are words taken directly from the catechism of the Catholic Church.

"And that's what contemplation is for," he continued. "That's what it's supposed to foster and nourish in us, is the ability to let go of our preconceived notions and our defenses, to actually be present, and to hear, and to commune with people of different races, different sexual orientations, different religions, and to be changed by that experience. That requires a lot of letting down defenses and only contemplation can do that."

Around the corner from St. Joseph's Church was the Still Mind Zendo, cofounded by Father Bob Kennedy, the Jesuit from whom Holleran had taken that course on Eastern religions back in college at Fordham. Kennedy had spent eight years in Japan and was now also a *roshi*, or senior teacher, of Zen Buddhism. It wasn't long before they reconnected and Holleran began studying Zen.

"It's amazing how that's happened throughout the years," he said, looking back. "I just get put in exactly the place I needed to be to move forward and to grow. Call that providence, synchronicity, or whatever, but it's quite astonishing." In 2009, the year Holleran's father died, Kennedy gave him dharma transmission as a sensei, or teacher, in the White Plum Asanga of the Zen tradition. That same year, Holleran formally transferred from the Carthusian Order to the Archdiocese of New York as a parish priest.

Holleran's decades of intense contemplation left him with the conviction, deep in his soul, that, as the great Hindu mystic Ramakrishna said, "God has made religions to suit different aspirants, times and countries. All doctrines are only so many paths."[24]

"I'm convinced, through experience and study, that they all do converge eventually, into the unknown, into the unknowable, into the un-sayable, into the immense mystery from which they all proceed and toward which they all merge," he told me. "We need to stop arguing about whose finger's pointing more directly at the moon and [say], 'Ah, come on, get over yourself, look at the moon.' Follow whichever path or paths help you to look at the moon and just be dazzled by that and be also subsumed into it."

Catholicism's mystic quest to gather knowledge from other traditions traces back to the Desert Fathers in the first centuries after Christ. The scholar Origen of Alexandria sought out the "wisdom of the rulers of this world"—from the Hermetic writings of Egypt to the teachings of the Chaldeans, Indians, and Greeks. Such "mystical, magical, occult tributaries" were "enthusiastically" embraced by "poets, painters and theologians" of the early and high Middle Ages, flowing naturally into "a unity of Christian contemplation," wrote Cardinal Hans Ur von Balthasar shortly before he died in 1988.[25]

The embrace of such tributaries had defined Michael Holleran since he emerged from his monastery cell. "I find substantial nourishment in other traditions," Holleran said of his spiritual journey. "We discover the splendor in many places. And the splendor reveals itself to us, in many places. And when we discover that they all work together towards one splendor, we are enthusiastic about it, and we want to share that." He considered it his "mission to spread the contemplative traditions of the world."

Since his teen years, Holleran, fluent in Latin, Greek, and Hebrew, had read widely and voraciously. When asked about his greatest influence, he was hard-pressed to answer. "I read Gregory of Nyssa on my own in the original Greek commentary on *Song of*

Songs back when I was in college," he said, referring to the fourth century Cappadocian saint. "But the influences have been so vast. Medieval influences, classical influences, fathers of the church." And then came Zen and the Kundalini practices of a Chinese-Filipino master of Prana healing, Choa Kok Sui, whose teachings he studied for more than a decade. "Eventually you make your own synthesis of all those things," he said, summing up his spiritual journey.

That synthesis ultimately led Holleran to become a practitioner of "double belonging," an approach championed by theologian and former priest Paul Knitter, in which the practitioner is "nourished" by more than one religious tradition, or, as Knitter puts it, learns "to be religious inter-religiously."[26]

To Holleran, there was no contradiction between being a Catholic priest and a Zen teacher. For him, the practices are synergistic. But he was careful to note that he had not gone through the formal steps of becoming a Buddhist, which involves "taking refuge" in the Buddha, the dharma, and the sangha, or community of Buddhists. "If you say a Buddhist is someone who follows the great insights of the Buddha, well, yes, that's true. I can say that of many traditions, but to consider myself formally in this world, institutionally, a Buddhist, that's not true. I'm a Catholic priest, and that's where I root. That's the trunk of my tree, at least in the worldly sense. I'm rooted in God." But he finds that Christianity is "high in inspiration, but low on technique; long on ideals and content, but short on method."[27] It is that search for method that sent Holleran into the embrace of Buddhist meditation.

"There's always a tension between people at the depths—people who have a deep, contemplative, prayer life—and institutional authority, because you can't control them," observed Sister Margaret Galliardi, the Dominican nun who also practiced Zen. She gave the example of Teresa of Avila and other Medieval mystics. "I think my experience of Michael is that."

So how had Holleran managed to avoid the crossfire? "I think he's under the radar because he doesn't have any kind of an academic position where he's out there in front, writing things," Knitter told me. "He's careful, but he'll stand up when he needs to."

Holleran said that while "I've traveled my own path in terms of the esoteric tradition," he had never been subject to any overt pushback from the Catholic Church leadership. "It's a *live and let live*, kind of thing," he told me. "They never saw it as straying." In fact, when he first started exploring Zen, he was sharing a parish rectory with the retired Cardinal Archbishop of New York. "He was interested in what I was doing." Even the incumbent archbishop, at the time we spoke, "certainly respects me and trusts me. He doesn't cause any difficulty. So officially, there hasn't been any opposition to me; I've been lucky that way."

At the end of the day, Knitter said, the reality was that what Holleran taught about the nature of Christ and the value of techniques and insights from other traditions "are views that are represented by a significant number of contemporary Roman Catholic theologians. The problem is, it's not getting through to the people."

A respect for Eastern thought is embedded in the modern Christian contemplative movement, which owes much to Buddhism and Hinduism. In the 1970s, in response to a flight from the Church of young Catholics who were exploring Eastern meditation, Pope Paul VI asked monastic orders to find ways to revive and popularize traditional Catholic mystic traditions that had suffered what Thomas Merton once described as "almost complete extinction" in the nineteenth century.[28]

Thomas Keating, abbot of the Trappist monastery where Holleran did a retreat as a young priest, invited Buddhist masters, Hindu holy men, and teachers of transcendental meditation, which is based on Hindu-Vedic traditions, to share with his monastic colleagues their techniques and experiences. These sessions inspired the monastics to reexamine ancient Christian approaches to contemplation, such as those described in *The Cloud of Unknowing*, which they distilled into what came to be known as the Centering Prayer. Keating would go on to host a series of interreligious dialogues—the Snowmass Conference—that would outline a set of principles that transcended religious doctrine, central of which was the premise that:

> The world religions bear witness to the experience of Ultimate Reality to which they give various names: Brahman, Allah, Absolute, God, Great Spirit; Ultimate Reality cannot be limited by any name or concept.[29]

At the same time, Eastern meditation provided the foundation for a corollary to the Centering Prayer movement, which came to be known as Christian meditation.

Hindu and Buddhist meditation is often based on the repetition of mantras, such as the ubiquitous "OM," popularized through yoga in the West, and the Tibetan mantra of compassion, *"Om mani padme hung."* Irish Benedictine monk John Main, who learned mantra mediation from a Hindu swami when he was serving in Malaysia, adapted this to Christian meditation; Buddhist and Hindu mantras were replaced by *"Maranatha,"* which means "Come, Lord!" and is the last word of the Bible's Book of Revelation.

A third link between Catholic and Eastern contemplative traditions is found in the "Interspirituality" movement, pioneered by Thomas Merton and Bede Griffiths, a Benedictine monk who travelled to India in 1955 and became a "Christian yogi." The movement is based on the idea of a "shared mystic heart beating in the center of the world's deepest spiritual traditions."[30]

Griffiths saw the signposts of religion as a two-edged sword. "As long as we remain in this world we need these signs," but it is "fatal is to stop at the sign, to mistake the sign for the ultimate reality," he wrote.[31] Holleran put it another way: "If you're clinging to a concept of ultimate reality, you can wind up an idolator, because that's not the reality," he told me.

Griffiths considered himself a *sannyasi*, which he defined as "one who is called to witness to this truth of the Reality beyond the signs, to be a sign of that which is beyond signs."[32] The term might likewise be applied to Holleran, whose talks are liberally seeded with references to great masters and obscure philosophers of the world's religions. Emblematic was a February 2022 *teisho* he gave in New Jersey. Holleran was presenting to a Zen audience a passage from Catholic mystic Bernadette Roberts, who wrote that at the ultimate stage of the mystic experience "oneness has gone—gone and taken the whole self-experience with It."[33]

"Physical perception remains, but it's not the self who is doing it," Holleran told those gathered at the Long Island zendo. "That sounds pretty scary. [Roberts] says, 'Fear is a function of your Self and so when there is no self, there is nothing to be scared of. There only remains the intensity of act.'" Holleran's tone of voice shifted; we were now hearing *his* insight: "It's way beyond the mind, that's why there's no mind. Only Buddha mind. So there only remains the intensity of the act. *Pure* doing,'" Holleran told the group, his quintessentially Irish face widening in wonder. "This is like *wu wei* and Daoism," he continued, referring to the concept of effortless action. "The Dao does nothing. There's no agent. No actor. No done. There's just doing. Pure doing. But everything gets done. The irony is that that's exactly the way scholastic theology and Aristotle and St. Thomas described God, describe the absolutely reality. *Pure act.*" What his voice, with its hint of a Long Island accent, lacked in natural power was made up in technique. Since his decades living largely in silence, Holleran had perfected a style of presentation that artfully used his intonation to capture the audience, hold their attention, and powerfully drive home his message.

He continued: "Losing self or being totally connected to God, that has everything 'that is,' as Roberts says—theologians would never understand that, but mystics would. God is everything that exists, you can look around and see that doesn't suppress perceptions, at all. It's not *your* sense perception anymore but it's there. And, of course, in Zen experience, we realize the experience to which its privy is everything. Totally connected! No self. No separation. As one of the great Zen masters, Shin'ichi Hisamatsu, puts it," Holleran's voice rose: "'The world! Formless and boundless! Nothing! No self, and no Buddha.'" He continued in own voice: "And what does that look like? It's just reality! It doesn't suppress the trees. Or the animals. Or individuality. It just suppresses the self. There's no more self, no more Buddha to be relative to the self. It's just reality. Pure! Dynamic. Moments of everything that is ..." He punched each word, his voice rising to crescendo, "... right NOW! Bernadette describes this ultimate reality as the smile. Not a smiler or a smiled at. Just *smile*. All spontaneous. That's the very nature of reality itself. Hmm? I'm reminded of Dogan's famous statement, 'In the beginning there are mountains and rivers, and later when you get enlightened, they just disappear. And in the end, there's just mountains and rivers that you can experience right now. No self anymore. It's just experience with a capital *E*."

Holleran closed the teisho by reciting one of the last poems written by the renowned Catholic monk Thomas Keating, author of the Centering Prayer:

> *Only the Divine matters,*
> *And because the Divine matters,*
> *Everything matters.*

"That's the great liberation," he told the group. "*Everything* matters. And *you're* everything. Because everything is God, and that's who you are. Nothing but Buddha."

Absorbing the insights of leading thinkers in other religions can add nuance, but religious teachers of many traditions have warned that to sample from a variety of religions is to court spiritual disaster. More than one has called it "spiritual promiscuity." To Holleran, it's all a matter of context. "I would say, do find a path and stick to it, yes. But that very path might open you up, or your own life experience may open you up to also investigating another path. I find substantial nourishment in other traditions." The key, he said, is being rooted in one tradition, then opening oneself to inspiration from others, rather than wandering through the spiritual supermarket and grabbing ingredients on different aisles. "It's more that we discover the splendor in many places. And the splendor reveals itself to us, in many places. And when we discover that they all work together towards one splendor, we are enthusiastic about it, and we want to share that."

"The Lord will surprise you. Turn your world upside down. He certainly did mine." Father Michael Holleran stood beside the altar in the Grotto of the Church of Notre Dame on New York's Upper West Side, forty-five years to the day since he had taken his vows as a Carthusian monk. The backdrop was dramatic. A statue of Mary perched on a pedestal high above his left shoulder, set against raw stone. The setting was appropriate. The chapel where Holleran was celebrating the Feast of the Presentation of the Blessed Virgin Mary in a midday mass was an exact replica of the Grotto in Lourdes where the Heavenly Mother is said to have appeared to St. Bernadette in 1858. About thirty students from nearby Columbia University sat on the pews facing him.

Holleran's homily focused on the teaching that Catholics must follow Christ, the Lamb of God, wherever he goes. "It's not as easy as you think," he told the young Catholics gathered before him. "Because you say, 'Oh, I know where the lamb wants to lead me.' It's all been paved out. I have all the documents and all the catechism I need. I know where the Lord wants to lead me." He paused. "No, you *don't*. You can't just follow where social media tell you to go or even the Catholic media tell you to go. He may surprise you.

He *will* surprise you. That's why you have to learn to discern his voice *in* you. His smile *in* you. His heart *in* you. So that you can let him be that in you. When you just follow your pious little self, that's not going to be enough."

The admonishment—"pious little self"—seemed a bit harsh. I asked him about it later, over lunch. The parishioners, he told me, were a group of what he characterized as "right-wing" Catholic students from Columbia University who were overly impressed by their own piousness. I told him that explained the rapturous smile that never left the face of the girl seated next to me during the mass. "Oh, yeah, that drives me nuts," he said, rolling his eyes. Holleran had only recently been transferred to Notre Dame as part of a consolidation of New York City parishes. The students knew about his role advocating for LGBTQ+ rights in the Church, and they weren't happy. "We're still trying to figure each other out," he told me. "I'm trying to figure out how to best reach them, and they're trying to get their heads around this priest who advocates for gays and preaches about other religions but spent twenty years in a monastery and sings Gregorian chants in mass."

The students embodied what Holleran saw as a growing conservative trend among young Catholics, encouraged by Opus Dei, the controversial, ultra-conservative movement. Emblematic of that encouragement, Opus Dei had recently made a large contribution to renovate Notre Dame and the attached rectory, where Holleran had lived for the past thirty years, forcing him to move to new, temporary quarters as he prepared for retirement. The move seemed symbolic: a literalist Church, where the written catechism silenced the voice within, no longer felt like home to this mystic insurgent.

I asked him if he regretted leaving the monastery so many years before. "No, the time was right." Just as the time was now right to leave the employ of the Archdiocese of New York and return to a life of contemplation. His hope was to establish a small retreat center or take up residence at an existing sanctuary, spending his remaining years among those who shared his joy exploring the ultimate unknown.

In his Catholic homilies, Zen dharma talks, and our many conversations, Holleran frequently quoted others: whether epistles from the Apostles, teachings of Buddhist masters, or the writings of modern mystics, weaving around them his own insights and elaboration. He rarely spoke of his own mystic experiences. But in one of our final conversations for this book, I asked him about a passing comment he had made years earlier about angelology—the study of angels—as being something that was "very powerful" for him. "Why?" I asked. His answer offered an illuminating perspective on Holleran's interior life.

"Once the spiritual world opens up to you and you discover the vastness and the energetic power of it, what you discover are these beings," he replied, almost matter-of-factly. "All of the traditions in one form or another attest to it, certainly the Judeo-Christian tradition, Islamic tradition, of course there are the *bodhisattvas*," Buddhist enlightened beings such as "Manjushri and Samantabhadra, these powerful forces. *You're there* and this is where they *live*," Holleran chuckled, recognizing how this would sound to someone who had not experienced a mystical encounter. "So, you're in communion with them, you meet them, and they become powerful companions, intercessors, aides, inspirers, encouragers, and then you share their own spiritual essence and power.

"So, it's just meeting the inhabitants of the various realms as you traverse them, and they become permanent ..." He paused, reaching for a word, "well, *friends* really, and companions on the journey, and it's just so wonderful because they're such magnificent beings. It's a shame that more people aren't aware of them and in contact with them and in communion with them because they are so powerful, and it becomes one of the great joys of life, you know? You have your human friends. You have your love of nature, et cetera, but this is ..." his voice trailed off, allowing me to imagine the mystical interactions. "They're friends and they're also nature at a higher level. So how can you not want to discover that and fall in love with it?"

Primary among these spiritual "friends," Holleran told me, was his namesake, the Archangel Michael. "Of course, even calling them by human names is an adaptation already on our part." He mentioned the Biblical story of Jacob wrestling with an angel. "Jacob asks his name, and the angel says, 'Why do you ask my name? It's too wonderful. You can't pronounce it.' So that's the first thing you have to realize; these are already adaptations."

The encounters, he told me, were wide and varied. "There are different species, different types of celestial beings. Of course, angelic spirits. There are also ascended masters, the ascended saints, and other celestial beings; they're not angelic, they're within our cosmic space and time but in different dimensions. These are all inhabitants of the spiritual world that you can meet, and I think I've met all kinds; and you can sense a difference; and it's also how they present themselves. So again, it's part of the wonderful explorations you can undertake."

Some of these beings, he explained, are encountered as the mystic moves through levels of consciousness. The connection with some entities can be triggered by a book or other forms of synchronicity. "There's an energetic exchange that you can sense when that happens. So, [the range of beings encountered] does broaden out as you go forward, but it's not like you're looking under rocks trying to find new ones. At the right time, in various ways, it gets revealed to you. In the end, all of these work together, and they're very selfless. They don't care who gets credit [for the insights they communicate] or whether they're named or anything like that. So that's an important element to understand. The authenticity of it's really humbling, you know?"

Holleran almost made it sound as if interacting with spiritual beings was an everyday occurrence. For him, it was. Each morning, he explained, he recited Carthusian rite prayers in Latin, sang Gregorian chants, then engaged in a *kundalini* practice he learned from a Chinese-Filipino Prana healing master that allowed him to raise his energies to a point where he could penetrate the thin veil between the physical and spiritual realms. He then recited in Hebrew the climactic conclusion of the Books of Psalms, which "has blossomed into this connection with all those spiritual beings."

At the end of the session, "I just wave to and, I hope, experience, the Dhyani-Buddha," he continued, referring to the five primordial Buddha families, "that I find to be very, very helpful and rich energies, which I integrate into my prayer every day. It's just part of my spiritual ascent and descent back down." He added, almost matter-of-factly, "And it's very, very nourishing and very, very satisfying."

This is an age when bookstores are filled with teachings channeled from angels, ascended "masters," assorted spirit guides, and enlightened aliens, as well as various supposed "conversations with God." "How does anyone separate the spiritual wheat from the opportunistic chaff, or worse?" I asked.

"The main way we discern the validity of it—and all of the traditions are unanimous on this—is by asking, 'Is it making us compassionate, joyful, and peaceful? Is it energizing us? Is it affirming us? Is it making us affirm others? Is it making us affirm the universe? Is it really transforming us in what we call in Christianity, the heart of Christ? Is it the fruits of the spirit, love, joy, peace? What is the effect that it's having on you, interiorly, and on your life?'" he continued. "And that's how you can judge what energies you're connecting to, because there are negative energies out there, which you can call demons or whatever you want. They are very real. You only have to look at history or look at your own life."

Father Michael Holleran had tears in his eyes. "I just learned that one of my closest priest friends, the pastor of a parish on Staten Island, died this morning of the virus," he said quietly, the words catching in his throat. "We thought he was recovering."

It was April 2020, the height of the coronavirus crisis in New York City. Father Holleran, then seventy years old, sat at the epicenter on the Upper West Side. His rectory shared a wall with Mount Sinai Morningside Hospital. Refrigerator trucks stood vigil waiting for the dead outside his window. He was on call to give comfort to the families of the dying.

"I'm able to stay calm and spiritually grounded," he told me in a soft voice, "but still, it's a terrible drain, emotionally and astrally. Plus, you're living with a specter; this could be you in a few days."

As he contemplated the suffering and death outside his rectory window, Michael Holleran saw Covid as "an initiation rite" that he hoped would be a harbinger of a radical shift in the perspectives of humankind. "We really have to engage in mutation, transformation," he told me. "None of this namby-pamby New Age self-actualization kind of stuff. We have to be mystically transformed. It's crucial. Not just for the happiness or the advancement, but for the survival of the planet, of civilization. [We have to] live at a level of depth where you not only assure your own happiness but assure the happiness of the whole community and the whole planet at the same time."

I mentioned the Buddhist prayer, "May all beings have happiness and the causes of happiness."

"Well, exactly," he responded. "That's what I dedicate my life to, that's what I consider my life's mission to be. That's what I'm here to share."

I returned to the death of his friend, wondering aloud why he was so sad, given his depth of faith and personal experience of the divine. "The sadness, if you like, it's part of the compassion, part of the sense of loss of the preciousness," he said quietly. "The most profound statement I ever heard is that there's only one joy, and there's only one sadness. And they're the same thing. That's what it feels like. That's God's way of being. So even God sheds the tears and laughs the laugh and dances the dance. And it's all one. Whether we don't get the virus at all or whether we die of the virus, resurrection will follow."

He paused for a moment, looking off into the distance, then replied with what might almost be considered a *koan*: "If you die before you die, you won't die when you die."

He gave me a moment to absorb that, then continued. "As St. Paul says, 'We should be in the habit of dying every day'; as Zen puts it, 'Dying is every moment.' So that when it comes to the physical death, that should be a piece of cake."

His voice was almost wistful. "Expansion into a whole new realm of consciousness …"

At the Feet of the Mother

Ram Alexander, Atmananda, and the joy of the Guru

"I am whatever you conceive, think, or say ... This body is the material embodiment of all your thoughts and ideas. You all wanted it, and you have it now."

Sri Anandamayee Ma

There is no relationship more fundamental to the spiritual quest in most mystic traditions than that of the guru and disciple. It is far more profound than that of priest and parishioner or Reformed rabbi and student. Like the priest or rabbi, the guru conveys spiritual teachings and models spiritual behavior, but practitioners of these mystic traditions believe it is through a direct psychic connection that the guru alters the energetic fabric of the student, enabling her or him to break through blockages and open the way to spiritual attainment.

On the most esoteric level, the guru represents an external manifestation of the Divine within the student, whether he or she calls it Brahma, God, Buddha, Allah, or simply the One. Spiritual seekers may have many teachers, but they will likely have only one true guru with whom, these traditions believe, they have deep karmic ties. Those ties bind the student to the teacher and, sometimes, the teacher's disciples to each other.

"When the student is ready, the teacher will come." It's almost a mantra, repeated across countless traditions. The phrase is part reassurance for the anxious spiritual seeker and part admonishment, reminding her or him that they must do the difficult work that prepares the ground for the arrival of the spiritual guide.

Seventeen-year-old Lee Alexander wasn't looking for a guru when he sat down beside the lake at his rural Texas boarding school in 1966. And he certainly wasn't planning a spiritual quest. He simply needed to knock out a school essay. Alexander opened his notebook and asked himself, "What is truth?"

"I was just going to write, 'Truth is blah, blah, blah,' finished," he recalled a half century later. "And very, very quickly I went into a state where I said, 'My God, I don't know what truth is.' And then I looked at my hand and I said, 'I have this hand. If I tell my fingers to move, they move. So, I'm going to call this thing me, this body, because I can control it.' And then I said, 'Oh my God, but then what's all this other stuff out there? Because it's not me, and I can't control it.' And somehow, I got into a state where I said, 'I don't even know if that's really there, because I have no control over it.'"

Idle teenage philosophizing soon gave way to a headlong plunge down an existential rabbit hole. "I was the One and the many simultaneously. And I could know anything because I was *That*," he said, using a term synonymous with universal consciousness. "But I could retain a separateness that wasn't really separate. So, I could know what a tree was. I could be the tree. I could be the inception of the tree from the moment of the Big Bang and how this tree came out. But it was all natural and organic. I could just know it, and I could be it. And so, I played around with that. I could know what Billy the Kid was saying to Pat Garrett at 2:45 in the afternoon in 1885, and I could be both Billy and Pat and myself, of course. But it was all one. And I said, 'Oh, that's all well and good, but what is that beyond which there is nothing more that can be known?'"

He perceived himself as a drop of water in an infinite ocean and then sensed he was going to die: "I said, 'No problem. I just want to know what's out there. And either I know, or I die. And either way, I win, because there's no point really in being here if you can't know what the ultimate nature of truth is.'"

Alexander instinctively crossed his legs into *padmasana*, the classic yogic lotus pose that he had once seen on TV. And then he blacked out. "It was a state of pure ecstasy." Eventually, he regained consciousness. As he began to walk back to his dorm, he heard a voice in his head that said, "This is the purpose of life. There is no other real purpose. The purpose of life is to know this. And every human being at some point has to know this to fulfill the purpose of life. All you can do is help in some small way whoever you meet, or whatever situation you're in, at that moment."

The tent pegs of his life uprooted, Alexander careened through the next few years. In the immediate aftermath of the numinous experience, his ego kicked in. "And it said, 'Hey, guess what? This doesn't happen to everybody, you know. You're special.' I said, 'Well, there's Moses, there's Jesus, there's Buddha, and me.'" High school seemed pointless, but he managed to graduate. He hit the road, bouncing between several universities, buddying up with a small-time drug dealer and pimp called "Cross Country Slim" in Washington, D.C., and ricocheting through a series of bad relationships. "I was nuts," he said, looking back. "I was schizophrenic. I

mean, I was losing it. I was going on manic highs and manic lows."
All the time, he was desperately trying to recreate his encounter
with the ethereal. To get back there, he cobbled together his own
form of meditation, thinking, "Yeah, well that must be how it works
somehow." At a party, he happened to run into a woman who was
a Transcendental Meditation practitioner. She invited him to her
apartment. In her bedroom, she lit some incense on a shrine to the
founder of TM and told Alexander, "I have a feeling this is what you
need, so I'm going to initiate you."

"And she did," Alexander recalled, but it wasn't quite in the way
he was hoping. "She gives me a mantra—I didn't even know what
a mantra was—tells me to repeat it, and she does the little *puja* [re-
ligious offering ceremony] and gives the initiation. And then she
says, 'That's it. If you want to, you can make a donation.' So, I went
back to my room. I mean, I was in manic depressive state. And I just
sat down, and I started saying that mantra for many, many hours,
maybe all night long, because I liked it. It worked for me. And all I
know is that I got rid of the depression and the manic stuff in twenty-four hours. And that was it."

In a bookstore not long after, Alexander picked up a copy of the
Bhagavad Gita, a classic of Hindu philosophy, along with the *Yoga
Sutra of Patanjali*, a second century BC compilation considered the
foundational text of yoga. "I read both of them just nonstop. And
I said, 'Wow, this is the whole show. This is it. I've got to find out
where this stuff comes from.'"

It was at the feet of a beautiful and charismatic young Indian
woman that Lee Alexander would find his path. The meeting took
place a few days after he arrived in India in 1972. Alexander wasn't
looking for a guru; he already had one. He had spent the previous
few years immersed in America's nascent yoga scene, eventually
becoming a yoga teacher and disciple of Swami Satchidananda

Saraswati, who founded a network of spiritual communities and yoga studios in the U.S. and was best known as the Indian yogi with the big cottony beard who opened the Woodstock festival. Alexander had also sampled the smorgasbord of spiritual and hallucinogenic mind candy offered in America in the early '70s, from Sikhism to a New Agey Scientology spin-off, even delving into past life experiences, which he said helped "peel the onion of 'Who am I?'" But he longed for something more. "I don't want to be whoever the hell I was in my past life. I want *moksha* [liberation from the cycle of birth and death]," he told himself. "I want that beyond which there's nothing more to know, and I'm going to India."

Alexander signed up for a university trip to Taiwan and scored one of those round-the-world tickets that were so popular in the '70s. After a stop in Japan, he headed to India with no fixed plan, other than to experience its spiritual energy for a few months, with plans to then head on to Kabul, Kathmandu, and maybe Damascus or Istanbul.

Most of that ticket ended up going unused.

Arriving in India, Alexander reconnected with an old friend who he considered a kind of spiritual mentor. The friend told Alexander to meet him at the ashram of a female guru named Anandamayee Ma on the banks of the Ganges. When Alexander arrived, no one was there, but "I had this deep feeling; at last, I'd finally come home." Back in New Delhi, he found his friend. Ma and her entourage had moved on to a remote village. "He told me, 'We're going right now, but before you go, you have to shave your head and you have to wear these robes,' which were sort of sheets," he recalled with a laugh. "Because this guy was a pro, a sort of *swami* who knew Ma quite well. He was a character."

Dutifully shaved and attired, Alexander and his mentor rolled up to Ma's ashram in a bullock cart at midnight after a long train journey. It was pitch dark. They wondered what they were going to do. And then they saw Ma, who was about seventy-six years old at the time, sitting on the side of the road with several other people, as if waiting for them. "So, we slam on the brakes and jump out, and actually I wasn't sure which one was Ma." His friend pointed and told him to go bow to her. "So, I did it. And she takes some red powder on her finger and gives me what's called a *tilak* between the eyebrows," he recalled, referring to a mark used to honor guests. "And she also gives me a towel." Only later would he learn that Ma rarely touched anyone—particularly foreigners—and that the towels, which she wore on her head, were usually reserved as blessings for those with whom she had a particular connection. At the time, Alexander thought, "This is an odd custom they have, but I've only been in India two days, so let's see what happens."

What happened was that Alexander was thrown into the spiritual deep end. Ma was in the village, a major Hindu religious site, for a festival in which she was the main attraction.

Born Nirmala Sundari Devi in 1896 in a small village in what is now Bangladesh, Anandamayee Ma, the *Joy-Permeated Mother* as she was known, is said to have radiated spiritual intensity even as a child. In her teens, it is said she would enter *samadhi*—deep meditation—for days on end. A local religious man announced she was an incarnation of the Divine Mother, the primal creator, also known to Hindus as Kali Ma. By the time Alexander met Ma, she had come to be hailed as a saint in the ranks of the greatest Indian mystics; her devotees included countless Indian luminaries, including Mahatma Gandhi, Jawaharlal Nehru, and many influential spiritual leaders.

The essence of Ma's teaching was that all things are an emanation of God or "the One," and that all religions are aspects of the Truth: "There is nothing save He alone; everyone and everything is but a form of God."[1]

Ma consistently spoke of her body as nothing more than a vessel of convenience. The great Hindu yogi Paramahansa Yogananda wrote that in their first encounter, "I had instantly seen that the saint was in a high state of samadhi.[2] He asked her to tell him something about her life:

"Father, there is little to tell." She spread her graceful hands in a deprecatory gesture. "My consciousness has never associated itself with this temporary body. Before I came on this earth, Father, I was the same. As a little girl, I was the same. I grew into womanhood, but still I was the same. When the family in which I had been born made arrangements to have this body married, I was the same. And, Father, in front of you now, I am the same. Ever afterward, though the dance of creation change around me in the hall of eternity, I shall be the same."

Vijayananda, a French devotee who first met Ma in 1951 said, "From the beginning I had the conviction that I was looking at the Lord Himself incarnated in the body of a woman."[3]

The event that brought Alexander to Ma's spiritual embrace was the annual Durga Mother Goddess celebration, which drew hundreds of devotees from across India. For the next ten days, he was caught up in a frenzy of religious zeal as devotees offered themselves to statues of the Goddess, an aspect of Kali, and to Ma herself, who was believed to be an avatar, or physical emanation, of the Goddess. Amid wild drumming, the trumpeting of conch shells, and hundreds of women ululating in adulation, the air was electric with spiritual energy. At its epicenter was Ma. "So, I'm sitting there trying to meditate, trying to figure out what's going on," Alexander recalled. "I didn't come to India to meet Anandamayee Ma; I already had my guru in America. But I'm here, so let's see what it's all about." One evening, meditating amid the frenzy, "My mind becomes filled with horrible thoughts. Like when I say horrible thoughts, I mean, more horrible than even I could ever dream of. And this goes on for a couple of days." Alexander knew enough about Eastern spirituality to recognize it as part of a purification process. "And after a couple of days of the most horrible, horrible thoughts, you come out the other end and now you're ready to meditate. Your *pranic* [energetic] structure is changed. And there's an ability to hold that energy of meditation you didn't have before."

A few days into the festival, his friend was invited to a group audience with Ma and asked Alexander to come along. At first, he said, "No thanks. I have no questions. I have my guru in America." At the last minute, he changed his mind. The scene at the audience was chaotic. "There are all kinds of people around. You want to ask the most important question of your life and people are saying, 'Hurry up, hurry up, most busy.' And so I knew I didn't have much time." Through a translator, he tried to tell Ma about his Texas meditative experience and ask how to retain that level of awareness. "And all she said was, 'Repeat your mantra.' And it was something like 45 *crore* [million] times." The people around were very impressed, since Ma rarely gave instructions to strangers, but they said, 'Why is she telling him to repeat his mantra? She hasn't given him a mantra.'" The attendants were trying to move him along. "Hurry up, hurry up!' And I said, 'Okay, Ma, grant me the grace to never forget you.' That was it."

Alexander stayed on in the village after the festival, taking a room next to a nearby temple. He found he was suddenly able to meditate for at least six hours a day. Looking back, Alexander believes his years with his guru in America and his other explorations had laid the spiritual foundation that prepared him for this transition. "And then with Anandamayee Ma I could really do it because she saw, 'Hey, if I press this button and that button, this kid could probably do what many others couldn't.'"

Ma rarely remained in one place for long. She crisscrossed India meeting with her followers. For the next few months, Alexander followed. It was about being in her presence rather than the teachings themselves, since Ma spoke only Hindi and Bengali, which Alexander did not understand. "I just wanted to look at her because it was this transmission of energy," he told me. But his innate wanderlust and curiosity about what other teachers might offer eventually made him decide it was time to move on.

"I mentally said goodbye to Ma in the ashram. I said, 'I'm going now, Ma, I want to see the rest of India. I have to get to Kabul, so who knows if we'll ever meet again?' I go back to my room and I'm sick as a dog. I can hardly stand up." A doctor was called, diagnosed hepatitis, and ordered Alexander to get on a plane for home.

Back in the U.S., his fever eventually broke. Waking up, he began to re-examine his body as he did in that first Texas experience. "'I can move my hand.' Now I'm looking at it, and I'm saying, 'This is new. This is 100 percent new. Every molecule in my body is new.' For about half an hour I just kept going like that and saying, 'What's happened? Every molecule is new.' Talk about being reborn!" In his mind, it was a continuation of the purification process he had begun at the festival. "I understood this had to do with Ma, had to do with India. And perhaps with the fact that I had been bathing in the Ganges every day for about six weeks. Hindus believe that you're immersing yourself in a goddess."

Rejuvenated, Alexander drove up to Connecticut to see his guru, Swami Satchidananda, who knew he had just returned from India. "These popular swamis, they have their big projects, and they have all their slaves for what they call *karma* yoga. And you work for the organization and for the greater glory of the guru," Alexander explained, his voice thick with cynicism. Satchidananda offered him the "opportunity" to be caretaker at his private retreat center. Alexander moved into the artist studio on the property and began meditating as much as ten hours a day. He furnished the house with a large picture of the Swami and a smaller picture of Ma. But over the previous weeks, someone had planted in his mind seeds of doubt about the Swami, which began to gnaw at him.

"One day I'm looking at Ma's picture, and just spontaneously out of my frustration, I point at her and I say, 'If you can hear me, prove it.'" It was summer, and the patio doors were open. "And at that second, a whirlwind comes through the door that's about four feet tall and three feet across. And it spun around and around me a couple of times and scared the hell out of me. And I said, 'I believe

you. I believe you. Go away, leave me alone.' Papers were flying
everywhere. And I heard this kind of wild Kali-like laughter in my
head. To make a long story short, I was on the next plane to India."

When Alexander arrived at Ma's feet in 1972, he was welcomed
by a German woman whose own spiritual quest had begun a half
century before when Vienna lay in ruins after World War One. The
conflict had devastated the capital of the defeated Austro-Hungarian
Empire. Sixteen-year-old Blanca Schlamm struggled to understand
the insanity that had engulfed her world. Looking for answers, she
turned to the writings of medieval mystics and contemporary esoteric philosophers like Tolstoy and Herman Hesse. Their works
triggered something deep inside. As she walked through a Viennese
park in 1920, she took the first steps on what would become her
lifelong spiritual quest.

> Suddenly, all matter—trees, rocks, the sky, water—was vi-
> brantly alive and filled with a divine light in which there
> was no separation between the seer and the seen, but only
> an ecstatic unity which was, by definition, eternal love. For
> one timeless moment all this was overwhelmingly revealed
> to her and this revelation was to be the driving force of her
> life from then on.[4]

Encouraged by her father, who would later perish as a Jewish refugee in Nazi Germany, Schlamm embraced Theosophy, the dominant mystic movement of those postwar years. Its belief system was
based on the writings of the late Russian spiritualist and Theosophy cofounder Helen Blavatsky, who claimed to have studied under
gurus in India and Tibet. The movement's leaders purported to receive direction from a set of Tibetan Masters on a higher spiritual
plane. Schlamm moved to Amsterdam to work at the organization's

European headquarters and later to South India, where she taught at a school at the Theosophy world headquarters. She became devoted to Jiddu Krishnamurti, who the Theosophists proclaimed to be the prophesied "World Teacher" after he was found on a beach near Chennai as a child and adopted by the movement's then-president.

"I have found my happiness and my tranquility. Krishnaji has opened my heart," Schlamm wrote in her diary in 1927, referring to Krishnamurti. "There I stand completely stripped, alone with myself. ... For I have touched the Eternal, for one moment I have quenched my thirst at the deep fount of Life, I have caught a glimpse of Truth." But two years later Krishnamurti renounced Theosophy, declaring, "I do not want followers. My only concern is to set men absolutely, unconditionally free." The move sent Schlamm into a spiritual crisis. She ultimately broke with Theosophy, studying for a time with another renowned guru, Mahatma Sri Ramana Maharshi. She was briefly introduced to Ma, sometimes addressed as "Mataji" out of respect by her followers, but it was two years later, in 1945, that Schlamm had her first private audience with the woman who would become her guru. It changed her forever.

> What She said was so completely convincing that there was no room for doubt. In fact, I felt it was not another talking to me, but my higher Self conversing with my Self. This cannot be explained. It was an experience beyond words, but all the more real for that. What Mataji said was only the outer expression of something that took place simultaneously on a much deeper level.[5]

By the time Alexander met Schlamm, she had been with Ma for almost three decades and had been given the name Atmananda, which meant Bliss of the Self, following a profound initiatic experience. The pair felt an immediate familiarity. He was twenty-three, she was sixty-eight, but it was like a reunion of old friends. She taught him to cook for himself over a kerosene stove and wash his *dhoti* robes. He would come to consider her his "big grandmother." If they had not known each other before, their karma would soon be linked. At Atmananda's first meeting with Ma, the teacher had instructed her to keep a diary. "This will in time become the account of a mystic," Ma told her.[6] In 1984, Atmananda asked Alexander to read the journals and decide if they were worth publishing. After her death the following year, he began to review the handwritten volumes and quickly realized: "Even though it's her story, as far as I'm concerned, it's my story. Everything I ever wanted to say about Ma was handed to me by Atmananda." He edited and published the diaries as *Death Must Die*, a classic exploration of the making of a yogi.

When tens of thousands of people gather in a football stadium to hear the Dalai Lama or the Pope, they are not all Buddhists or Catholics. Nor have they necessarily come to learn about the religion. Whether consciously or not, they are there to bathe in the presence of these spiritual beings; to receive their blessings.

For Hindus, exposure to this spiritual energy is called *darshan*. "The profoundly magnetic spiritual presence of the Guru activates the spiritual center within the disciple, making him aware of the transcendent divinity within himself," Alexander wrote in *Death Must Die*.

The guru, Alexander told me in one of our many conversations, "isn't just a guy or a woman who happens to know a lot more about the topic than you do. This is a transformed individual who has brought that realization down into the molecular structure and then horizontally transmits it" to the student. To be in their presence triggers "a fundamental, energetic, molecular shift" that transforms the individual at the level of the DNA. "The external manifestation of the Saint awakens your own interior connection with divinity."

Back in India, Alexander immersed himself in Ma's darshan. Words were almost superfluous. "This silent communication [through her very presence] was Her principal teaching and this was not something that could be learned from a book," Alexander recalled. "It was an experience of overwhelming intensity which powerfully entrained the mind in the grooves of meditative absorption."

She gave him the name Ram, an incarnation of the god Vishnu whose mission was to annihilate evil. "Living and traveling with her ... one came to understand that energy can be transformed and 'divinized,' [and] the immense importance of wholly transformed individuals and sacred places of power that make up the mystic body of Mother India." That energetic integration with the guru is what produces the total surrender that non-practitioners find so hard to understand. "I just want to be an atom of Her body, so as to be with Her all the time. I am aching to be with Her, nothing else," Atmananda wrote in her diary. "I feel like crawling inside Her and ceasing to exist."[7]

"You met someone that's more you than you are yourself," Alexander explained. The guru, he told me, reflects your essential personality structure, rather than the superficial personality you have come to know. Students who, knowingly or not, have a deep spiritual connection with a teacher often find tears come to their eyes at the very thought of the guru. "You cry because you always knew it was there, but you never actually saw it face to face before. It's archetypal and it's utterly entrancing. It's the nature of divine love."

"But then who is the guru?" Alexander asked rhetorically. "It's the job of the guru to tell you who the guru is. And the guru is *you*, and the guru is who you truly are. And a *true* guru will never keep that a secret," he laughed. "That's their *job*. They may make you so attached to them that you can't sleep. You leave your family; everything goes because you're so madly in love with them. And then they will break that attachment completely and leave you with the truth of what the Hindus would call *Satcitananda*," the belief that all things are part of a single universal consciousness.

"They say, 'When the disciple is ready, the guru appears,' which is true, but the guru is always there, because it's sort of built into the whole show," Alexander said, punctuating the comment with a laugh that conveyed that it was all so obvious.

The act of *pranam*, bowing to the guru or a sacred image, is an outer display of that surrender. But on an esoteric level, pranam is also much more. Alexander recalled that Ma "often pointed out that in the act of bowing down, particularly to an exalted spiritual personage, a profound transmission of spiritual energy takes place—something utterly beyond the mind—that is the antithesis of anything debasing or humbling."

Ma told one group, "To pranam means to give one's mind to Him," meaning both the guru and God, "and to give oneself so that there should be only the 'one' and not the two; no other."[8]

"There is nothing but God; everything and everyone is only a form of God," Anandamayee Ma told her followers. "We can cry out to God but even that is actually done by God."[9] This is the notion of nonduality; there is no "you" and no "me." No student and no teacher. There is only *That*. It is *every* thing and it is *no* thing. Or in the words of the classic Vedic meditative inquiry, "Who am I?" *Neti neti*, Not this, neither that.

"I always said I wanted to do something called Atma *jihad*," Alexander told me, displaying his irreverence, "with the battle cry being 'neti neti' as you swing your saber and charge." Truly recognizing nonduality, Alexander continued more seriously, "When you understand that the true meaning of 'neti neti' means nothing exists except God, he said, "You see very clearly that the most important thing you can do for the benefit of all sentient beings is to spend your entire life cultivating this alchemical transformation, transforming matter into spirit via your own molecular structure so that you too can transmit better. You may never leave your room and maybe those awakenings are the greatest ones. It's not just that the transformation does good. It does the *supreme* good."

The vast majority of Ma's followers were Hindu and the Hindu dharma was at the heart of Ma's approach. But her true teachings, her followers believed, existed at a level far above religious doctrine. In fact, even her use of the label "God" was a device. For her, the "personalized gods" of organized religion—whether Brahma, Buddha, Allah, or "God the Father" of Christianity—were "like ice, different forms of what is really only [the] pure formlessness" of water: "When you become attracted and get in touch with a particular Divine form, as you become more absorbed in it, you one day find out that He is indeed the formless. Then you see that He is *sakara* [with form] as well as *nirakara* [without form], as well as beyond both."[10]

An Irish journalist once asked Ma what she would say to those who insisted their religion was the right one: "He is infinite, there is an infinite variety of conceptions of Him, an infinite variety of paths to Him. He is everything, every kind of belief and, also the disbelief of the atheist."[11]

When visitors from other traditions came to see her, Alexander and others reported, Ma had an uncanny ability to give them spiritual instruction specific to their belief system. "Her path was all paths," Alexander said. "Her mantras were all mantras. The way that she opened up for you was simply your way. Somehow, she knew exactly what your *sadhana* [spiritual practice] was when she looked at you. And she saw who you were on a spiritual level and what your background was. And she simply facilitated that to the max." As Melita Maschman, a German Ma devotee and contemporary of Atmananda, put it, "She wants everyone—inside or outside Hinduism— to follow their own path but to follow it to the ultimate goal." [12]

When he returned to India, Alexander immediately made his way to Ma. He wanted to tell her about the experience with the whirlwind in Connecticut. "As soon as Ma saw me, she said, 'I know all about it. I'll give you initiation in two weeks.'" He stayed with her for several months, reveling in her darshan and deepening his spiritual practice. Eventually, he decided it was time to go back to the U.S. He asked her for an audience. "I go to Ma and ask to speak with her privately. And this time it's like, 'How long do you want to talk? I'll give you six hours if you want.' I mean, it was just like the opposite of the first time. So," through a translator, "I asked her so many technical questions about meditation, and this, and this, and this, until I can't think of anything else to ask her. And then I say, 'Ma, I'm going back to America now.' And she says, '*acha*,' which is Hindi for okay. As I'm standing up to leave, I ask, 'Ma, is there something I can do for you in America?' And she says, 'If you want to do something for this body, stay here, and you can make a room for yourself in the new ashram we're building.' And then she says, 'But don't tell anybody I told you because this is an orthodox Brahmin ashram. It's not going to be easy for you, by the way.'"

Thus, began what Alexander calls his "radical surrender" to the woman he now recognized as his guru. "I ended up staying there for the better part of eight years. I would meditate seven, eight hours a day, every day. I loved it. You live beyond death, that's all I can say. You're doing this chronic purification. You're living with something that is beyond imagination at every second."

Fundamental to that purification was the process of stripping away the ego. "What does God do?" Ma was once asked by a follower. Her reply: "He eats the ego." This death of the ego is essential to penetrating the duality that prevents the student from a recognition that the True Self—the universality of existence—is buried beneath the false façade of the smaller Self, the *I*. "This ego death entails abandoning all of one's beliefs and concepts that make up one's passionately held idea of who one is," Alexander wrote in *Death Must Die*. Where conventional religion offers comfort, this process "sweeps away completely our conditioned identity and makes it seem as a corpse. ... This is not a placid mindlessness, but a state of radical clarity."[13]

It can be a painful process lasting years—or lifetimes—as the individual battles what Alexander called "the unceasing tricks of the ego as it desperately fights for its survival."[14] This is where the role of the spiritual guide is essential. "The transformative presence of a living guru is by definition a great threat to the status quo of the ego," Alexander told me.

The rigor of life in an ashram was the shared experience of a generation of Westerners who spent time in India's retreat centers in the twentieth century. "Ashram life is hell! It's *five* hells—five! And I can name them all," Simonetta Colonna de Cesaro, an Italian duchess and follower of another respected guru, Swami Chidananda Saraswati, told an interviewer in 1980. "Lack of running water, [the] cold, [the poor] food. The animals we have in our rooms; monkeys and famished dogs trying to get in; ants, scorpions, cockroaches, and flies already installed inside; mosquitos having feasted to their fill, waiting to get out." And then, she added, there is also a "much subtler hell ... having to live with other people" and, conversely, "the loneliness of ashram life."[15] It was precisely those "laboratory conditions" of the ashram, according to Alexander, that facilitated the alchemical transformation the guru sought to achieve.

When she invited him to move into the ashram, Ma warned Alexander that it was "not going to be easy" for him as a Westerner. While Ma had other Western students who would come for a few teachings and leave, Atmananda and Alexander were among a total of just five foreigners who lived within the ashram walls. There they faced a unique form of racism that had as much to do with their culture as the color of their skin. At root was Hinduism's highly developed esoteric science of vibrations. It is a much more conscious and systematic version of the Western notion of being "in tune" with one's surroundings, loved ones, or friends. Just as the guru's darshan—vibrational field—influences the disciple, so does everything from food to those with whom she or he comes into contact. For the sanyasis, the orthodox Hindu Brahmin renunciants who had gone into retreat behind the ashram walls, it was critical for everyone and everything to be vibrating at the same frequency, which facilitated intense meditation and the psychic connection with the guru. Anything that undermined that resonance was a threat to their spiritual attainment. Foreigners were fundamentally out of tune—in a literal sense—with this ethos.

Strict diet and extensive religious rituals were "believed to have a physiologically alchemical effect on both them and their environment, rendering them pure channels for the higher spiritual forces which maintain the equilibrium of their culture," Alexander told me. In such an environment "there is simply no place in this for the foreigner, who comes from completely outside the cosmological structure and whose physical presence is felt to disturb the spiritual harmony and thus to be, literally, polluting."

The foreigners living in the ashram were in a perpetual state of siege. "We all knew that Ma used these things for our purification," Alexander explained. "There was not the slightest doubt. Nevertheless, the people could be vicious at times," he said, laughing at the painful memory. "I mean they were hardcore racists, but Ma knew that. It was useful for her to let the Hindus vent their frustrations on us," he laughed again. "That was all part of our ego purification. I understood that, but most Westerners, you know, would not put up with it," which was why most just showed up for an occasional audience with Ma and then left.

The one saving grace for Alexander was that he didn't speak the local languages. Years before Ma had instructed him not to "waste his time" learning Hindi or Bengali, and instead focus on his sadhana. "That means I couldn't understand all the gossip about me," he said, smiling.

For Atmananda, a lone Western woman who moved into the ashram long before other Westerners began arriving on the scene, the strictures imposed on her by the Brahmin renunciants led to many conflicts and heartache, exacerbated by the fact that she *did* speak the local languages. "I cried my eyes out on the eve of my birthday," she wrote in her diary in 1947. "By mistake I set my foot on the veranda in an area where I am not allowed and thus polluted the eating arrangements of the sanyasis."[16]

But by 1952, she had come to recognize the ordeal as part of the process of stripping away her ego. "This evening somehow the whole humiliation of these seven years that I have lived in orthodox Hindu society arose before my eyes and I felt sore all over, like someone whose whole body has been scalded. How have I been able to put up with this, day and night, for all these years? But evidently it was necessary for me." She remembered what Ma had recently said: "How can you become Atmananda unless you can endure? You must have the power to bear what comes." Eventually, she would empathize with her tormentors. "To have three Europeans here quite upsets me," she wrote in March 1950, when visitors arrived. "I have become so attuned to the subtleness of the Brahminical vibration that I find the Western one quite jarring. For the first time I realize how these orthodox Hindus must be feeling when they have me there mixing with them."[17]

As Ma predicted, the ashram hierarchy had fought a rear-guard action to prevent Alexander from moving in, but finally construction on his tiny room inside the walls of the new ashram was about to begin. And Alexander was having cold feet, not just because he knew what Atmananda had endured. "I thought, if I move into this ashram, this is like being a Carthusian monk. They're gonna lock me in there and throw away the key basically. And even though I've been preparing for this for years, you know, I'm not sure I'm ready. You know, I'm not!"

He went to Ma and told her. "And she said, 'Look, wherever you go, whatever you do, your home will always be here.' And she meant herself obviously, but I think she also meant this place. I was completely disarmed. There was nowhere to go. There was nothing else to be done. That was it. We built the room. I moved in and then I started leading a much more focused, contemplative life. And I loved every second of it. And you know, after about two weeks, I was in the groove." Like that of the Carthusian monk, the day for a monk in Ma's ashram was largely devoted to meditation, reading scripture, and contemplation, with short breaks. There was one meal a day, which Alexander prepared for himself: "It's a very Brahmin thing; you don't want to eat something with someone else's vibration."

Alexander took to the ashram "like a fish to water," but when he hit "a dry spot" in his meditation, "you could just go and find her and be with her for a while." It was the ultimate energy reset. "Each time one went before Ma, it was a wholly new and original experience, a mini ego death in which one stood naked before the Eternal Truth of Being."[18]

If the guru is essential to the process of killing the ego, she is thus the greatest enemy of the ego. And the ego's greatest weapon against the guru is doubt.

"I have doubts about Ananadmayee. Is she really completely divine? It is impossible for me to know," Atmananda wrote in her diary in September 1945. "Yesterday, I felt Mother to be like the Christ, then it crumbled into doubt," she confessed the following spring. Even after Atmananda took a one-year leave from her job as a teacher to immerse herself completely in her sadhana, or spiritual pursuit, her ego retained its powerful grip. "I revolt and revolt. My ego doesn't want to be killed and I want to remain as I am." A few months later, she wrote, "I get periods of great faith and adoration followed by rebellion and reaction." And then, "There is a severe cancer in my mind. ... Against all reason and experience, I doubt Mother."[19]

By 1953, a full eight years after her first real meeting with Ma, Atmananda was beyond despair.

> At times I feel quite mad. I don't know anything anymore—who or what Mother is, though it cannot be denied that whenever one looks at Her one feels overwhelmingly: This is truly God. One can't help feeling it. In any case at least I know that I love her. But how can I even say that when I don't know what love is or what She is. How can I go on living like this? Until one truly knows oneself—the I—one cannot know anything at all. Lord have mercy upon me! How many times has one to wash one's feet in the blood of one's own heart. No, this is the last time. I realize that what I have done up to now is basically to deify my own ego and call it Mother. I mistook the picture I made of Her for the Reality that she is.

What Atmananda was enduring was what Alexander described as the "profound psychological catharsis" that "ruthlessly reveals the fundamental falseness of the conditioned conceptualizing mind through which one defines oneself and the world." Alexander blamed what he called "the supreme evil" of monotheism—"kill everybody that doesn't worship your goddamn ego's idea of the One True God"—for deifying the mental concept of God, and thus duality, thereby cementing the ego's hold on the mind in a *He* vs. *I* dichotomy. And as Alexander knew firsthand from his Texas experience, without the guru to beat back the ego, even a genuine spiritual revelation was likely to be hijacked: "The ego grabs a hold of it and says, 'Oh, this happened to *me*. It didn't happen to anybody else. I must be special.' That is death." It was the reason so many gurus gave the same instruction as Ma: "If you have any experiences in your meditation, don't bother about them."[20]

Like Atmananda—and virtually every spiritual seeker—Alexander also battled to keep his own doubts in check. Though Atmananda had studied under several other leading gurus in India before devoting herself to Ma, Alexander had only known the swami back in the U.S. In India, he realized saints seemed to manifest like mushrooms. But because he had gone straight into Ma's spiritual embrace, he had no one to whom he could compare Ma. Locked in his tiny room, Alexander sometimes couldn't help wondering if he had truly found *his* guru.

Sitting in a garden with Ma and a few attendants one day, he began to meditate, as he often did in her presence. "I was just absorbing this *rasa*, this divine nectar, and that's all I cared about, you know? And at a certain point I went into this timeless state in which I had this thought," he recounted. "Ma," he told her silently,

I've been with you now for several years and it's been wonderful. It's been an utterly divine adventure, but maybe there's something else out there. Maybe there's a better adventure. And at that point, I went into this state, this very subtle, gentle, altered state, where I experienced every desire and every adventure I could possibly ever imagine having, and I actually lived through each adventure in a timeless moment. I exhausted myself with adventures and Ma was in my head and she said, "Come on, come on. Think of something else. I want to get all of this out. You must have one more desire, one more adventure, just do it. You know, let's do it together."

Eventually, Alexander opened his eyes. Darkness had fallen. Ma stood up with her attendants and Alexander fell into step beside her. "I'm in kind of a daze," he recalled. Ma was holding a flashlight, "and she shines it right in my eyes, and she asks, '*Theek hai?*' meaning, 'Is it okay?' And [she] burst out laughing. That's what she used to do," Alexander chuckled. "Nobody else had a clue what was going on. But I had this understanding that all adventure, all desires, are the nature of the mind, and that the ultimate adventure is beyond the mind. And that Ma held the key to that adventure."

On August 27, 1982, eighty-six-year-old Anandamayee Ma left her body after a slow physical decline. The woman one leading yogi had called "the most perfect flower the Indian soil has produced" was no more in the physical form. "Death means changing one's apparel," she had often told her devotees.[21] Thousands, including then-Prime Minister Indira Gandhi, flocked to her funeral on the banks of the Ganges.

For Alexander, the months that followed were a time of transition. He missed the physical presence of his teacher, but he took to heart her teachings; disciples who pined for their guru after her death had missed the whole point. He knew that the very idea of death must die.

Alexander's life had also taken a new turn in the form of a relationship with a young American woman, who he would eventually marry. She was the student of a guru who lived not far from Ma's ashram. Alexander doesn't think he could have remained at the ashram without Ma's physical presence if he had not met Parvati. "Maybe Ma set me up. I don't know. I've never worked that one out," he said, grinning.

With his long white hair, unruly beard, and irreverent laugh, Alexander came across as an aging surfer meets trickster. Ma taught that all existence was just *leela*, theater. The elf-like mischievous glint in Alexander's eye and permanent hint of amusement in his high-pitched voice four decades after the death of his guru telegraphed the sense that Alexander saw life as a play conducted for his entertainment. None of it really mattered and he was just here to enjoy the show. Regaling a listener with tales of stumbling on The Beatles' rock-star-status guru alone in his empty ashram—"he vibrated like a used car salesman"—or riding elephants with fifty

stoned yogis clad in nothing by loincloths, it was clear that his inner
Deadhead was bemused by what a long, strange trip it had been.

For someone whose self-proclaimed "job" was to shed his ego,
Alexander still retained a healthy dose of *Self*. But he was self-
aware enough to make light of it. Serious yogis are often reticent to
share much of their interior experiences. One person I had hoped to
interview for this book refused, saying, "God knows my story, and
he's probably bored with it." Alexander had a slightly different take:
"I always thought it was a kind of secret and you're not supposed
to talk about these things, but now I'm so old and I don't care about
secrets anymore." He paused and laughed. "I'm ready to spill the
beans." He thought Ma would approve. "She kind of wants me to
shoot my mouth off a little bit at this time in my life. So, I can be
a little more garrulous than I would normally be," though it's hard
to imagine an Alexander who was not garrulous. But he did have a
motive for speaking to me: Having been nudged down his spiritual
path by books at various times in his life—from the *Upanishads*
to the Medieval Christian *Cloud of Unknowing*—Alexander knew
the power of books to help influence others on their journey toward
"radical surrender," and the will to "generate that passion to act"
which, he said, "is the whole show." Some of his comments might
be misconstrued as boasting, but they were framed by a deep sense
of gratitude for the opportunity he had been given. "To be with her
was to be in another dimension all the time. And it's like for almost
ten years, my feet never touched the ground. You had to pay; she
put you through a lot of tests before she let you in to actually stay
there with her. And you had to be more or less stark, raving mad to
pass the test, and I qualified."

There was a certain awe in Alexander's voice as he thought back
on his years in Ma's ashram. "I had this training that most people
can't imagine, because most people aren't gonna do it because in
order to get it; you have to pay a serious price to get through the
door," he said with a self-depreciating laugh. "And there's a lot of
testing to see if you're that mad enough that you're really gonna

put up with it, and your ego gets just trashed to the limit on a daily basis. And on the other hand, on a daily basis, you are encountering and entering into this extraordinary relationship with divinity. And that's a big part of the training, this kind of attachment to divinity rather than to your own ego." He paused in thought. "I'm not about to say that I lost my ego, but I let go of it."

His guru no longer in the flesh, Alexander eventually left India. After short stays in Wales, California, Washington state, and Hawaii, he and Parvati found themselves wandering through Europe visiting Catholic shrines. "I could go to these shrines, especially to Mary, and I felt this tremendous *shakti*," he recalled, using the Hindu term for divine power, "and it was just like being with Anandamayee Ma. I became addicted to these shrines, and I just wanted to go from one shrine to the next." In Assisi, home to the great Catholic mystic Saint Francis, they met someone who offered them the unlimited, open-ended use of a fifty-acre farm set in an isolated valley facing Mt. Subasio, the holy mountain where hermits have stayed for centuries. They eventually settled in the stone farmhouse. "The dharma provides and protects," Alexander told me with a grin. That had been the case since the day back at the ashram when he went to Ma and told her he wanted to give her everything he owned. "I was at the peak of my devotional fervor to Ma and radical renunciation to where I just couldn't sleep. It was so intense. It wasn't a mental idea. It was more of a deep, emotional intensity that was part of this whole process. I said, 'Ma, I want to renounce everything.' And I said, 'One day I may have some inheritance. I don't want any of it. I don't wanna know anything about it, and I want you to take it.' And she probably saw that I was never gonna take no for an answer, and I might do something extremely rash. And so, she said, 'Okay, I accept it, but now I want you to look after it for me; you're the custodian.' So ever since then, I've never had any financial problems. Invariably, whenever I'm about to go under financially, I'll get a phone call."

Despite his decade at Ananadmayee Ma's ashram and the many years of practice since, Ram Alexander considered himself a failure. The way he saw it, he "slipped on a banana peel" on his spiritual path. That banana peel was Ma's death. Even though he continued to feel deeply connected with Ma; even though he had internalized the teaching that there is no individual, there is only That; even though he was completely convinced "Ma is not other than one's Self—the most essential and true part of all of us";[22] he missed the anchor and inspiration of her physical presence.

"I didn't get there in terms of my initial desire to be a, you know, Milarepa," he told me with a self-depreciating laugh, referring to the famous Buddhist yogi. "But yeah, you really need the protection of the guru not to go off on a tangent, especially as you get more advanced in the sadhana process." In some ways, Ma had become his crutch. "This is the problem with the great Saints. Their presence is so powerful that they can radiate it to a large number of people and those people are really in the light while the guru is physically present, because it's so powerful. You almost get spoiled by having such an accessible deity right next to you. And then they go away, and people get lost again. You fall back to earth. It's not, it's not fun," he said, his face clouding. "In my case, at least I had somebody, I had a companion to be lost with. Maybe that's why I went to the direction I went in," he said of his relationship with Parvati, "because the guru was definitely going and what was I gonna do when the guru wasn't there?"

If Ma had not died, Alexander was convinced he would still be meditating in his little room in the ashram, but he was philosophical about the direction his life had taken. "I've reached a point where I do feel very connected with all of these things that I did, spiritual things, and that it all kind of falls into place. It's just that I, um, I'm not quite as flashy as I would've liked to have been," he laughed. "You know, radiating light."

"More than anything else I wanted to, you know, become a perfected yogi, or something along those lines. Maybe that was the problem. I want it to be a perfected yogi rather than an absolute nothing. There are a few egos bigger than that of the perfect yogi."

Still, Alexander considered himself "a successful failure. I'm accepting that now in the twilight years. Yeah. You know, it could be a lot worse." I asked what success might have looked like. "Well, losing all sense of *I*-ness. It's incredibly audacious and ambitious. Like when I was young, I said, *anybody* can be a rockstar, *I'm* gonna be God. It's God or nothing, take it or leave it, you know?" he laughed at our shared recognition that he wasn't completely joking. "It's tremendously ambitious on a certain level, but then you have to learn how to do it. And it's a real trade."

Alexander said he has no interest in taking to the spiritual speaking circuit like some who have harvested the teachings of the East. While he recognized that some disciples were sharing wisdom at the behest of their gurus, he had contempt for the rest. "This whole thing of the successful monk, the successful contemplative, this has always been a painful dynamic because the world demands that you have something to show for your money: Write a book, go on the lecture circuit. To aspire to that kind of material success is idiotic. That is the antithesis of what needs to be done if you are true to what you're trying to do in the first place."

There was a time, he said, when he would not have been comfortable with even having conversations like ours. Still, he wouldn't completely rule out the idea of quietly teaching at some point, if the time came that it "just happens spontaneously."

As for his relationship with Ma, Alexander believed it remained as strong as ever. "I think that she really grabbed me and she's not gonna let go. I have this interior connection with her. She used to say that you may forget me, but I'll never forget you. And now that I've kind of blown it, you know, in terms of my initial desire to be a, you know, Milarepa," he smiled gently, "I can at least fall back on that. I feel confident that I'll be back with her soon enough."

As for that initial numinous experience in Texas that started it all, after several years with Ma, Alexander had again asked her about it. By then he had recognized his rapture to be an advanced meditative experience, which was usually the result of guidance from the guru in the presence of the divine. But, he told Ma, he didn't understand how that could be because at the time he had no guru and didn't believe in God.

"She said, 'God is always there,'" he recounted. "And then she said, almost *sotto voce*, 'And it was known to this body at the time.'" Alexander laughed. "And I've been pondering that ever since …"

The Yogini and the Scribe

*Jetsunma Tenzin Palmo and Nick Ribush. All paths
lead to Buddha.*

*"View all traditions and views as non-contradictory,
and as true expressions of the Buddha's teachings."*
Dilgo Khyentse Rinpoche, *Heart of Compassion*

The Yogini

I first met Tenzin Palmo in Bali in the late '90s. Indira and I were
hosting a week of teachings by a renowned Tibetan lama, and it
was hard not to notice the obviously Western woman who wandered
into the gathering wearing the maroon and saffron robes of a nun in
the Tibetan tradition of Buddhism.

When I approached her, I was greeted with a warm smile and a
strong British accent. She was just plain Ani Tenzin back then; *Ani*

being the Tibetan term for a nun. *Jetsunma*, an honorific for the
most revered and accomplished teachers, would come much later.

There was a comforting magnetism about Anila. As Indira and
I spent time with her over the next few weeks, we came to know a
gentle, down-to-earth, almost ageless woman whose peaceful de-
meanor brought a calm equilibrium to those around her.

It would soon become clear that this was no ordinary nun. Tenzin
Palmo had spent twelve years in a cave on a Himalayan mountaintop. And she had made a vow to continue to be reborn as a woman
until reaching enlightenment.

The Scribe

You have probably never heard his name, but if you've ever
picked up a book about Buddhism, Nick Ribush has had an
impact on your life.

These days, chains like Barnes & Noble have entire aisles devoted to Buddhism. But back in the 1970s, when this Australian
doctor helped publish the first compilation of his lamas' teachings,
the selection in most mainstream bookstores didn't extend much
beyond Herman Hesse's *Siddhartha*.

"From my first involvement [in Buddhism], I had shown a couple of tendencies," Ribush told me, seated in his home office in the
Boston suburbs, surrounded by Tibetan thangkas and photos of his
teachers. "One is to want to very strongly share those teachings with
other people, and the other is the medium of editing."

That first involvement occurred in Nepal, where Ribush attended
a one-month course led by two Tibetan lamas who were among
the first to teach extensively to Western students. The course had
barely finished when Ribush was already hard at work editing the
transcripts. "I told Lama Yeshe that I thought this was a real treasure
and my life had changed as a result of these teachings," Ribush said
years later, referring to Lama Thubten Yeshe, who, like his chief

disciple, Lama Zopa Rinpoche, had fled the Chinese invasion of Tibet and established a monastery in Nepal. "So, I wanted to make it into a textbook for future courses." Pictures from the time show a thin, balding, deeply tanned young man with an enthusiastic grin.

Buddhist teachers talk of planting seeds. That text planted the seed for much of what eventually blossomed on the shelves of Western bookstores. Within two years, Ribush had guided into print a book entitled *Wisdom Energy*, the cornerstone of what would become Wisdom Publications, one of the preeminent publishers of the teachings of Buddhism—known as the dharma—in the world today.

"Nick was really the prime force behind Wisdom," actor Richard Gere, one of the best-known Western students of Tibetan Buddhism, told me in a phone call. "In the English language, all the really serious translation work has been done at Wisdom."

Perhaps as importantly, Wisdom helped spawn a huge dharma publishing industry that has moved firmly into the mainstream. "Wisdom is part of the fabric of it all," said the Venerable Robina Courtin, an Australian Buddhist nun who also played a key role in Wisdom's early years. "It was an integral part of bringing Buddhism to the West."

The Tradition

Buddhism came to Tibet from India in the seventh century, as prophesized by Shakyamuni Buddha ten centuries before:

> *For a long time in the future,*
> *Buddha's speech and teachings ...*
> *In the country of the Land of the Snows,*
> *Will spread and flourish.*

Its foothold in "the Land of the Snows" was cemented with the arrival of two Buddhist teachers, Shantarakshita, the abbot of a major Indian Buddhist university, and Padmasambhava, known as Guru Rinpoche, a meditation master said to have subdued the local spirits who were fighting a rearguard action against the imported religion. That division of labor—the scholar and the yogi—characterizes the two main streams within Tibetan Buddhism to this day.

Nick Ribush found himself drawn to two lamas whose lineage was that of the scholarly Gelug tradition, founded by the fourteenth century religious philosopher Tsongkhapa, who is credited with building the three great monasteries of Tibet. "If the lamp of true learning does not illuminate the darkness," Tsongkhapa told his monks, "you cannot even know the path. ... Therefore, I studied closely all the books." Therefore, the Gelugpa, as the Gelug followers are called, emphasize philosophical analysis and monastic discipline over intensive meditation.

Tenzin Palmo would walk a very different path, inspired by an eleventh century poet and yogi called Milarepa, one of the founders of her Kagyu lineage. Milarepa was a murderer who turned to Buddhism, spent much of his later life meditating in a cave, and is said to have been the first person to reach enlightenment in one lifetime, telling his students in a spontaneous song,

Deep in the wild mountains,
is a strange marketplace,
where you can trade the hassle and noise of every-
day life,
for eternal Light.[1]

Following his example, the Kagyupa prioritize intensive meditation practice over textual knowledge.

In many ways, Ribush and Palmo were polar opposites, save for their dedication to serving others through the teachings of the Buddhist dharma. "Some people are devotional; others are intellectual,"

Palmo said in one of her many teachings to groups around the world. The "huge dharma supermarket" of Tibetan Buddhism "contains skillful means to deal with all kinds of personalities and needs. … They all work."² As the Dalai Lama emphasized, while the approach of each school is different, they all lead to the same place—enlightenment.

Diane Perry was raised by a spiritualist mother, her London fish-monger father having died when she was young. Seances were a regular event in Perry's home. They opened her mind to the idea that there was something beyond the physical world; perfect preparation for her future encounter with a religion in which there are no boundaries.

It was a book that brought eighteen-year-old Diane to Buddhism. *Mind Unshaken: A Modern Approach to Buddhism* by John Walters had just been published. "I still vividly remember what an outstanding revelation it was to learn that there was a perfect path already set out and that it embraced all the things I already believed in," she recalled a half century later. "Buddhism was a path which led inwards, rendering any notion of an external creator God totally superfluous."

Diane told her mother, "'I'm a Buddhist,'" and she replied, "'That's nice dear. Finish the book, and then you can tell me all about it.'" London's tiny Buddhist circle in those days was dominated by the Theravada tradition of Buddhism found in South and Southeast Asia and the teachings of an eclectic British lawyer and spiritual seeker named Christmas Humphreys, who established Britain's Buddhist Society and was a proponent of his own unique interpretation of Zen Buddhism. For Diane, none of it felt quite right. Then, buried in Humphreys' book *Buddhism*, she found a chapter on the Tibetan tradition. It described the four schools of Tibetan Buddhism, one of which is the Kagyu. Diane instantly knew. "A voice inside me said, 'You're a Kagyupa.' And I said, 'What's a Kagyupa?' And it said, 'It doesn't matter. You're a Kagyupa.'"[3]

She went to work at London's School of Oriental and African Studies so that she could begin to learn Tibetan. Through that job, she met a young lama named Chogyam Trungpa, who was studying at Oxford. Trungpa, ultimately a very controversial figure, would go on to help pioneer Tibetan Buddhism in the West, founding the Shambala network of Buddhist centers and the first Buddhist university in America. But in the early '60s, few people in the UK were interested in Tibetan Buddhism. At one point, Trungpa said to her, "You might find this difficult to believe, but in Tibet I was quite a high lama, and I never thought it would come to this, but please can I teach you meditation? I must have at least one disciple." Diane replied, "Sure, why not?"[4]

Trungpa's meditation instruction was an important step on her path, but Diane knew deep in her being that she was meant to be in India. In 1964, at age twenty, she boarded a ship. Her destination was a school for young Tibetan boys run by an Englishwoman in a region of India settled by recent refugees from Tibet.

Reincarnation is central to Tibetan Buddhism. So, too, is the idea that highly realized teachers consciously choose rebirth in a certain time and place to help others achieve enlightenment. They are identified by other high lamas through what are considered miraculous signs associated with their birth. Such individuals are known as *tulkus* and are specially trained to *resume* their role as teachers. The Dalai Lama is the best known tulku, but more than one thousand such lineages have been recognized within the religion.[5] The place Diane volunteered was a boarding school for tulkus.

Closely tied to the Tibetan Buddhist belief in conscious rebirth is the concept of the *tsawai* lama, or heart teacher, with whom a student is said to have a karmic connection that stretches back to previous lives. Those studying Tibetan Buddhism may take teachings from many lamas, but, according to this belief system, the heart teacher "has vowed and committed to take the disciple to enlightenment in this or future lifetimes."[6] As one senior Tibetan lama put it: "Meeting one's Root Guru isn't like a date but occurs spontaneously. While one treads the path to mental refinement, one matures and then spontaneously meets and recognizes one's Root Lama."[7]

For Diane Perry, that meeting took place on her twenty-first birthday. News of the impending arrival of a senior Kagyu teacher had come in the mail a few weeks before. The letter was signed, Khamtrul Rinpoche. "As soon as I read the name, faith spontaneously arose, as they say in the books," Palmo recalled.[8]

When she was introduced to him, "there was a sense of recognition, like meeting an old friend you haven't seen for a long time. At the same time, it was as if the very deepest thing inside me had suddenly taken external form."[9] It was a reference to the idea that the root teacher is an external manifestation of the nascent Buddha that resides within all of us.

Diane asked, through a translator, whether Khamtrul Rinpoche would allow her to take refuge with him, the formal ceremony of becoming a Buddhist. Of course, Rinpoche replied, as if the idea was never in question. She became his student and secretary. Not long after, she was ordained as a nun, only the second Westerner to do so in the Tibetan tradition, taking the name Tenzin Palmo.

At Khamtrul Rinpoche's monastery, life was sometimes lonely for the young nun. She was the only Westerner and the only nun living with eighty Tibetan monks. One day, Rinpoche acknowledged that the situation was challenging. "Previously I was always able to keep you close to me. But in this lifetime, you took form as a female so I'm doing the best I can, but I can't keep you close forever because it's very difficult."[10]

Eventually, he sent her to a remote monastery to do a series of meditation retreats through the long winters. But after six years, Tenzin Palmo decided her tiny retreat hut in the hills above the monastery grounds was still too full of distractions. She found a cave far up the mountain. She would stay there for the next twelve years.

Nick Ribush stole his first book about Buddhism. It happened in
Thailand. Ribush had put on hold his career as a medical doctor in
northern Australia and hit Asia's drug-infused "hippie trail" with his
girlfriend, Marie Obst. The plan was to begin in the surfing mecca
of Bali, then wander through Southeast Asia and parts beyond. The
trip was meant to last a couple of years, so, to make their meager
savings last, they survived on a dollar a day for food, transport, accommodation, and dope. In Bangkok, they decided to head to Laos,
then Burma, and eventually, India. Ribush figured he should know
something about the local culture along the way, so they hit a bookstore—literally. "There was no book budget, so we did this heist,"
he recalled, laughing. "I'd put rubber bands around my thighs under
my jeans and while my girlfriend distracted the bookshop owner, I
shoved a book about Buddhism into my pants."

And with that, a Buddhist was born. The stolen book was *Buddhism* by the British author Christmas Humphreys, the same book
that led Tenzin Palmo to conclude she was a Kagyupa. Ribush
started reading it the next day.

"We were staying in some hippie hovel, and we went to the market and bought a sheaf of dope for about ten cents. The market was
full of ducks hanging on these hooks, so we bought this already
cooked duck and ate that, and smoked dope, and I started reading this book. As I was reading it, it was like I had this stirring
in my heart, and the thought came: 'Good God, this sounds true.'
He was talking about karma, he was talking about ultimate reality,
about emptiness. I don't know exactly which part grabbed me, but
I couldn't get enough of it."

Even a nonbeliever might be tempted to conclude that the fact
either Ribush or Palmo were inspired by Christmas Humphreys'
book probably said more about their karmic connections than the
author's portrait of their future religion. Back in 1951 when it was

first published, Tibetan Buddhism was also known as "Lamism," for the lamas that led it, and Humphreys was beyond dismissive. "Nowhere save in Tibet is there so much sorcery and black magic, such degradation of the mind to selfish, evil ends," he wrote in the chapter on Tibetan Buddhism. "Primitive Lamism may be defined as a priestly mixture of Sivaite mysticism, magic, and Indo-Tibetan demonology, overlaid by a thin varnish of Mahayana Buddhism."[11]

Nevertheless, Ribush was intrigued. Over the coming weeks, he would visit Buddhist shrines in Laos and Burma and, from Buddhist pamphlets he picked up along the way, endlessly read aloud to Marie, a lapsed Catholic. "She wasn't quite ready to pick up a new religion. She hadn't got over the old one yet, so she was kind of rolling her eyes."

It was a drug deal that got Ribush to Kathmandu, and a cheap room that brought him together with the Tibetan lamas to whom he would dedicate his life. Before he and Marie left Thailand, Ribush was approached by an occasional traveling companion, Lars, who had run out of money and was planning to smuggle a suitcase of Thai weed to Europe. "He wanted me to stake him on the trip, buy his ticket. I mean, basically put it on my credit card, and then we'd rendezvous in Kathmandu, and he'd repay me with interest. So, I was like, 'Oh, okay. That's cool. We'll do a little business on the road. Why not? Probably get the money back before I even have to pay the credit card bill.'" The pair crafted a false-bottom suitcase from a couple of Samsonites and agreed to meet up in Kathmandu in a few weeks' time.

When Ribush and Marie reached the Nepali capital, Lars had not yet arrived. They ran into another friend who recommended a cheap hotel. As an aside, he mentioned that there was a meditation course starting at a local monastery the following week. "I was like, 'Oh yeah, I meant to find out about Buddhist meditation. Maybe we should check it out.'"

Kopan Monastery, the site of what was once the royal astrologer's home, sits on the peak of a steep hill on the edge of Kathmandu, with a commanding view over the city. It is today the spiritual heart of the Foundation for the Preservation of Mahayana Teachings (FMPT), one of the most influential Buddhist organizations in the world. A lavish prayer hall stands amid buildings that house more than 350 monks and staff. Magnificent statues of Buddhas and elaborate stupas containing sacred relics decorate the grounds. But when Ribush ventured up to the monastery in 1972, Kopan was a far more modest affair, with a few small buildings and a handful of huts.

"Nobody was around" when he and Marie visited to check the place out, he said. "The Westerners who were organizing the course were downtown buying supplies. I didn't see any monks or anyone. It was very quiet." On the bulletin board was a notice for the course. "There was food, accommodation, tuition, the whole thing. Ten bucks or whatever. A fraction of what it would've cost to stay in Kathmandu." Ribush, whose family were Eastern European Jews who emigrated to Australia, chuckled as he recounted the story. He "had to listen to [my] inner Jew" and go for the cheap option. However haphazard the decision may have seemed at the time, the implications were profound. "That's where my medical career finished, and my Buddhist career began."

Within a year, he was kneeling at the feet of the Dalai Lama at Bodhgaya, said to be the site of the Buddha's enlightenment, being ordained as a monk, among the first Westerners to take such vows. "His Holiness laughed, looked at us, and said, 'Well, I hope it lasts.'"

Tenzin Palmo's cave was little more than a stone outcrop. It sat at an elevation of thirteen thousand feet, a few hours hike above the monastery where she had spent six years. With the help of some workers, she bricked in the open front of the cave to block the blizzards that raged through the long winters, creating a six square foot space with a sitting meditation box in which she also slept. Supplies were brought to her when the weather cooperated, and she managed to grow a few vegetables and potatoes in the short summers. One year the supplies didn't come for six months, and she nearly starved. After one particularly brutal storm, the cave entrance was completely buried, leaving her trapped inside and convinced she was going to die. Palmo thought of Milarepa, a famous yogi who was the eleventh century founder of her lineage. He had aspired to die meditating in his cave; she prepared herself.

Buddhists consider the entire realm of existence as samsara, an endless cycle of birth and rebirth mired in *dukkha*, suffering. One spring as the snows melted, the cave flooded. Sick and soaking wet, Palmo sat in her meditation box examining her plight. "I was thinking, 'Yes, they were right in what they told me about living in caves. Who wants to live in this horrible wet?' It was cold and miserable and still snowing. Then suddenly I thought, 'Are you still looking for happiness in samsara? We're always hoping that everything will be pleasant and fearing that it won't be." Suddenly, she realized, "'It doesn't matter. It really doesn't matter. Samsara is dukkha. There's no problem. Why expect happiness? If happiness is there, happiness is there. If happiness isn't there, what do you expect? It really doesn't matter.' When I felt that in my heart, this whole weight of hope and fear just dropped away. … It was an enormous relief. … Why do we make such a big fuss when we suffer? It doesn't matter. We go on."[12]

For the final three years of the retreat, the British nun remained in total isolation. She considered it one of the greatest learning experiences of her life: "There was an infinite amount of time without external distractions just to see how the mind functions, how thoughts and emotions arise, how we identify with them, how to disidentify with them and to resolve all the thoughts and emotions back into spaciousness. I was very fortunate to have the opportunity to do this."[13]

To a Western eye, a twelve-year retreat might seem the ultimate act of selfishness. Rather than working for the benefit of others, as

Tibetan Buddhism constantly preaches, Palmo retreated from society and focused on herself. But for her, it was ultimately an act
of self*less*ness. "I felt that if I was ever going to be of any benefit
to anybody, I could only do it by really realizing the dharma in my
heart. When I, myself, was in a state of ignorance and confusion,
how could I help others? And it seemed to be that the perfect way
to do that was to be in isolation."[14]

You might expect someone who had spent twelve years meditating in a cave to be a bit disconnected from reality. Ani Tenzin Palmo
was as grounded as anyone my wife and I had ever met. And ego-
less. It took days of probing before she began to tell her story. I immediately sensed material for a book. Anila, as everyone called her,
told me that author Vicki Mackenzie had beaten me to it. *A Cave in
the Snow*, the story of Tenzin Palmo's life, was being prepared for
publication as we spoke.

In Bali, as we discussed Buddhist concepts and practices over tea
one evening, Anila suggested that I try a technique for internalizing
the teachings. One of the things that differentiates Tibet's *Vajrayana*
or *tantric* approach from other branches of Buddhism is the use of
meditation practices that involve complex visualizations of specific
Buddhas, which represent aspects of our subconscious. There are
mantras, or sets of sacred syllables, associated with each practice.
For example, practitioners meditating on Chenrezig, the Buddha
of compassion, will chant, "*Om Mani Padme Hum.*" The mantra
reinforces the practitioner's focus on compassion for other beings.

Anila suggested that I try constantly repeating a mantra throughout the day, not just during meditation. No matter what I was doing,
I should silently repeat the mantra. Reading, talking, making dinner.
The mantra would always be there. She explained that the mantra
repetition would eventually shift from being something I had to
consciously tell myself to do, to something that was subconscious,
moving from the mind and settling in the heart. The Tibetans say
that the spiritual evolution of an individual dictates the level of
teachings for which she or he is prepared. Clearly, I was not ready

for this one. Despite my best efforts, each time I tried this technique over the years that followed, my conscious mind would eventually be distracted and forget about the mantra, while my subconscious was, apparently, not evolved enough to pick up the task.

Such background mantras had literally been the soundtrack of Tenzin Palmo's life. She had instinctively adopted the technique long before she ever had a teacher. When she read about mantras as an eighteen-year-old back in London, she assumed she was supposed to repeat them all the time. Palmo was working in a library and couldn't say her mantra aloud, so she began repeating it silently in her heart. "Within a very short time, my mind split and there was this quiet, calm, spacious mind with the Om Mani Padme Hum reverberating within it, then there was this peripheral mind with all its thoughts and emotions. The two minds were detached from one another. This gave great poise to my mind and the ability to exercise far more choice over my thoughts and feelings because I was no longer immersed in them."[15]

Nick Ribush was an unlikely candidate for dharma scribe. Unlike Tenzin Palmo, with her upbringing in a spiritualist household, Ribush was the son of a "card-carrying atheist" and grew up reading Bertrand Russell. "In our house, science was supreme, the universe was a series of random events, the human race was a chemical accident, and the object of life was to enjoy yourself as much as possible," he recounted with a wry smile. "When you died, it was all over."

It was no surprise then that Ribush became a doctor. But even as he spent the next six years training to be a kidney specialist, he found something missing. "I felt that doctors were a bit like boxers' handlers: The patients would come reeling into the surgery from the ring of life and you'd patch them up and throw 'em back out into the same circumstances that made them sick in the first place," he recalled in an Australian accent that remained thick.

To cope, he made the most of his off-hours. "I led a kind of Jekyll and Hyde existence—straight young medico by day, drug-crazed hippie by night. I don't know," he continued, arching his eyebrows, "it worked for me." In retrospect, Ribush marveled at how emotionally empty he and his fellow doctors were. "Knowing the little I do about Buddhism, it's odd that seeing a roomful of dead bodies laid out on tables didn't induce in any of us, as far as I'm aware, a sense of mortality."

His first encounter with the lama who would, as Ribush later put it, "completely put an end to life as I knew it," was less than auspicious. Dr. Nick, as he was known at the monastery, was summoned to treat Lama Yeshe, who had an infected wound. But when Ribush tried to administer an injection, he failed to tighten the syringe. "The needle was stuck in Lama Yeshe's holy buttock, and I'd sprayed penicillin all over the wall," he told me, laughing. The lama turned, his face crinkled into the broad, gap-toothed smile Ribush would come to know so well, and said, "Maybe you should come back and try again tomorrow."

Those first teachings that Ribush attended had a profound effect on the shy young doctor. "After the course, we had a group photo on top of the hill at Kopan, and then I went up to [Lama Zopa] Rinpoche and said, 'Rinpoche, thank you for changing my life.' He kind of laughed and held my hand, and we started to walk down the hill holding hands, but I was too shy, and I pulled away. It was pathetic."

Later, he raised the issue of the course materials. "I told Rinpoche, 'This is a life changing text, but it could use some work,' and he said, 'Oh yeah, well it was just put together by the students. I've actually got quite a few ideas how I'd like it reworked. If you want to help, you're welcome.'" Ribush did want to help. He and Marie were soon hard at work editing the rough primer that students in the first two courses had compiled, making changes requested by Rinpoche, and trying to turn it into something presentable. Rinpoche told them that they needed to liberally correct what he called his "breaking English." "Whenever you publish my teachings, you make sure you edit them properly. Don't make me sound like a Himalayan gorilla," he instructed them with mock severity.

In those days, long before the age of computers, they had to duplicate the edited versions on wax stencil machines. It was an exercise in patience. "You take the ribbon out of a typewriter, and you reel a wax stencil into the typewriter, and you type on it," Ribush explained. "The keys cut the wax. It is quite tedious, and if you make a mistake, you have to paint over it with nail polish and then wait for that to dry and try to line that letter up again, and you hit it again and it cuts through. Where there is a mistake, it comes out blotchy because it doesn't cut cleanly."[16]

There was no electricity at Kopan, so to even operate this rudimentary system they had to go down to Kathmandu. The lack of electricity also meant that teachings by Lama Yeshe and Lama Zopa Rinpoche couldn't be recorded, so Ribush and others initially took notes and combined them afterward. But the burgeoning scribe soon realized they were missing too much.

In the fall of 1973, "at the fifth course, I sat down right in front of the throne with a big, fat Indian notebook and started writing" he recalled. "For the whole month, I wrote down pretty much everything he said, making up abbreviations as I went along, writing in my best medical student scrawl."[17] Luckily, his girlfriend was able to make sense of the notes and type them up for Ribush to edit. Eventually, an American student brought a tape recorder and batteries from New York, taking the process out of the Dark Ages. From then on, every Kopan course was recorded. Those tapes would become the raw material from which Ribush would build his life.

In those early years, the two lamas each played a different role in the Kopan teachings and in Ribush's evolution as a Buddhist. Lama Yeshe was the senior among the pair, but Lama Zopa had been recognized as the incarnation, or tulku, of a renowned yogi. He had fled Tibet as a child and ended up at the school where Tenzin Palmo was a volunteer at the time. It was there that Lama Yeshe took him under his wing. "I think that's because I had been guided by Lama Yeshe in many lifetimes, just as you have," Zopa Rinpoche told Ribush and a group of his fellow Western monks and nuns in 1982. "So, even though I had no strong wish, there was a strong force, karma, between Lama Yeshe and myself. ... He hasn't only helped and guided me in this life, but he planted seeds in my mind in many past lifetimes."[18]

Both lamas spoke English, which was rare for Tibetan teachers in those days, barely a decade after Tibetans began fleeing the Chinese invasion of their homeland. This set them apart from the many other lamas in exile. "The word was really getting out in India and Nepal amongst all the freaks and hippies and spiritual seekers and everything, that these remarkable lamas were teaching in English at this monastery near Kathmandu," Ribush recalled. "You had to go a long way to find a lama who spoke English in those days."

Zopa Rinpoche took the lead in the teachings, while Lama Yeshe supervised the development of Kopan and a second monastery in an area of Nepal where Zopa Rinpoche's previous incarnation lived. "Lama [Yeshe] was always the boss, and he was always the one who told me what to do. I related to him more on the administrative level," Ribush recalled. But he considered Lama Zopa Rinpoche to be his principal teacher. "I always regarded them as two sides of the same person," he explained, reaching into Tibetan mysticism, "two aspects of the omniscient mind manifesting in their aspects in order to benefit me and the others around them according to our karma. That's sort of a traditional way of putting it."

Those complimentary personalities were also reflected in their respective styles of teaching. Lama Zopa Rinpoche presented a traditional approach to the ancient texts, while Lama Yeshe often counseled his students to place Buddhism within the context of their own culture. "What I mean is you don't need to do all those Tibetan rituals—the prostrations, the prayers, those things," he told students at a 1983 retreat. "In my opinion you don't need to do any of these at all. What you should do is the essence: really learn true love and how to technically practice it, and how to practice true wisdom."[19] This was the heart of what came to be known as his "Big Love" approach to Tibetan Buddhism.

Very early on, Lama Yeshe tasked his young Australian convert to play an important role in the development of what would become the global FPMT organization. "He said to call it the Council for the Preservation of the Mahayana Tradition," Ribush recalled, "Mahayana" being the term for the broad group of Buddhist traditions that prioritize compassion for other beings. It includes those found in Tibet, which fall into the subcategory of *Vajrayana*, employing complex, esoteric meditation practices said to provide a fast-track to enlightenment. "We said, 'You can't market that,'" Ribush recalled, referring to the name suggested by Lama Yeshe. "It's too long. But, in fact, it was kind of a mission statement. He said, 'What are we trying to do? We are trying to preserve the Mahayana tradition, to prevent it from dying out, like it's dying out in Tibet and like it died out in India.'"

Ribush had already—somewhat inadvertently—brought the Tibetan Buddhist teachings to Australia. After that first month-long course with the lamas, Ribush did a one-week meditation retreat in one of the little cabins on the monastery's property. "I wasn't, and I never have been, a particularly good meditator, and so the way I'd meditate on the teachings was, I'd visualize my mother or my brother or some of my friends and I'd be explaining the teaching to them, and they'd be arguing against it, and I'd be refuting their argument. I'd have this conversation in my head, and I'd always win," he recounted, with an ironic smile.

It was a highly unconventional, mono-Socratic approach to Buddhist analytical meditation. "I was so fired up by this victory of the dharma over my friends' wrong views that I'd write a letter explaining what was going on here. You're not supposed to write letters in retreat, but for me it was kind of like recapping my meditation," Ribush told me. By the end of the week, he had written about twenty letters, which he quickly mailed. "And they'd finish up with, 'Look, I don't know how to explain it to you. If you really want to find out, you've got to come here yourself.'" When it came time for the lamas' next course, the participants included many of Ribush's family, friends, or friends of friends who had flown up from Australia, including his mother: "They then went back and spread the word. That's how dharma really got started in Australia."

By the spring of 1974, the semiannual course was attracting more students than Kopan could handle. The lamas decided it was time to take their teachings on the road. The first stop was New York, where Lama Yeshe thanked all the automatic doors and Zopa Rinpoche said going up in an elevator was just like the rising of attachments in the mind. From there, they headed to Australia, where no Tibetan lama had previously taught. Not long after the trip, Ribush and Marie donated to the lamas a piece of land they owned outside Brisbane to create the Chenrezig Institute, the lamas' first dharma center in the West.

And, you could say, Ribush also donated his mother, who married Lama Yeshe to get him an Australian passport. Like many Tibetans, Lama Yeshe had fled Tibet and was a stateless refugee. The Western students had managed to buy him a Nepali passport, but they were nervous about him traveling on a document of dubious origin. So, someone came up with the idea of a marriage-of-convenience to Ribush's mother, who had converted to Buddhism after attending the teaching at Kopan. "It was obviously such a fake marriage. Lama was giggling and laughing through the whole thing," Ribush recalled of the ceremony. "I never asked but I think it's pretty safe to assume it was never consummated." Within a month of the sham wedding, Lama Yeshe was an Australian citizen, free to travel the world.

The world of Tibetan Buddhism is patriarchal. "There is definitely arrogance, there is definitely some sort of chauvinism," Khandro Rinpoche, one of the few Tibetan women recognized as the incarnation of a revered teacher, told me in 2001. Thirteen centuries before, Padmasambhava had declared, "The awakened state of mind is neither male nor female."[20] That was what the texts may have said, but the reality was that many in modern Tibetan society still believed men were superior. "We have terms that women have a lot of difficulty with, such as 'the lower birth,'" Tenzin Palmo said, shaking her head in dismay.

Until the late twentieth century, there were no women lamas. Traditionally, nuns were not even allowed to take part in ritual practices or receive the same level of ordination as their counterparts in other branches of the religion. Lama Yeshe, who Tenzin Palmo had met at the school for tulkus when he was a little boy, was recognized as the incarnation of the abbess of a nunnery, but because his previous life was as that of a woman, he was never honored with the title Rinpoche.

Tenzin Palmo rebelled against those strictures. With her teacher's blessing, she went to Hong Kong to receive the full bhiksuni ordination in a Chinese order. She subsequently dedicated her life to making women full partners in the religion. Before she began her retreat in the cave, her teacher, Khamtrul Rinpoche, asked her to take on the task of reviving a famous lineage of yoginis, female practitioners who lived in remote locations and focused exclusively on advanced meditative practices. Their male counterparts, the *togden*, with their distinctive matted dreadlocks and white tunics, still survived; but the *togdenma*, the women yogis, had faded away. Time was of the essence. In Tibetan Buddhism, specific practices must follow an unbroken line of transmission from teacher to teacher. Only a few individuals were still alive who held the togdenma transmission.

When she emerged from her twelve years of solitude, Tenzin Palmo wanted nothing more than to go back up the mountain, but she took on the task of creating a nunnery and making nuns full partners in the dharma. In the fall of 2024, Palmo presided over celebrations marking the fiftieth anniversary of Dongyu Gatsal Ling Nunnery, which by then housed more than 120 nuns from across the Himalayan region. At least ten nuns had followed in Tenzin Palmo's footsteps, completing twelve-year retreats.

"Once the nuns become educated, they begin to think for themselves," Palmo told a podcast interviewer. "They begin to get a sense of self-worth. They stop praying just to be reborn as a male so that they can get on with it. They recognize that even in female form, there's nothing that they cannot do if they're given the opportunity."[21]

Her center has been at the forefront of nunneries creating a new culture within the religion. "Things have really changed a lot in the last twenty or thirty years, which is good for all Buddhism, not just for the women," Palmo said proudly. "Before [the nuns] were like a rosebud, and because they were not watered, the soil was very hard, there was no sunshine of approval. There was no watering of the teachings. So, they lived and died as withered buds. They never opened. Whereas now they're opening up and showing how beautiful they are, and the scent of the dharma is just wafting from all these nunneries now."[22]

Even in her eighties, Palmo still believed her task was just beginning. One of the things that differentiates Tibet's Buddhist tradition from other schools of Buddhism is the bodhisattva vow taken by some practitioners, in which they promise to work through endless lifetimes for the enlightenment of all beings. Palmo's commitment included a vow that she would do that in each lifetime as a woman.

"Male teachers are like stars in the sky. So, therefore, it seemed obvious that there were already more than enough males out there. What we needed was to travel the path as a female—as many females as possible out there—showing that there's really no difference. Buddha nature's not male or female. Women are absolutely as capable of realizing the path as the males. And the only way to do that is to be a female and realize the path."[23]

Buddhism is all about losing the ego. But to the Western ear, a public declaration from a British-born nun who believes she can consciously reincarnate in a certain time, place, and body to help lead all beings to enlightenment might seem like the epitome of egoism. Palmo helped put it in context for an audience at an American Zen Buddhist center: "We are not autonomous beings. We're not separate little bubbles. We are all interconnected. We are responsible for each other," she told the group. "So, our motivation is not just for this hard little ego sitting here. It's very vast, very expansive, going through endless eons of time. We have vowed to be with sentient beings for endless eons, not just in this lifetime, the next lifetime, and the one after that, but endlessly, infinitely. Not as *I*. I mean, I, Tenzin Palmo, am not going to come back in the next life. Something else will be here, but this stream of consciousness and this energy force will be part of it."

Drugs got Ribush to Kathmandu and drugs helped fund Kopan. When we were chatting one day about the prerequisites for becoming a monk, Ribush mentioned that there were certain negative actions that could get you disqualified. These included such things as killing your mother or father, drawing blood from a Buddha, and creating a schism in the religious community.

"But dope smuggling is okay?" I wryly interjected.

"Oh, yeah," he responded with a broad grin. "In fact, it was encouraged. If it weren't for dope, we wouldn't be having this conversation. The monastery would probably not exist and certainly, I don't think these publications would exist," he motioned to the piles of books of the lamas' teachings published by his archive. "So, weed has a lot to recommend it."

"Because it got all those people out to Kathmandu, you mean?" I asked.

"Yeah, for many people, it was the way they supported themselves or supported the monastery. Absolutely."

When Ribush's would-be partner in crime, Lars, finally turned up back in Kathmandu, it was without the money he had promised. His explanation was compelling. He and his friends smoked the weed he had smuggled, instead of selling it. As compensation, he handed Ribush another false-bottomed suitcase, this one lined with hashish, far more valuable on the Western market. "Now we're square," he told Ribush, who stashed the suitcase in his room. When a student attending one of the teachings heard about it, he offered to smuggle it to Australia and split the profits with Ribush. At the time, Kopan was being largely funded out of the salary of an African American nun known as Max, who taught at the local international school. Because Nepali banks were unreliable, Ribush told the student to wire his half of the profits to Max's European account to benefit Kopan. The monastery never saw the money. The kid had no issues at customs, but when he turned up at the bank, the problems began. Max's real name was Mary Jane, coincidentally a nickname for marijuana. "Here's this barefoot, long-haired kid with no visible means of support, with $5,000 cash he wants to send to a bank account in Switzerland in the name of Mary Jane." The bank called the cops, and they confiscated the money, though the smuggler wasn't charged.

One more of what Ribush wryly called his "adventures with marijuana" went almost as badly. Dope smuggling from Kathmandu in those days was so common that dealers would build crates with false cavities for their foreign customers. Hashish would be packed into the walls, then the crate would be filled with local curios as cover. One of Ribush's fellow foreign monks wanted one built but didn't have time before he was scheduled to go abroad. Ribush agreed to handle it for him. He dutifully sampled the various varieties of hash, selected the best one, and commissioned the crate. Because of a series of mishaps, he ended up dragging the thing with him from

Kathmandu to New Delhi and halfway back again. The crate eventually arrived in Australia, but his friend called to say the hash was terrible. The dealer had done a bait-and-switch with the good stuff. Ribush decided he had better stick to his real job.

About a year after he arrived at Kopan, Ribush was editing Zopa Rinpoche's teaching on the requirements to become a monk and realized he ticked all the boxes. Not long after, he was at the house he shared with Marie and several other Westerners and answered a knock on the door. "There was this Tibetan guy, and he had all these things that he was selling, including some beautiful monks' robes from Tibet made out of yak wool. Very high quality," Ribush recalled. "I bought it all and I was feeling, 'Well, you know, even if I don't need the robes, I can sell them in Kathmandu for profit, so this is a deal.'"

When Marie returned, he excitedly told her about buying the robes. "She was like, 'You what?' So, then I started explaining the benefits of getting ordained, being a monk or nun and why we should take advantage of the opportunity, but she wasn't that convinced." Eventually, he asked Lama Yeshe about the idea of becoming a monk. "His immediate reaction was to fall back on his bed, laughing uproariously at the idea. But then he said, 'Okay, well, let's see.'"

The following winter, January 1974, Ribush and nine other Westerners knelt in front of the Dalai Lama and took their vows as monks and nuns. Among them was Marie, who Lama Yeshe gave the name Yeshe Khadro.

She had been immersed in some of the highest and most secret practices of Tibetan Buddhism, yet Tenzin Palmo brought a distinct irreverence to her approach to the dharma: "There's no celestial Buddha up there with a thunderbolt glaring at us if we go off track a bit," she told those struggling with meditation.[24] "Nobody, including the great saints, were ever on an eternal high."[25]

She could expound about the complexities of visualization practices and the most esoteric aspects of the Tibetan cosmology, but a moment later she was stripping all that away. "If Buddhism ever had a slogan, that slogan would be, 'Let go.' Let go of the ego. Let go of grasping to people and things. Let go of negativity.' The whole of the Buddhist path is about transforming negative emotions into positive ones."[26]

"We can start by befriending ourselves, being a little more tolerant of ourselves and that will help us be friendlier and more tolerant of others," she told all who would listen.[27] Palmo likened meditation to riding a surfboard. "An unskillful surfer will just go, *sploosh*, back into the water again, and that's mostly what we do."[28] And she told students who were concerned they had not met the right guru that spiritual guidance appears in many guises. "It may not come in the form of high spiritual masters radiating lights or sending out brochures ahead of time to tell us they're enlightened," she said teasingly.[29]

Westerners, whether religious or not, Palmo argued, "were brought up by our culture to think that somehow we are basically sinners." Buddhism rejects that. "We are NOT innately sinful," she said with emphasis. "[W]e are inherently perfect. ... All of us have intrinsically the perfection of wisdom, compassion, purity, and power." The problem, she continued, was that "[o]ften in the West, we grasp at our negative qualities and forget our positive qualities."[30]

At the heart of the Tibetan Buddhist worldview is the idea that we are tied to the physical world—experiencing samsara, an endless cycle of birth, death, and rebirth—because of our attachments and greed. "It is like pornography that gets increasingly explicit, gross, and vicious in order to regain that frisson of excitement and pleasure," she would explain, getting her audience's attention. "There always has to be more and more and one is enslaved. It becomes an obsession, and addiction, which is very sad."[31] We have no one to blame except ourselves. "[On] the wheel of life and death, there are no chains, there are no ropes. We are holding on with both hands."[32]

Because our consciousness is cluttered with the physical and emotional detritus of our attachments, she believed, we cannot see that everything around us is shaped by our minds. "We are all projecting our own movie," she told one audience.[33] But she quickly emphasized that Buddhism was not saying it is all just a bad dream. "If I hit somebody with an object, that person would certainly feel it. So, it's not that it's all our illusion on a relative level."[34] She cited recent discoveries in physics to illustrate this concept. "When the Buddha said there is no Self, he didn't mean that we don't exist," she told a gathering at Deer Park, the place the Buddha gave his first teachings. "Of course, we exist. But fundamentally we do not exist in the way we conceive ourselves to exist. Just as if there is a table made of wood and this table is solid. Look tomorrow and it will still be a table and it will still be solid. Nonetheless, we know that from the point of view of quantum physics for example, the table does not exist at all as it appears. In fact, it is energy/space."[35]

For those who found that a bit too esoteric, she brought Buddhist beliefs back to the fundamentals. Perceptions shape reality. "Everyone has experienced how mood swings seem to alter the world around us," she explained. "We are feeling depressed, and everything seems grey and heavy. We fall in love and the gloomiest day is bathed in sunshine."[36]

"The thoughts, the feelings and the memories are not the problem," she told another group. "The problem is that we identify with them, and we believe in them, and so we are controlled by them."[37] We also need to take responsibility for ourselves, and "stop blaming our parents, our society, the government, etcetera."[38]

"We need to see that memories are just mental states, emotions are just states, feelings are just states, the thoughts that come into our mind are just mental states. They're like bubbles. They arise, they expand, and they burst, to be replaced by other bubbles. This is not who we are."[39]

Achieving *realization*, in the Tibetan context, involved breaking through the illusion of who we are and glimpsing the "sky-like" nature of the mind, a vast energy of which all sentient beings are a part.[40] "The nature of the mind is like a huge, blue, endless sky, very clear, very, very, very deep and stretching in all directions. It's vast and infinite and clear and empty and transparent and luminous."[41]

"We are all thinking me, me, me. But when we touch the nature of the mind, which is our true nature, our Buddha nature, then we see that, of course, we are actually all completely connected. The sky is not one sky and then there's another sky and then another. There's just sky, and it is infinite and vast. It is not my sky versus your sky. It is not my Buddha nature versus your Buddha nature. It's just Buddha nature. There's just Mind. Therefore, we are all very intricately interconnected with each other," she says.[42]

Unlike many teachers, Palmo demystified the process by using her own experiences. During meditation, "there sometimes appears like a gap between the previous thought and the next thought. ... A momentary opening. ... At that moment, we might perceive the nature of the mind." In her cave, she recalled, "Suddenly, I saw the whole thing. It was a moment of clarity and understanding. In that moment ... something inside dropped away and never reformed again."[43]

Central to Tibetan Buddhist meditation is the cultivation of loving kindness and compassion for others—*bodhicitta*—and the aspiration to help all beings reach enlightenment. This is achieved through systematic mind training (*lojong*) that strips away the focus on the practitioner's own ego. Those on this path will take a bodhisattva vow to defer their own enlightenment until they have helped all other beings achieve enlightenment.

A traditional Tibetan Buddhist prayer, *The Four Immeasurables*, implores:

May all beings have happiness and the cause of happiness.
May they be free of suffering and the cause of suffering.
May they never be disassociated from the supreme happi-
ness which is without suffering.
May they remain in the boundless equanimity, free from
both attachment to close ones and rejection of others.

"Traditionally we think to ourselves, 'May I be well and happy. May I be free from suffering! May I be peaceful and at my ease,'" Palmo told one audience. "Loving-kindness means 'May all beings be happy,' and compassion means, 'May they be free from suffering.'"

Such meditations, she continued, have a visceral effect on the world. "There are many stories of monks [in the jungle] coming out of their meditation and finding themselves faced with a cobra or a tiger sitting there gazing at them tranquilly." She had experienced it herself with a pack of wolves that lived near her remote cave. "Sometimes when I was sitting outside, they would come close but just friendly and curious. They would stand there looking at me and I looked at them and it didn't occur to any of us to feel threatened."[44]

Such stories might come across as someone trying to impress an audience, but Palmo consistently emphasized that those glimpses of insight are within the reach of everyone. "Being enlightened means uncovering our infinite potential for wisdom, compassion, purity, and power in the sense of infinite energy. We actually possess all of this. We just have to uncover it and discover what lies within us. The way to do this is to meditate."[45]

There is no magic involved: "Some people imagine that they are going to sit and meditate for a while and then, in the space of one minute, they're suddenly going to get this big breakthrough full of bright lights, trumpets, angels, and flowers falling. It's not like that."[46] It takes perseverance. And humankind, she says, is inherently lazy.

"I, myself, have had so many opportunities, so how come I'm not a Buddha yet? It's because of my laziness. There's no other excuse."[47]

In 1983, after traveling the world as the lamas' attendant, establishing a dharma center in New Delhi, heading the growing organization of Western monks and nuns studying with Lamas Yeshe and Zopa, and serving as Wisdom's editorial director, Ribush was asked by his teachers to move to the UK and head up the financially faltering publishing company.

"Lama Yeshe would simply give a task to Nick—start Wisdom Books, set up a center in Delhi—without any backup, no facilities, no contacts, no money, and he would get it done," said Salim Lee, a board member of the FPMT. "It was incredible. Within the FPMT, he's legendary."

To save the publishing operation, Ribush and his small team set up Wisdom's own direct-mail operation to cut out the middlemen and expanded the publications list far beyond the teachings of Lama Yeshe and Lama Zopa. "We realized it would be very easy to slot in other Buddhist books and become the major source of English-language Buddhist books," he said. "His Holiness [the Dalai Lama] encouraged us to publish and distribute all Buddhist traditions. His Holiness' words were, 'It shows the whole picture.' That set our philosophy."

For Nick Ribush, life in London in the 1980s was a world away from a monastery in Nepal. "You go to a realtor, you go to a bank, they didn't know what Tibetan Buddhists were. They see someone with a shaved head wearing funny-colored robes and they think you're going to shove a book in their hand and demand five dollars." And, there was the fact that life seemed so normal.

Lama Yeshe, who died the year Ribush moved to the UK, had seen it coming. Originally, the Australian monk was supposed to be based at a monastery in England's rural Cumbria region, where Wisdom's editorial arm was headquartered. But circumstances led to the consolidation of operations in the London business office. "When I told Lama that we were going to set up in London, Lama shook his head and said, 'London is a bad place for monks and nuns.' If I had been stronger, I could have done it," Ribush said, his voice tinged with regret. "Living a life which was more like the life I led in Australia, I started to think more and more like a lay person. It got to a certain point where I wanted a girlfriend." Monks and nuns take a vow of celibacy, so once he and Marie were ordained, their relationship had changed to one of spiritual friends. Eventually, after several years of internal struggle, Ribush decided he had a choice: return to the monastery or return his robes. He chose to be "a good person rather than a bad monk."

"That was the obvious call," he said, reflecting back on his decision to disrobe after twelve years. "There was more benefit developing Wisdom Publications, which was at a crucial stage."

One of Ribush's last acts as a monk was to carry a fifteen-month-old Spanish child on his back up a steep hill to meet the Dalai Lama, who would confirm that little Osel Hita Torres was the tulku—the incarnation—of Lama Yeshe. Lama Osel Rinpoche, as he would be known, was the son of a Spanish couple who were students of Lama Yeshe. They had established an FPMT retreat center near the Spanish town of Granada. Not long after Osel was born, other lamas began to suspect he was the tulku of Lama Yeshe, who had died the previous year. One stage of the process of recognizing a tulku involves laying out ritual items, such as a bell and prayer mala, which belonged to the previous lama and mixing them with similar items. The toddler Osel chose Lama Yeshe's items from amongst the others.

Four years would pass before Ribush met the young monk again, this time in Australia. I asked him if he felt anything being in the presence of the child said to be the tulku of the man to whom he had dedicated his life. "No," he said firmly and without a hint of hesitation. There are many stories of other students of Lama Yeshe claiming they had an immediate, emotional reaction on seeing Osel, but that was not the case for Ribush. "What I go on is that His Holiness and Lama Zopa say he is the continuity of Lama Yeshe, so what do I know?" he told me.

He was careful to use the phrase *continuity* of Lama Yeshe, rather than *reincarnation*, an important distinction that underlines the Tibetan concept that the tulku is an aspect of the mind of the person, not the rebirth of the identical "soul," which does not exist in Buddhist beliefs. "You sort of have this idea that the incarnation is going to have the same personality or be basically the same person in a small body again, but it doesn't seem to work like that at all," he observed.

Lama Osel would ultimately rebel against the confines of life as the tulku of a high lama and, at age eighteen, leave the monastery where he had been sent as a six-year-old child. He spent years on the beach in Ibiza, making music, and studying to become a documentary-maker. "I got a huge amount of letters and phone calls, and people coming to visit me, just telling me that I made a big mistake, that I lost a huge opportunity, that was my destiny, my purpose, blah-blah-blah, whatever," he told the BBC in 2012.[48]

Lama Osel eventually embraced his role and slowly began to offer teachings, a few of which Ribush watched online. While he didn't relate to the young lama, who insisted on simply being called Osel, he did see the similarity to his late teacher. "The way he talks is much like Lama Yeshe used to talk. It's very fluid and you don't quite know where he's going. I always found after Lama Yeshe's talks that they were fantastic while you were listening but when I came out, it was hard for me. 'What did he talk about?'" With Lama

Osel, "I can't follow sometimes what he's saying. To that extent I can see a similarity to Lama."

He also found another similarity; both were monastery drop-outs. Lama Yeshe left the monastery before finishing his Geshe teaching degree. "Lama always used to say, 'I'm a Tibetan hippie, I dropped out,'" Ribush said with a laugh.

That antiestablishment streak appeared to be strong in Osel, who, by his early thirties, had firmly embraced his role as a nontraditional teacher who considered himself "a radical free thinker," defined his "One Big Love" philosophy as a "fusion" of Lama Yeshe's "Big Love" and Jamaican reggae artist Bob Marley's song "One Love," and called on his students to be "warriors of clear light."[49] The bio on his website had a photo showing him with scruffy long hair and goatee and wearing a hoodie, leather jacket, and a necklace with a pentagram, accompanied by the caption, "Tenzin Osel Hita: A Different Way for This Future Generation."[50]

While Ribush was open to the idea that a new version of his old teacher had simply taken his "hippie" approach to dharma one step further, the eighty-something former monk preferred to stick to the tapes and transcripts of the original lama in the archive and leave Osel to the new generation of practitioners: "I don't really relate to the way he presents stuff. I'm fairly traditional in my thinking about Tibetan Buddhism."

Tenzin Palmo's experience with her teacher was much different from that of Ribush. The child identified as the tulku of the eighth Khamtrul Rinpoche was born less than a year after Palmo's teacher died in 1980. Based on letters from two high lamas, his tulku was quickly located, tested, and confirmed as the ninth Khamtrul Rinpoche.

"And so, he was taken to a monastery when he was eighteen months old and enthroned," Palmo told me with arched eyebrows and a bemused tone in her voice. "I mean, he was still wearing his nappy and drinking from a bottle. And there he is sitting up on the throne with all this brocade and a hat on and everything."

She had been devasted when the eighth Khamtrul Rinpoche died. "It was like traveling in this desert, and suddenly my guide had gone, left." But she found herself initially reluctant to meet his spiritual successor. "I thought he'll look at me and burst into tears, this weird looking White woman." The Tibetan toddler's response was completely unexpected: "He just looked at me for a moment, and then he laughed and laughed and said, 'Look, look. It's my nun. It's my nun. It's my nun.' And he was jumping up and down, 'Oh, it's my nun.' And he was just so happy," Palmo recalled with a broad smile. "And his attendants said, 'He never acts like that. He's very shy with people he doesn't know.'" The toddler climbed down from his throne, "and we just spent the whole morning playing together. I was crying because I was amazed at how absolutely delighted he was to see me."

Forty years later, according to Palmo, the incarnation of her teacher was still "introverted, sweet and gentle," in contrast to the eighth Khamtrul Rinpoche, who, she said, had a "powerful presence." "You felt, whatever happened, the sky could fall down, and Rinpoche would deal with it." But that contrast did not surprise her. "They're all different," she reflected of the high Tibetan lamas. "I mean, every incarnation is very, very different. [For example], with the Dalai Lama, you had the strong, political fifth Dalai Lama, and then this playboy sixth Dalai Lama," she said, referring to the historic predecessors of the fourteenth Dalai Lama. "I mean, you never know what you're going to get. It's like they play different roles. Comedy, drama, tragedy, all kinds, just to get the range of how it is to be a human."

Complicating things further was the fact that, in some cases, more than one child would be recognized as the simultaneous incarnations of different aspects of a senior teacher. Some of that was dharma politics; controlling the assets of major monasteries meant money and power, leading to rival claimants. But, in other situations, each tulku was believed to embody a different aspect of the personality of the previous incarnation, such as compassion or wisdom. In the case of Khamtrul Rinpoche, Tenzin Palmo remained close to that little boy who came down from his throne to greet her, but there was also a second boy born the following year who was also recognized by the Dalai Lama as another incarnation of her teacher.[51]

I asked Palmo how she explained all this to Western non-Buddhists. "We don't exist the way [non-Buddhists] think we exist as an entity, solid, enduring, unchanging, separate," she explained. Buddhists do not believe in a soul in the Western, Judeo-Christian sense. "It's not like that at all. The consciousness is moving. It's like a river, right? It's not like a monolithic stone. It's a river, which is constantly flowing, and therefore, it's always in change. And that is what keeps going on," she said, referring to rebirth.

In the Buddhist belief system, consciousness is *nondual*. In other words, there is no individual consciousness or ego; it is all part of a sky-like interconnected consciousness that encompasses all sentient beings.

"Space is all-prevailing, right? The idea of a self or soul separates us from everything else. The idea of *me* or *mine*. But the nature of the mind connects us with everything, not just humans. I mean, the whole of nature. Our sadness is that we don't recognize our interconnection and we cut ourselves off, which is why we destroy; we destroy everything, ourselves, others, the whole planet, because we live in this duality of separation.

"The difference between tulkus and ordinary people," she continued, "is that they die consciously. And therefore, they're able to get reborn consciously and choose where they're going to get reborn instead of just being reborn in accordance with karma."

Buddhism is not about blind faith, Tenzin Palmo insisted. Questioning is a vital part of the process. Western students, she argued, tend to be "too trusting" and "too gullible." Palmo did not hide her view that some Tibetan lamas teaching in the West are just on "a power trip," surrounding themselves with "adoring acolytes waiting for every nectar-like word he speaks."[52]

"It's a bit like, 'Hit me harder, ouch, it hurts, it must be good for me,'" she said derisively of students who blindly follow an abusive teacher.[53]

Several leading Tibetan lamas who taught in the West have been accused of sexual exploitation by female students. Prominent among them was Chogyam Trungpa, the lama who taught Palmo meditation in Britain when she was nineteen years old. Palmo had seen firsthand how easy it was for Western students to be seduced. She and her mother visited with Trungpa every weekend and, "Let's say he didn't act in an appropriate manner for a monk," she told an audience in New York in 2012. "He kept presenting himself as this pure monk who, until he met me, had never been tempted." Palmo paused and rolled her eyes. "And I thought, 'Yeah, right.'" But, in retrospect, she said, the situation drove home how easily Western students can be misled. "I thought he probably was a pure monk because he had just come from India, he never had any opportunities. I didn't realize he had already fathered a child."[54] Trungpa would go on to become a hugely controversial figure. While he built one of the largest Buddhist networks in the West, he propounded a doctrine of "crazy wisdom" that involved heavy drinking and womanizing. He was accused of physical assault by students and died of complications of alcoholism in 1987. In contrast, Jamgön Kongtrul Lodrö Tayé, the nineteenth century scholar considered one of the greatest masters in Tibetan history, once described himself as "someone who merely maintains the appearance of a guru in this degenerate age."

By 2020, Tibetan Buddhism had been roiled by a wave of accusations of physical, sexual, and psychological abuse by several prominent teachers, leading Tenzin Palmo to ask the Dalai Lama about the problem in a public session. "That is why the texts say for twelve years you must examine your teacher before [committing to him]," His Holiness told her.[55]

"Are you meditation-shaming me?" Nick Ribush asked, with more than a hint of irritation in his voice. I had just challenged his contention that he was "not much of a meditator." As Ribush himself had said during an online meditation class he led, "The main thing Buddhism deals with is the mind, and the only way to really examine and understand the mind is through meditation."[56]

Of the four schools of Tibetan Buddhism, the Gelugpa, to which Ribush and his teachers belonged, prioritized scholarship over meditation. In Tibet, while the yogis of Tenzin Palmo's Kagyu tradition spent their lives in meditation on remote mountaintops, the Gelugpa founded renowned universities where monks spent decades studying Buddhist teachings, philosophy, logic, and debate to obtain the vaunted degree of Geshe, essentially an advanced PhD. Even today, while they take part in religious rituals, many Gelugpa monks have only the most glancing familiarity with meditation.

But I also knew that Ribush taught a particular form of meditation called *Tummo* or Inner Heat, an advanced meditation practice in which the person visualizes a red-hot ember at the naval, then manipulates internal kundalini energy to raise the body temperature. Tenzin Palmo once told me that at the monastery where she did her initial six-year retreat, during the winter she could tell which of the unheated huts contained monks doing tummo practice because the snow on the roofs had melted from the heat generated by the meditator.

Lama Yeshe had instructed Ribush to teach tummo to recovering drug addicts, the idea being that the sensory experience might give them a new focus. "I can teach it, but I don't practice it that much," Ribush said, when I explained what I meant in questioning his claim that he wasn't much of a meditator. "The only time I do it is when I'm leading a meditation of other people. Maybe saying I'm not much of a meditator isn't the best way to put it," he added on reflection. "I never had an *affinity*. I find it much easier to publish books than to concentrate my mind." He paused, reconsidering, thinking back to the four-and-a-half-month retreat he did in a remote cave shortly after becoming a monk. "It was tough, but I really did get into it there, and it was a wonderful experience. By the end, I didn't want to come down. I wanted to stay there." A few years later, he was able to do another six-week retreat. But ultimately, he recognized that his role in serving the dharma did not involve a life in a cave. "I was always given these jobs. 'Go and start a center in Delhi, go to London and run a publishing company.' And so, publishing and doing this external work has really been my path."

After years helping to run Wisdom, which he moved to Boston and helped grow into a company publishing a broad range of Buddhist books, Ribush quit to return to his roots, exclusively publishing the teachings of his beloved lamas, Zopa Rinpoche and Lama Yeshe. He established the Lama Yeshe Wisdom Archive, which has produced scores of publications since it was set up as a separate publishing company in 1996.

When he had first decided to serve the lamas, Ribush told a Western nun at Kopan that he didn't have any money and didn't know how he would support himself. "And she looked at me as if I was a bit simple, and said, 'Oh, well, you know, if you give yourself to the dharma, the dharma will always look after you.'" It did just that. At each juncture, some donor stepped up to cover the cost of publishing a book, paying for an office, or keeping a roof over Ribush's head, even if it was only a Nepali hut without plumbing or a one-bedroom London squat shared with others.

The first time we first met in the late 1990s, shortly after the Archive was founded, Ribush and his wife, Wendy Cook, were living in a comfortable guest house on a property in an upscale neighborhood outside Boston. It was both their home and the headquarters for the Archive. The property was owned by the daughter of the cofounder of Intel and her husband, both doctors. They provided the house as a donation to the dharma, just as they had previously provided Nick and Wendy with a condo. When the Intel heir decided to sell that property, Ribush and Wendy moved to another house that was subsidized by that owner, and when he decided to sell, Ribush reached out to a wealthy Malaysian donor and asked if she would purchase the house, so they didn't have to move. She checked with Rinpoche, and he said it was a good idea, but told them to find a better house. Ribush did and "she wired us a million bucks and we bought this," he said, spreading his arms to encompass the beautiful, spacious building.

"The dharma will provide" also applied to the Lama Yeshe Wisdom Archive, which he set up when he left Wisdom Books. Instead of producing a brochure to drum up support, Ribush compiled three of Lama Yeshe's teachings into a little pamphlet and mailed it out to his lists. "I was just overwhelmed by the response." Giving away the dharma became his business plan, tapping into an ancient practice: "Buddhists have created merit for centuries, if not millennia, by sponsoring the publication of books that were given away free."

"What that does is keep everyone's motivation clean," Richard Gere, one of the project's funders, told me. "To keep that ancient pledge that you can't buy dharma; you can't charge for it."

"People liked it—people supported us with money, and people sponsored books," Ribush said. Books were often sponsored in memory of loved ones who had died. "And then of course we developed the website," he continued. "And now we're reaching far more people online than you ever could in print, and it's just so much more cost effective."

By 2021, the Archive had more than a million books in print, and had just released *Big Love*, the 1,500-page biography of Lama Yeshe, who a noted American scholar of Buddhism called, "one of the most influential lamas of the 20th century."[57]

Asked if he was proud of all he had achieved, Ribush, then in his eighties, with a white beard and wild fringe of white hair framing his balding head, demurred. "I don't know, I think I tend more to look at my mind as it is today and think, 'Shit, I made no progress whatsoever.'"

"When I became a monk, I envisaged leading a life of study, meditation and teaching—I wanted to be just like my Lamas and help people in the way they did. Clearly, that was not to be," Ribush wrote in 2002.[58] Twenty years later, he told me, "Honestly, I think of the time I've wasted more than what I've done."

His lamas would disagree. In a 2006 talk at Australia's Chenrezig Institute, on the land Ribush and his girlfriend donated so many years before, Lama Zopa Rinpoche looked back at the role played by Ribush and that small group of early devotees.

"It all started with the sincere hearts of the young students who came to Nepal and India looking for a spiritual life and a guru," the FPMT co-founder told the audience. "These young people broke their fixed ideas about a materialistic life and about there being just one life." Even though they weren't businesspeople, he said, they persevered and built a worldwide organization that spread the teachings of Buddhism. "There is a huge difference, like the difference between the earth and the sky, between working in a factory and offering service. There's a huge difference when you think about the benefits that sentient beings receive, and it makes so much difference to your own life."[59]

Tenzin Palmo did not believe Tibetan Buddhism has a monopoly on *Truth*. It may be *her* path, but it is not the *only* path, she told me a quarter of a century after we first met.

"The analogy of walking up a mountain is useful because you go up the North face or the South face or the East face, West face, and everybody's walking up the same mountain, but we don't recognize it because the scenery is very different. Very, very few people actually get to the top and get a 360-degree view. But even if they do, they're going to come down the same way they went up. So, therefore, they're not going to recognize that other paths would actually lead there, too," she continued. No matter the doctrine that puts them on their path, those few who do reach the top, she believed, all encounter the same Truth. "I think that there is ultimate reality within us. And if it's the ultimate reality, it cannot be different for different religions."

In her 2012 talk at Deer Park, she told the audience, "All genuine spiritual traditions are trying to deal with the little self so that it can dissolve and open up into something much more."[60] In such teachings, she frequently used the analogy of a cloud-covered sky to describe the challenge of glimpsing that ultimate reality. "When you look, all you see are clouds, but if you keep looking, then eventually the clouds might clear for a short time. Then suddenly you see there's the sky. It's not clouds." Even when the clouds come back, she said, we still know the sky is behind them. So, too, that glimpse of ultimate reality. "And so that can happen for anybody. It doesn't even have to do with religion, per se. Many people have a sudden glimpse of something beyond me, which they recognize as being their true nature."

Religious doctrines provide the framework to contextualize that glimpse, whatever name they may give ultimate reality. But for those who do not have a spiritual path, she warned, such glimpses can be disorienting, or worse. "Quite ordinary people suddenly get it, but then they have no context in which to place it. And that's very, very frightening. Especially if you have no container for that kind of understanding. It disorientated their whole lives, because they saw that what we regard as being a reality, is not genuine reality at all."

"Then each religious doctrine is just a tool?" I asked her.

"Throughout history, humans have always created some kind of structure on which to hang their innate feelings of something beyond themselves, however they want to frame that."

But doctrine alone, she said, cannot reveal ultimate Truth. "That's why all spiritual paths have some elements of meditation or silent prayer, and so forth. It's to allow our consciousness to deepen and gain some kind of inner recognition that we're not just our surface."

Palmo had come away from her interactions with counterparts on other non-Buddhist spiritual paths convinced that they shared the belief that it is ego that prevents us from recognizing our true nature. I asked her why so few in any religion immerse themselves in the mystical side. "Because it's hard. The principles are very simple, but simple doesn't mean easy. The ego resists because it knows it's the death of the ego. The ego ultimately doesn't exist, but in the meantime, it seems very powerful."

In Tenzin Palmo's Kagyu tradition, advanced meditation practices are the priority. That isn't the case in other religions, where mystics through history have found themselves outcasts for pressing beyond the strictures of doctrine. "They reached to that which was beyond dogma, and that's very threatening to the establishment," she said. "Like with St. Francis of Assisi, he was very, very careful, because so many of his time were not only repudiating the wealth of the church but also recognizing that God was something that they could apprehend for themselves. They didn't need an intermediary of a priest. That was dangerous for the Church."

In the West these days, many people in search of meaning in their lives become spiritual grazers, sampling the many offerings on the religious landscape: a "mindfulness" retreat this month, a Sufi sema the next. Palmo believed that while those paths all have the potential to bring their students to a place of realization, that can only happen if one full path is traversed.

"People expect instant results. They learn one meditation, they sit there, nothing happens, they hear somebody is teaching something else, and then they rush off and they start doing that. That is a problem. When you do a little bit of this, then a little bit of that, a little bit of that, you don't have anything central. The example would be if you're in the desert, but you know underneath there is an underground lake. So, you're trying to get to the water, and you dig a little hole, but it's still very dry, so you try another little hole, and then you try another little hole, and in the end, you end up just with a claim full of holes."

A few years after Tenzin Palmo became a Buddhist and left for India, her mother did the same. She spent a year with Palmo before returning to England, but she continued helping to support her daughter. Friends told Palmo that her mother prayed that in their next life she would again return as Palmo's mother, because she was afraid other parents might not understand that her daughter needed to lead a *special* kind of life.[61]

Nick Ribush was a reluctant teacher, as is fitting for a scribe. His dharma talks revolved around the teachings of his lamas, not his own interpretations. "I couldn't speak extemporaneously like Lama Yeshe did and like Lama Osel does," he replied when I asked about his reluctance. "When I have to talk, I just follow the quite traditional teachings."

In his articles and responses to questions from students at FMPT events, Ribush would almost inevitably quote Lama Yeshe or Lama Zopa Rinpoche, rarely straying from the many books of their teachings that he had published. "Rinpoche taught us that motivation is everything; it is motivation that determines whether an action will be positive—the cause of happiness—or negative—the cause of suffering," he wrote in one article. "[T]he principal cause of happiness and suffering lies within, in our own minds, not externally, in the material world or other people."[62]

On one of the rare occasions when he offered his own perspective, Ribush made it clear he didn't expect that suffering to end anytime soon.

"Although personally I believe that only Buddhism, purely practiced, can offer true peace and happiness to the world, it's not going to happen. The world is getting worse, not better. Society is far too deluded and immature for Buddhism to gain wide acceptance. The planet is grossly overpopulated, and there are too few resources and far too many powerful and dangerous weapons in the hands of ignorant, angry people. The main problem, of course, is that we believe that happiness comes from external phenomena; we don't understand karma, and how peace, happiness and satisfaction are created by the mind. All we can do as individuals is to control our own minds, avoid negative actions and practice virtue to the best of our ability. The opportunities we have today might be the best we'll have for a long time, and we should take full advantage of them while they last."[63]

In an online teaching to mark the thirty-third anniversary of Lama Yeshe's death—which Tibetans call *Parinirvana*—Ribush was asked what he learned in his decades with the lamas. "I certainly learned that I had completely the wrong worldview until I met the teachings on Tibetan Buddhism; and the main lesson really is that happiness comes from your own mind." His tone was that of a student responding in a measured, almost rote, manner, as if ticking off the Dharmic boxes. "And suffering comes from your own mind. And external circumstances are merely secondary. Positive karma brings happiness and negative karma brings suffering. That was kind of the main thing I learned."

I later asked him to strip away the formal language and reduce what he learned to its essence.

"The bottom line really is that happiness comes from your own mind, not from external phenomena. People, or material possessions, or nice scenery, or flashy cars—a lot of things I used to chase after. If you work with your mind, it's easy to be content."

He paused and added, "I fully believe it is possible to achieve a cessation of suffering, I don't think I have come even close to it."

Like many Tibetan teachers, Tenzin Palmo frequently emphasized that life is about preparing for death and what comes after. But she tended to frame it a bit differently than more traditional teachers, telling one audience, "As Professor Dumbledore advised young Harry Potter, 'For one with a well-organized mind, death is but the next great adventure.'"[64]

She told another group that the best we can hope for as we approach the moment of death is to be able to look back on our lives and know that we have done something to benefit ourselves and others. "Maybe you are not radiating lights from a lotus twenty feet above the ground, but you have made some progress with this life."[65]

Palmo's "progress"—her unique impact on Buddhism—was recognized in 2008 by the head of her spiritual lineage, who conferred on her the rare title of *Jetsunma*, which loosely translates as venerable master, and is the counterpart to the title *Jetsun* that was bestowed on her spiritual inspiration, Jetsun Milarepa.

Palmo and Ribush were both in their eighties when we last spoke for this book. Their dharma paths had been very different, but neither believed they had much choice in the matter.

"This is not how I thought my life would turn out," Ribush told me in 2021. "I didn't leave Australia in the early '70s on a spiritual quest. I left looking for a good time."

In contrast, Palmo *did* leave Britain on a very focused, very specific spiritual quest to find her Kagyupa guru, but in other ways, she, too, was surprised by where she ultimately found herself. When she asked the Dalai Lama in the 1990s whether she should build a nunnery, as her teacher had asked, or return to her cave, "He told me, 'Well, of course, to start a nunnery is very good, and you should do that. But don't give it much of your time. One or two years is enough. Then go back into retreat because for you it is most important to serve beings by being in retreat.'"[66] One month in retreat each year was all she was able to manage in the three decades that followed as she built the nunnery, traveled the world six months a year giving teachings and raising money, and led several international Buddhist organizations.

The Jetsunma was accepting about it all; she believed it was simply her path that led her up the mountain and then to the gates of her nunnery. "I really feel this is what I was meant to do, because as soon as that I was asked to do it, everything came together," she told me. "It all just was meant to happen."

Ribush felt the same about his own journey from the hippie trail to the dharma path. "One way is to say this all happened by accident," he told me. "But I could also look back at all my years before I left Australia and how my medical career didn't quite develop as I thought it was going to and I could see Lama Yeshe kind of reeling me in. Not that I really think that he was aware of my existence or that I could at all be useful, but there is a way of looking at it where you could see somehow it was gradually bringing me step by step closer to the lamas."

He thought back to that Nepali cave where he spent four-and-a-half months so many years before. "The happiest I've ever been was when I was doing retreat in '74. I didn't want to come out of there. I wanted to stay there for years; as long as I could." But he knew his path, in this lifetime at least, lay in a different direction. "I had to help Rinpoche. Otherwise, maybe I'd still be there." Ribush shook off the reverie. "Books got me into this at the beginning, they've kept me going, and I hope they'll be there at the end. I would like to continue editing and publishing dharma books for the benefit of all sentient beings until the day I die. It sure beats being a boxer's second."

What happens in the next life, he's not so sure.

As for Tenzin Palmo's vow to endlessly reincarnate as a woman until all beings have reached enlightenment, the Jetsunma gave herself some maneuvering room: "I mean, if it ever happened that the females were all in charge and the men were not listened to anymore, then maybe to come back as a male, to help the boys. But that's not happening very soon," she said with a knowing smile. "So in the meantime ..."

The Jewish Bard

Jill Hammer, who lives between the sacred words

"*The physical world in which we live ... is only part of an incon-ceivably vast system of worlds. Most of these worlds are spiritual in their essence ... they exist in different dimensions of being.*"
Rabbi Adin Steinsaltz, *The Thirteen Petalled Rose*

She had me at Lilith.

My children are the souls of yours [Lilith told Eve]. Until there are bodies for them, they cannot remain in the world.
...
We are meant to scatter our sparks in the world. You must bear the bodies for the souls that are waiting. You must begin the story, Eve.

It all made so much sense. Adam and Eve weren't tossed out of the Garden of Eden because Eve messed up and ate the forbidden fruit. It was all part of *our* plan. God wanted to see himself; *we*—sparks of His being—wanted to taste the physical to experience, learn and grow. We weren't going to get that in some Paradise.

> So, Lilith came to Eve in the Garden of Eden and set it all in motion.
> Without that task, we are not alive [Lilith continued]. And so you must begin death, and hope, and children.

This is not an ancient tale found on some rediscovered scroll. The words come from the inner life of a relatively obscure university professor living on the Upper West Side of Manhattan, who also happens to be a rabbi, priestess, poet, shaman, and cofounder of a movement to rebirth the feminine in Jewish practice, and whose influence, according to the Jewish magazine *Moment*, "can now be found in many of the foundational institutions of American Judaism."[1]

Her name is Jill Hammer, but if you don't venture into the corners of Judaism where the Goddess dwells, you have probably never heard of her.

> Somewhere between the Talmud and the Zohar, I came across the story of the Divine Mother. I met her again in the words of my ancestors, so powerfully She burst out of the world of ideas and out into the open sea. Now I live out there.

That passage in Hammer's 2016 compilation of prose and poems, *The Book of Earth & Other Mysteries*, weaves together the threads that shape her worldview: a deep reverence for ancient esoteric Jewish teachings, a profound connection to the Divine Feminine, and a level of mystic insight that, as one admirer put it, runs in her DNA.

A Jewish colleague heard I was writing a book about under-the-radar mystics and suggested Hammer, an ordained rabbi on the faculty of the Academy of Jewish Religion. I was immediately captivated.

Havdalah (Separation), Hammer's retelling of the story of the poisoned apple, was one of the first pieces of her writing that I read. To Hammer, Lilith is no she-demon, as depicted in the Bible (Isaiah 34:14), or spurned first wife of Adam, as described in Medieval Jewish texts. She is the spiritual mother of us all; Eve's ethereal alter ego, whose divine mission is to embody the Word and give birth to the world.

> "And disobedience," said Eve quietly after a long moment. "I must begin that as well."
>
> Lilith smiled, her dark eyes glowing with the firelight. "You may find that even in rebellion, you are following the sound of the Voice."

The tale is an example of *midrash*, reading between the lines of ancient texts for deeper wisdom. Skeptics might call it fiction—an alternative fairy tale made up by its author. But for practitioners of midrash, and others familiar with mystic experience, it is a form of inspired writing. Not necessarily "channeling" in a literal sense, but a method of tapping other ways of knowing; to revisit and perhaps recapture the truths behind ancient spiritual tales that may have been misinterpreted or corrupted through the ages.

As Rabbi Zalman Schacter-Shalomi, a founder of the Jewish Renewal movement, wrote, "This is not a world of pure imagination, but a place where worlds or realities meet and coalesce."[2] Hammer described it as filling in the white space between the lines to "uncover the voices that the text does not hold."[3]

> She did not make evil; that was God. She has been framed.

"There's something of the shamanic in the midrashic process," Hammer told me in the first of our many conversations. "This was probably true of the rabbinic creators as well, that they had a sense that something spiritual was happening as they were creating these stories."

Religious scholars have been using midrash to interpret and explicate sacred texts since at least the sixth century. Among those who study esoteric Judaism, the process is called White Fire Torah. Jewish sages teach that the words of the Torah, the first five books of the Hebrew Bible, or Old Testament, were written with mystic black fire, representing truth that is clear and indisputable. But they believe there is a second higher form of Torah hidden in the white fire—the spaces between the words—that is discernable only to those who look deeply.[4]

Some experts argue that the Bible itself is midrash, a compilation of sometimes conflicting versions of the same events, interpreted and reinterpreted. One expert describes midrash as "our persistent attempt to create meaning" from the ancient texts. It "can be didactic, moralistic, subtle, and even subversive."[5]

"Through midrash," Hammer explained in one of her books, "each generation can add its own wisdom and experience to a fixed text and makes it dynamic so that it does not reflect a single era but every era in which it is read. A holy text can remain holy only if it stretches into the lives of its readers."[6]

For Hammer, the glimpse into Lilith and Eve's alternate Garden dug at the roots of the patriarchy and misogyny she saw as molding centuries of Jewish doctrine, and it tapped into the earth-based feminism and Jewish mysticism at the heart of her worldview: "I write midrash to give biblical women the honor that is due them as prophets, rulers, and teachers of Israel and to carry on their legacy," she wrote in *Sisters at Sinai: New Tales of Biblical Women*. "Not everything we have inherited from the Rabbis is just or beautiful."[7]

It is that unveiling of the feminine hidden between the words that has so entranced a growing number of students whose path she has crossed. "I can't remember the exact moment, but as I became more and more engaged with progressive Judaism and mystical Judaism, there was a growing sense that this was a luminous figure in that landscape," recalled Rav Jericho Vincent, the daughter of an Orthodox rabbi, who considers Hammer one of her most important teachers.[8]

Midrash also gave Hammer a chance to commune with these historic figures. Her process often involves meditating on specific Biblical matriarchs. "There is something magical about it, you know," she told me with wonder in her voice. "There is a sense of ancestors wanting to talk to you, wanting to come through in some way."

"[T]he muse comes like the wind, invisible but tangible, and nearly knocks one over with its force," she wrote in *The Book of Earth*.[9] Her journeys took her to "a mythic space where our ancestor's spirits can sustain us and give us hope for the future."

It is a place where "the imaginal and the oceanic meet."[10] But she is careful not to put a name to what was going on. "I don't know that one can say with any certainty what part of this is my own imagination and what part of it is inspiration from something beyond myself. Is this me or not me? I feel like that's an open question, and I prefer to leave it an open question."

In one such meditative encounter, Hammer recounts receiving a teaching from Leah, one of two wives of the Biblical patriarch Jacob. In the esoteric teachings of the Kabbalah, Leah is associated with divine wisdom. In the encounter, she seemed to reinterpret a passage from Deuteronomy to remind Hammer of the role of midrash:

> "The mother bird is Torah," Leah said, "and the nest holds the traditions of the Jewish people. Sometimes it is necessary to climb the tree and take the eggs, to find something in the Torah and use it in a new way."

"Midrash is always surprising, both when it comes from others and when it comes from within. My encounter with Leah taught me an important lesson," Hammer recalled. "Interpretations change; what we believe to be revelation also changes over time, although that uncertainty may be disturbing."

Some lessons conveyed in midrash are complex. At other times, there is a sudden flash of insight, as she wrote in *Sisters at Sinai*:

> To make midrash, in any age, is to become a character in the action, to wrestle a blessing from the words, to receive a sacred challenge and a powerful gift.

There are many voices in Hammer's midrash. At times, as in the tale of Lilith and Eve, it is third person; in other stories, as when Lot's wife recounts her woes, it is the character herself who is telling the story:

> When I heard we had to leave Sodom I was thrilled. I hated the place. No good yogurt was to be found.

Hammer is both respectful and subversive in her retelling of the ancient tales, never hesitating to eviscerate Biblical orthodoxies, as in a story narrated by the Angel Gabriel:

> In the days just after the creation of the world, certain angels, others among my kind, lusted after human women and pursued them.

Hammer's academic credentials as a PhD and director of spiritual education at the Academy for Jewish Religion in New York, coupled with her encyclopedic knowledge of the Torah and other Jewish scriptures, lends a critical level of authenticity to her mystical analyses. "She is always going to the tradition which has many branches and bringing it back to herself and then going out again and coming back again. And that is part of what makes her work so important," said award-winning poet and midrashist Alicia Ostriker, winner of the Jewish National Book Award. Rav Jericho Vincent agreed: "She had the clarity and the *chutzpah* to be able to look at this wall of patriarchal texts and to notice that there were glimmers of our mother's voices that patriarchal culture had tried to ignore."

"She was born to do this," said Ostriker, "she was born with a mystic DNA."

A self-described bookworm, Hammer grew up in the Hudson River Valley town of Fishkill, New York in the 1970s, playing in the woods and streams surrounding the town and reading nonstop in the well-stocked library.

It was decidedly not a religious upbringing. Hammer was adopted when she was a baby, and her birth parents were not Jews. Her adoptive father was what she called "reflexively Jewish"; he acknowledged his Jewish identity but wasn't particularly religious. Her adoptive mother was a German refugee who converted to marry Hammer's father, a soldier she met in Germany at the end of World War II. As Hammer described it, her parents went through the motions of the religion—occasionally going to synagogue and sending her to Sunday Hebrew school—but it wasn't really something that interested them.

"They thought it was weird that I loved Hebrew school," she recalled. They thought it was even more weird when she enrolled at Brandeis University, founded by Jews for Jews after the war, and dove headlong into what she described as the school's "playground" of Jewish philosophy and identity.

At Brandeis, Hammer avidly connected with her religion. She kept kosher, observed the Sabbath, and prayed three times a day. But she quickly found herself pushing back against the strictures of the male religious hierarchy, including by laying tefillin during prayers, strapping onto her arm and head black leather boxes containing Hebrew scrolls, an act traditionally prohibited for women.

Even as, in class, one of her most distinguished Brandeis professors railed against the concepts of the divine feminine, Hammer immersed herself in the work of Jewish women poets. She quickly concluded that something had been lost in the centuries of male domination of Judaism. As she later wrote in *Book of the Earth*:

> I have found a river that flows beneath the Torah and sometimes rises to irrigate its words.

Hammer felt a sisterhood with the ancient women called to be "midwives of spiritual consciousness" and came to understand "that I heard the same calling, the same holy wind. I was becoming a pipe for music that had not yet been heard."[11]

She eventually earned a PhD at the University of Connecticut. Somewhere along the way, Hammer had convinced herself that she needed to be a social psychologist—"I have no idea why"—but by the time she finished the degree she knew she had a different life path and enrolled in Rabbinical School at the Conservative Jewish Theological Seminary. The inspiration was a dream of God as a pregnant woman who offered her a lamp. She was wise enough not to share that in her admissions interview.

It was early days for women in the Rabbinical ranks, and they were not warmly embraced by all. "There was a sense among some of my teachers that, well, you know, we're letting women in now and we're gonna let you be rabbis, but don't break anything." That didn't sit well with Hammer. "I was like, that's not an okay deal to make with us. You've been excluding us for two thousand years. You can't just decide that we're not allowed to touch anything," Hammer said, rolling her eyes and laughing. "So, a lot of my work has arisen out of a desire to make sure that women and other marginalized people are included in this religious tradition. And our histories are included." Looking back, she told me, it was clear this was where her ultimate path began to be sketched. "It wasn't really 'til I got to rabbinical school that I became a little radicalized around not only feminism, but mysticism and earth-based stuff, because I was confronting directly the patriarchy of the ancestral texts, many of which did not feel good to me as a woman and as a queer person."

A spiritual insurgent even back then, Hammer's hope was to seed a "virus" that would "replicate itself" within the rabbinical ranks to elevate the role of women. But her other agenda was to make sure that spiritual experience took its rightful place at the heart of Jewish practice, because, she said, without that, "it's just boring and stultifying."

The night before her first Talmud class, Hammer had a dream that she walked past the seminary gates and entered a witch school. Looking back, she was convinced "the dream was telling me something that I wasn't yet ready to hear. The kind of spiritual leader I was becoming had a past, and it wasn't in a rabbinical academy."[12] As she would later write in *The Hebrew Priestess*:

> The old temple of Western religion is burning. ... We are seeking a new temple, one that links our inherited traditions with our forgotten ancestors.

The Goddess is a constant presence in Hammer's life. She has dived deep into the ancient texts, finding evidence of the Goddess everywhere.

> She is the numinous, genderless cloud of glory hovering over communities of prayer, sickbeds, and the Temple; and sometimes She is the wife of God, the mother of the Israelites, weeping over their exile.

Lady Wisdom, who Proverbs describes as "a tree of life to all who cling to Her," echoed the prebiblical goddess Asherah, variously known to other peoples of the ancient Middle East as Ashtoreth, Astarte, and Ishtar. She was considered God's consort and was so influential in early Judaism that she was represented in the First Temple in the form of a tree or pole, since she, too, was known as the "tree of life." Asherah, in turn, carries in her the spirit of Tiamat, "the Babylonian goddess of the primordial sea, whose body was torn apart to create the world." She would emerge as the Shekhinah in the teachings of the kabbalists, "the wife of God, the mother of the Israelites."[13]

According to the Zohar, the canonical text of Kabbalah, "The Holy Shekhinah comes down and spreads Her wings over Israel like a mother embracing Her children."[14]

An underlying theme of kabbalistic teachings is that the separation of the Shekhinah from the masculine aspect of God reflects a fragmentation of cosmic unity that can only be restored by human action. Hassidic Jews begin some prayers with the dedication, "For the sake of the unification of the Holy Blessed One with His Shekhinah."[15] Hammer quotes the Baal Shem Tov's teaching: "Prayer is a form of intercourse with the Shekhinah."[16] She argues that "for much of Israelite history, goddesses were still active divine entities in the lives of the Israelites," until the advent of Rabbinical Judaism system wiped the Feminine aspect of the Creator from Jewish religious history.[17]

Yet, she insists, the divine feminine is "hidden ... in plain sight" in the texts, in the menorah, and in ritual: "The Torah, dressed in finery and then undressed during the Torah service for a ritual of learning and knowing, is an image of a woman."

This, said Rav Jericho Vincent, is Hammer's special talent. "She's like an oyster diver. She's able to go very deep into the esoteric text and find that one line that on which you can build a castle. The way the Jewish tradition works, it's so anchored in text, and there's this problematic need for there to be a verse that a man said a thousand years ago that says that this is okay."

It was during a 2004 retreat that Hammer glimpsed her *real* calling. As candlelight reflected off the walls of a womb-like cavern in upstate New York and Hammer's future wife, Shoshana Jedwab, pounded out a hypnotic beat on her *djembe* while chanting an invocation to the Divine Mother-Father, twenty women cried out in an ecstatic release of existential pain. Hammer stepped into the center of the circle, knee-deep in a pool formed by an underground river, to preside over the culmination of the ritual. Each woman cast away a stone representing all that they wanted to shed from their lives, then immersed herself in the cold water. "It was one of my first conscious moments of priestessing: escorting the larger force of the universe into the realm of the human."[18]

She had been growing into that role since childhood. "I read about princesses; that wasn't me," she told me, shaking her head, as if confirming that to herself. In the fantasy novels to which she was drawn she repeatedly encountered mythical priestesses. But the moment she saw the High Priestess card in a tarot deck, she had a shock of recognition and knew the priestess would be integral to her life.

"I wasn't, I wasn't beautiful in, uh, you know, in," she hesitated, discomfort visible on her face, "in the way that people found, you know, beautiful in a, you know, in a ..." she trailed off, remembering the pain. "And I certainly wasn't passive. I was interested in ideas and in creating things. I probably came off as a know-it-all." She laughed. Then her face turned serious again. "I remember, I was probably nine or ten feeling old, feeling fundamentally different than many of my peers," she continued, looking off into the distance.

"And I remember feeling that the social world in which many people moved was not a world that appealed to me, or that I even really knew how to participate in. I had friends, but the easeful social connections that some people had were not open to me. It was the other worlds that most pulled me, and where I felt most at home and most alive. So, although I didn't really discover mysticism until I was in my teens, I think I always did feel between worlds."

In 2005, Hammer brought her worlds together when she and another Jewish seeker, Holly Taya Shere—known today as Taya Mâ Shere—formed the Kohenet Hebrew Priestess Institute, dedicated to, as its website proclaimed, "embodied, earth-based, transformative, Jewish ritual." The name was derived from the ancient line of Jewish priests—the *kohen* or *cohen*—who traced their bloodline to Aaron, brother of Moses.

Shere's journey had taken her to Brazil, where she had immersed herself in an African-Brazilian spiritual tradition. "I came into presence of Goddess through moon, through earth, through body, through blood," she told an interviewer. From there she moved to a community of priestesses in Philadelphia engaged in ritual practices celebrating the lunar and solar cycles. Eventually, she was drawn "home" to her Jewish tradition, and discovered that, "What mattered to me, in terms of honoring the moon and honoring the earth and honoring the sacred feminine, was all there in Judaism—just not the Judaism I was handed growing up."[19] She visited a leader of the Jewish Renewal Movement, who gave her a blessing for a *shidduch*, usually a romantic match. But this blessing held a very different meaning. Not long after, she was introduced to Jill Hammer and the seeds of the Kohenet Institute were planted.

In Kohenet, Hammer and Shere sought to reconnect with the priestesses of Jewish history. "There was what you might call shamanic practice, earth-based practice, indigenous type spirituality happening" before and during the first Babylonian exile of the Jewish people, Hammer explained. She pointed to biblical tales of King Saul consulting the Witch of Endor and archaeological evidence of priestesses at the Holy Temple. But by the time the Jews returned from their exile, Hammer told me, they had become a very book-based culture that had lost its mystic underpinning. Lost also was the role of the Divine Feminine.

"The Middle East was a place where deity was generally multi-gendered. What the Bible did that was quite unique was to eliminate the whole idea of reproduction as part of creation, and if you read the book of Proverbs, which was written later, you still get this sense of the desire for God to have a feminine witness, helper, partner, advisor," Hammer explained.

That feminine alter ego is called Wisdom; she emerges in the Talmud as Shekinah and is then brought to mythic level in the Kabbalah, which presents God as multi-gendered yet part of a singularity. Hammer pointed to the fact that "El" was one of the renderings of God's name in Jewish religion. "El was a very important Canaanite god whose partner was Ashera, believed to be an early form of Shekhinah. That name *El* got borrowed and used by Hebrews to mean 'One God.' It's a function of patriarchy that we're able to absorb the name El, but not the name Ashera, because one is male and therefore is consonant with our view of deity, and one is female."

By presenting Shekhinah as a female aspect of God, the sages who transcribed the Kabbalah were not creating a polytheistic universe, but rather a richly textured idea of unity. "They thought that was kosher. And I don't think I'm saying anything different from them really."

When Hammer encouraged the women in that New York cave to release their anger in a primal scream, symbolically cast away their fears in the form of stones, then cleanse their souls by immersing themselves in the crystal waters of the underground pool, she was enacting the kind of ritual that would become central to the Kohenet Institute.

"I'd had powerful ritual experiences before that, but nothing like that," she told me. "Just the sense of timelessness and the voices and the stone and the feeling of the water, and it really inspired in me a sense of, 'This is what it means to do spiritual work, to be in service to this elemental truth that contextualizes all of our lives.'"

In the coming years, hundreds of Jewish seekers would flock to the teachings and retreats of the Kohenet Institute, many enrolling in the eighteen-month course that would culminate in ordination as a *kohenet*—a Hebrew priestess—in the tradition of Israelite women who fulfilled sacred roles as far back 800 BC.

Ritual was combined with study of Torah, Kabbalah, and the histories—and midrash—of the female ancestors whose sandaled feet had tread the spiritual path they now sought to follow. They learned of the many roles of sacred women in Jewish and pre-Jewish history: the Temple weavers who created the holy curtains and shrouds, the shrine keepers, prophetesses, midwives, witches, and many more. As Hammer wrote in *The Hebrew Priestess*, the sisters of Kohenet "build shrines together, pray together, dance together, go on spirit journeys together, and create ritual together. We commit to an embodied, earth-based, and ecstatic practice, and to rediscover Shekhinah in our lives in whatever way that makes sense to us."[20]

Liviah Wesseley, who was raised by a scientist, arrived at a 2016 Kohenet retreat a firm agnostic in search of an answer to the question, "Is meditation a thing Jews do?" The answer she found was yes, and a lot more. Her first impression was, "It's all weird and crazy and very *woo woo*. And I am not a very woo woo person." She and her roommate for the retreat started rating things on a scale of "woo." "We had a 'woo-ometer,' and we'd be like, 'That was just off the scale.'"

And then the *really weird* things started to happen.

Dreamwork was one important tool the Kohenet Institute used for opening the minds of these women thirsty for spiritual insight, firm in the knowledge that biblical prophets such as Abraham, Jacob, Joseph, and even the Pharoah, had paved the way. "These dreams [related by the prophets] are some of the first revelations within the Torah itself," Hammer wrote in *Undertorah: An Earth-Based Kabbalah of Dreams*. "We might say that dreams are the poems we and the Divine send to one another." Hammer quoted the Zohar in reminding her future priestesses, "Prophecy in the world is male, but the dream in the world is female."[21] Dream circles became a fixture of the retreats along with online "dream baskets" where, when they went back home, community members could deposit and discuss their dreams as a tool of healing and spiritual growth. "Dreams do not speak from stone tablets in voices of authority. They whisper in fragmented images, like a mosaic. They show us facets, faces, shards of the real."[22]

For Wesseley, this was all firmly in the world of woo. "Jill had suggested, 'As you're falling asleep, ask the goddess to bring you dreams and see what happens.' And I went, 'Yeah, sure.' I thought, 'This is the dumbest thing I've ever heard.'" But she did it anyway. The result was the first in a series of mystical experiences that grew in intensity. "It moved me to the point where I am now to some extent as woo woo as they come," she told me, laughing. Wesseley would go on to play an important administrative role in the institute and serve as a guardian priestess, filling the role of one who physically and energetically protects the community.

"I still feel a little like a little kid at her feet. She's just a remarkable intellect. And she seems to know everything about everything. She has a way of knowing. And I think part of it is intellect, but I think there's also a spiritual, mystical—I don't know—connection that she has to Judaism that I think is just extraordinary. I am blown away by her presence. I mean, she is a human, and I've seen her be quite human in moments, but sometimes it's hard to remember that she's a human, just so amazing." She paused, reflecting, then repeated, "She's amazing."

Such sentiments left Hammer nonplussed. I once asked her about how she felt about her role as a spiritual teacher. Her eyes welled with tears. "It's hard for me," she said with a self-deprecating smile. "I mean, many people come up to me to say, 'You've changed my life.' I … it's … it's a thing that happens to me … um … that I feel … I feel very weird about." She paused, her eyes welling with tears. "It's very humbling to be told that by people, you know?" She looked me in the eye then looked away. "It, it's very, very humbling to be told that. I still don't really know what to do with it. You know, I just, I just try to think of myself as, you know, some kind of—I'm gonna use the word 'channel,' although I don't really like that word. It's some piece of the universe that decided to come through me, and we don't know why about those things."

Caves hold a very special place in Jill Hammer's mystic worldview. For her, caves are a "return to the womb" and "the sense of non-separation." Because she was separated from her mother at birth, Hammer said the kabbalistic notion of healing the sense of separation from the Godhead was particularly powerful for her. She invoked Jewish feminist Bonna Haberman, who wrote, "The inner sanctuaries of the Jewish people are uterine."[23]

Back in that cave in New York state where her inner priestess emerged, Hammer had the sense "of not only descending in space but descending in time. I was going back into an ancestral experience. There was just something about the surroundings that made it feel like I had entered a portal into an ancestral moment." In the coming years, she would walk in the footsteps of the Greek goddess Persephone and her mother Demeter, the Mesopotamian goddess Inanna, and the Prophet Elijiah in their exploration of the spiritual descent, and feel kinship with the Greek nymph Heuresis, who proclaimed:

> The underworld draws me in
> like a child into a lap,
> as if there has never been a search,
> as if reunion has no need for words.[24]

"I have a certain fascination with myths of the underworld, which in some way, to me feels more compelling than going to heaven in the sky," she told me. "It feels more interesting to me to be going into the earth."

"Men do mountaintops, women descend," Alica Ostriker teased me when she heard the title of this book. "That's true of Jewish spiritual writers and particularly true of Jill."

Hammer agreed. "I think of the world of the poet, the world of the mystic, the world of the prophet, as *under* rather than up. The first Israelite conception of the afterlife is under the earth. Jung says that's the vertical dimension; whether you go up or down, it's the same. Right? And I tend to be a down person, like in my dreams, I find the entrance into the basement."

In the caves of Israel, Hammer found a new and visceral connection to the Divine Feminine of Judaism. She experienced Her in the "primordial birth canal" of Hezekiah's Tunnel, an eighth century cistern carved beneath Jerusalem; in a cave in Wadi Sorek, "with underground stalactite formations like breasts"; and in the hot springs of Tiberias, which was "like being in the womb of some immense being."

"I began to find that the Goddess would not stay safely in contemporary feminist poetry. She was in the land and I saw Her everywhere."[25] Hammer embarked on spirit journeys that led her to even more profound insights into the connection between the Divine Feminine and the very Earth itself. "That year in Jerusalem really contributed to my earth-based approach later on, because I had been largely taught a Judaism that took place in temples and synagogues and books, and having these experiences changed my view of what a spiritual life could be."

Hammer's rootedness in caves, her connection with the Divine Feminine, and the earth-based spirituality that draws on the Celtic blood she inherited from her birth parents, came together during a pilgrimage to Ireland's Oweynagat Cave, said to be the entrance to the underworld and residence of The Morrigan, a goddess associated with war, destiny, and fertility.

At the time of the visit, Hammer was nursing her daughter, Raya, and had not had a menstrual period for several years. But when she left the cave, Jill immediately started to bleed. "And not only did I start, but my partner started," she told me, amazement in her voice at the memory, "and not only did she start, but our babysitter, who was a trans man, started to menstruate. It was extraordinary. And we just felt that we had been in the presence of a massive feminine life force that had just triggered all of our uteruses. It was extraordinary."

As I was writing this chapter in a Scottish fishing cottage at the mouth of the North Sea, Hammer's spiritual ties to the energies of the Celtic goddesses and my own seemed to entwine. The Picts, the tattooed aboriginal tribes of northeast Scotland, are believed to have worshipped some of the same gods as the Celts. The goddesses of the Pictish faith were said to be particularly powerful. Among them were Macha and Badb, both said to be aspects of The Morrigan, whose cave had such an impact on Hammer. So the Jewish mystic was very much on my mind as my wife and I took a few days to explore this powerful spiritual landscape, walking the perimeter of a remote stone circle and gazing in admiration at Bennachie, a range of hills nearby that was the site of what was once a Pictish fort. And then, in a wooded knoll, we came upon a monumental sculpture of Persephone, incongruously standing in a glade.

Persephone, the Greek goddess whose ties to the underworld so influenced Hammer. At the feet of this towering figure, carved from a single 8.5 ton block in 1961, worshippers had laid pomegranate seeds which, according to the legend, she ate to seal her marriage to Hades. Her hand held a mirror. Its presence was perplexing. But then I learned that it pointed to the Maiden Stone, an eighth century Pictish monolith covered, Janus-like, in nature symbols and a Celtic cross a few hundred yards away. Legend has it that the daughter of a local laird made a wager with a stranger. If he could build a road up Bennachie before she could bake enough Bannock cakes for her wedding, she would marry him instead. The stranger turned out to be the Devil. And when she ran, he turned her into the Maiden Stone. The chip in the ten-foot-tall monolith, they say, is where the Devil grabbed her. In Persephone's mirror, we were seeing the dance between the Divine Feminine and the Devil play out in the mists of Scottish history.

"The Goddess really is everywhere," Hammer responded when I sent her to photos, "in so many different forms."

At the foundation of Hammer's mystic worldview are the teachings of the Kabbalah, a set of doctrines and practices that emerged in the twelfth and thirteenth centuries. The sages who brought forth the teachings of Kabbalah believed mystics tap "branches of cosmic knowing, prepared especially for that individual because they are attached to the very root of that person's soul."[26] Humankind—all of existence—is God incarnate to these sages, part of the "overflowing infinite light" of *Ein Sof*, the unfathomable Ground of Being;[27] "the divine power that is intertwined and combined with all the separate atoms of all beings."[28]

This is a nondual God; we—humankind and every animal, rock and tree—are Them, not separate from Them. As the Ba'al Shem Tov, the renowned seventeenth century founder of Hasidic Judaism wrote:

> No existence has existence other than the self-existence of God. Hence even that which at first glance seems as separated and sundered from divinity is itself absolute divinity.[29]

The soul, thirteenth century Spanish kabbalist Abraham Abulafia taught his followers, is part of the "cosmic stream of life," and our ultimate goal is to "untie the knots" that keep us bound to the physical and "liberate ... these sparks to restore them to divinity."[30] But mystics—and religions—are shaped by time and place. Kabbalists believe Jewish esoteric doctrine itself went through phases reflecting the time and place: "each an appropriate expression of the highest and most integrated levels of spirituality available in that period."[31]

The centerpiece of Hammer's scholarship is *Sefer Yetzirah* (*The Book of Creation*), a highly esoteric pre-Kabbalah text that dates at least to the sixth century A.D. It posits all of existence as an infinitely large temple suspended in the void with the Godhead at its center. Existence was created through God's breath; holy letters from the Jewish alphabet were the tools used to create the ethereal edifice, an echo of Hebrews 11:3: "By faith we understand that the universe was created by the word of God, so that what is seen was not made out of things that are visible"; and the New Testament: "In the beginning was the Word, and the Word was with God, and the Word was God" (John 1:1).

"It is the story of the cosmos as an unending ritual," Hammer told an online class about the text, before leading the participants, a collection of rabbis and serious students of Judaism, in a meditation in which they repeated the actions of God to "seal" all of existence. "God as cosmic architecture," she called it in *Return to the Place*, her study of the text. Since the Torah's name for God is YHWH, which can mean "Becoming One," she added, "We might even say God *becomes* creation."

In this divine cosmology, the physical plane—the world of action—is the farthest from the center, with four levels of awareness above, each veiled from the other. A web of connections is woven through the fabric of time and space, and a set of ten *sefirot*, cosmic orientation points or inscriptions that define the boundaries of the universe, representing both physical attributes—such as *self, vibration, manifestation*—and psychological characteristics, such as strength and kindness. The sefirot, sometimes also portrayed as angels, are constantly in motion, and there is an eternal coming and going of energies between the levels.

Hammer was drawn to the text from the moment she opened its pages. "The sefirot, the engaged pathways of divine creative power, are the end of the creative process, yet they are interwoven with the beginning, which is God," she wrote in *Return to the Place*. Via the sefirot, "divine energy interpenetrates creation." God is "a divine scribe engraving the sefirot and the letters upon the surface of reality."

This image of God manifesting mystical letters on the face of the void as an act of creation is consonant with Jewish myths of the Torah as an eternal teaching that existed before time began. The act of *sealing* space and time to create an otherworldly temple with the Godhead at its center sees its physical form in the Holy Temple of Jerusalem. It is, writes Hammer, "cosmos as both book and temple."[32]

Hammer saw in this ancient text a foretelling of modern physics. "It has this eerie parallel with contemporary science and philosophy, this sense of indeterminacy that sometimes we see in Sefer Yetzirah," she told her online class. "It's almost like a quantum. Is it a particle? Is it a wave? Are the sefirot like *this* or are they like *that*?"

"Like neurons firing in the brain," suggested one student. She smiled and nodded.

Hammer sees the concepts of Sefer Yetzirah as an invitation to "shift our egoic awareness to a consciousness in which we are channels for divine energy" and become "vessels for creative potency."[33]

While many aspects of Sefer Yetzirah can be found in later kabbalistic texts, it offers its own unique version of Jewish mysticism. Where the Zohar, a kabbalistic commentary on the Torah, describes levels of God or levels of existence that extend from the transcendent to the physical, which itself is a veiled illusion, and describes the soul's ability to move between these levels, Sefer Yetzirah posits this *running and returning* as taking place within us.

"You're not running to another world. You are connecting to the divine reality that is at the root of this world," Hammer told me. "Ultimately, we're empty space that God is filling with God's imagination, but we're also real too."

The visual expression of this spiritual geography used by both the Zohar and Sefer Yetzirah is the iconic image of the Sefirot, the mystical Tree of Life, which contains a multicolored map of the celestial order that carries a strong resemblance to the system of chakras in Eastern religions, and finds its counterpart in the "Cosmic Tree" of Christianity, "that stands at the center of heaven and earth, firm support of the universe," and its earthly manifestation the cross, "the Tree of Life planted on Calvary."[34]

Sefirot are the stuff of many dueling interpretations within the various schools of esoteric Judaism. Hammer's friend Rabbi Jay Michaelson called them "a nest of cosmological, theological, and literary speculation" that "may be understood intellectually, emotionally, physically, and spiritually."[35] There are even contradictions within Sefer Yetzirah itself. Hammer explained that it may be that Sefer Yetzirah incorporated a variety of even earlier texts, but, as she told her class, "it's also possible the book intends to confuse us that there are two different versions precisely because the book does not want us to become too certain about how God created the world."

At the heart of Sefer Yetzirah's account of creation stands Wisdom, also known as Sophia, a feminine aspect of the divine found in the biblical book of Proverbs, synonymous with the Divine Logos. Wisdom, Hammer wrote, is "a multiplicitous womb within which God creates the infinitely varied substances of the world." She "comprises a web of channels by which divine creative energy becomes created beings."[36]

Hammer weaves into this ethereal belief system what one scholar has called "kabbalistic shamanism,"[37] reaching back to the ancestors and plunging down into the earth for spiritual succor, awakening to the fact that, as one of her influences, ecologist and philosopher David Abram has written, "our sentient bodies are entirely continuous with the vast body of the land."[38]

"We experience the energies of the world as multiple and alive," Hammer told me. "One of the things that happened when people went from a more traditional Jewish community to the contemporary Jewish world is that a lot of what they believed in, ancestors and angels and house spirits and all kinds of things, were swept under the table because that was embarrassing and it wasn't scientific. And God became very abstract. But the original Jewish view of the metaphysical realms was very complex and populated."

There is plenty of archeological evidence to support Hammer's contention that the Divine Feminine played a significant role among at least some sects of ancient Judaism. This includes statues and ancient sites of worship of Yahweh and the Canaanite goddess Asherah—God and His wife—scattered across the Negev and Sinai. But the victors get to write, and rewrite, history.

"I think that Jill's heretical, pagan Judaism is much closer to the likely historical truth than anything resembling Orthodox Judaism," said Rabbi Jay Michaelson. "It's funny. She's simultaneously much less authentic and I think more authentic as a representation of what people were actually doing and believing before one Jewish sect prevailed over the other."

Hammer's earth-based, ritualistic approach to Judaism is an extension of the work of a handful of pioneering Jewish women who either left what they saw as a patriarchal Judaism that could not be reformed, such as Starhawk, a former Jew whose 1979 book *The Spiral Dance* helped launch the feminist, neopagan Goddess movement, and others, such as Rabbi Lynn Gottlieb, who in 1981 became one of the first women to become a rabbi in Jewish history.

It is also shaped by the rediscovery of meditation by a previous generation of Jewish seekers. As with the Christian meditation movement, the rebirth of Jewish mystic practice owes much to the East. In the '60s and '70s, Jewish seekers like Rabbi Zalman went to India and Southeast Asia and studied with Buddhist and Hindu masters. Some returned to the U.S. and are today among the most influential leaders of Buddhism in America. Others, as Hammer put it, became "spiritually bilingual" and led a renewal and rediscovery of Jewish meditation and mysticism.

If Hammer was Buddhist, one might say her early "discovery" of esoteric practices could be written off to karma. I mentioned this in my conversation with Reb Vincent and they reminded me that reincarnation has a central role in kabbalism, which teaches that souls continue to return to the physical until they have completed their role in healing creation. Only then can they reunite with the Godhead. Each prayer, each act of kindness—a *mitzvah*—creates an angel and strengthens our connection to the higher worlds. Jews call this *tikkun*, repair. Conversely, each act of malice or evil creates a bad angel, who are "parasites" pulling humankind away from God. "The more evil a human being does, the more life-force do these angels draw from him for their world," according to renowned Talmudic scholar Rabbi Adin Steinsaltz. Those who fulfill the task of "raising the level of the universe ... can wait after death for the perfection of the whole world" which will manifest what we know as Heaven. But those who fail to contribute to the repairs are fated to incarnate again and again.[39]

Reb Vincent told me that the teacher they shared with Hammer, Rabbi Zalman Schachter-Shalomi, taught that some Christians who converted to Judaism were Jews who perished in the Holocaust and had returned to complete their tikkun. When evaluating a person who wanted to convert, he wrote, it was important "to check whether we are dealing with a recycled soul, one who in a former life was a Jew."[40]

But not all souls have returned to complete unfinished work. The sages wrote of great teachers who, like the bodhisattvas of Buddhism, return again and again to help others complete their tikkun, "until the world will be filled with knowledge, bringing the nearness of completion."[41]

A subtext to Hammer's spiritual identity is that of the dragon, warranting an entire section in one of her books of midrash. When she was a teenager, Hammer had a dream of riding a dragon. "That dream is probably one of the formative experiences of my life, because it was like, 'Oh, this is what it feels like to be fully realized,'" she recounted, wonder in her voice at the memory. "For me, the dragon, although it's a mythological being, says something about the fire of being alive."

For Jewish women awakening their spiritual power, such dreams also upend traditional Jewish images of the dragon as embodying the demonic feminine. "Dragons appear as powerful, erotic, sacred figures that 'queer' the divine feminine by offering a norm-upending vision of what the feminine is and does," Hammer wrote in an academic article.[42]

But back in everyday reality, the dragon provided Hammer with a foil through which to see the world, whether pondering good and evil, being jostled on the New York subway, or lying exposed on the gynecologist's table.

The gynecologist has good news for her:
Her caves are just like boxes, all in order.
She feels obscurely angry, violated.
When he is not watching,
She eats his speculum.

As I began my conversations with Hammer in late summer of 2023, she was picking up the pieces of the Kohenet Institute, which had imploded just weeks before. It was a painful transition, one part financial, another personal. Like rock stars who had recorded their last album together, Hammer and Shere found themselves taking different forks, even as the priestesses they trained were being pulled between the various philosophical threads that made up the Kohenet tapestry. "It feels a bit like burying a friend who may not in fact be entirely deceased," Liviah Wesseley, who helped with the transition, told me sadly.

Many factors contributed to the demise of the organization, but the bottom line was simple: mystics are human too. "There was the tension between me and Taya," Hammer told me cautiously, reluctant to probe the wound too deeply. "We were very different. We came to love each other very deeply, but we didn't see eye to eye on everything." Ultimately, they came to the breaking point. "We were beyond burned out. Some people were really understanding and supportive, other people were really demanding. There were also political tensions in the community around Israel-Palestine, among other things." She paused, "*Mostly* around that actually."

In some ways, it was a blessing that Kohenet quietly disbanded. The tragedy of October 7, 2023, and subsequent war in Gaza, may well have torn the institute asunder. "Because Kohenet was a more radical community, we had a larger percentage of anti-Zionist Jews as well as people who would not embrace that label," Hammer told me. Left unsaid by Hammer was what would likely have happened if Kohenet was still functioning on October 7th. Wesseley filled in the white space between the lines. "If the institute hadn't fallen apart already, this would've done it."

The October 7th slaughter of her fellow Jews, and the Israeli invasion of Gaza, deeply shook Hammer and her wife Shoshana, whose father survived Auschwitz and fought in Israel's war of independence. Hammer looked drawn and exhausted when we spoke a few days after the massacre. I asked if there was anything in her belief system that would allow her to digest what had happened.

"In the Kabbalah, the world is a broken place," she said almost forlornly. "And the whole idea of tikkun, repair, which is at the heart of Kabbalah, assumes that our world is broken. And it makes the mystical assumption that the small acts of repair that we do are a way of slowly piecing back together that broken world. I don't think that's a bad way to look at the human condition."

As we spoke, thousands of human beings were being killed each day by other human beings. Divine intervention was not the answer, Hammer explained sadly. The onus, she said, was on us. "The

Kabbalah assumes that there isn't some deity looking at this from some perfect realm, but that the transcendent is *itself* implicated in all of this brokenness and also cannot escape it. And for me, that's a much more appealing theology than there's some God in some perfect space who could fix all this if only God would bother."

Hammer's spiritual ties to the soil of Israel ran deep, but compassion for all the human suffering then taking place had left her nerves raw.

"I'm a pessimistic idealist. I have a lot of desire to see a world that is built on compassion and justice, but not necessarily a lot of hope that human beings are going to get to that right away. I do see life and death as part of that reality, and neither is something to regard as evil. There can be acts that are evil ..." she trailed off, leaving the rest unsaid. After a pause, she added, "Everybody is here to fulfill their own tikkun. And that could be true of nations and peoples as well." It was almost as if she could see the parasitic angels of evil descending on the Middle East.

I asked what she was praying for, expecting something like "peace in the Middle East." Her response surprised me. In essence, she said, prayer has its limits. "I don't think of it as the kind of thing where I would intercede with an indifferent God to say, 'Please pay attention to my people.' Of course, I feel it that way sometimes, but theologically, that's not really how I think about it. Surely if God were already inclined to do the right thing, God wouldn't need my advice."

I could see a change in her face as she tried to compartmentalize her human pain and reconnect with her spiritual self. "As long as we live in bodies, there is the potential that we will fight over things, that we will hurt each other." The Kabbalah taught this was the inevitable result of imbalance between *gevuruh*, strength, and *chesed*, loving-kindness, in the world. Strength without compassion, she explained, was the root of evil. "It's like a cancerous growth that comes out of gevuruh. Then you get acts of ego and cruelty and separation."

But it was on the idea of Jews as the "chosen people" that she parted with her beloved Kabbalah. "I certainly feel the Jewish people have a unique history and perhaps destiny, but the Kabbalah's argument that Jews are engaged in this work of tikkun and other people are at best neutral and at worst agents of brokenness, that's not a thing I would want to adopt." That view just fueled narcissism and the quest for strength without compassion. Peace might be out of reach, but restoration of balance—which would be the first step—was at the center of her prayers. "I understand that there are things that may not move in response to my prayer, but maybe there are some things that can."

Even as the legal and financial structures of the organization were being unwound, Hammer was hard at work sketching the outlines of what would take its place. *Beit Kohenet*, Kohenet House, was already taking shape, offering classes, holding retreats, providing community for at least some of the 137 kohenot—the priestesses—its previous incarnation ordained, and considering whether ordination had a place in its future. While sensitive to how the kohenot may be perceived in the absence of the institution that created them, Hammer was optimistic. "I don't think that this is going to wreck the idea" of priestesses. "It's a blow. There's no question. But I think the idea will move on in new ways," she said in the spring of 2024.

"The institute has closed, but the movement has just begun," Liviah Wesseley told me. No matter what happened, the institute had made its mark.

Back in the '40s, Gershom Scholem, considered the founder of modern academic study of the Kabbalah, concluded his book, *Major Trends in Jewish Mysticism*, with the observation that the esoteric side of Judaism had largely faded from view: "Under what aspects this invisible stream of Jewish mysticism will again come to the surface, we cannot tell—that is the task of prophets not professors."[43]

Eight decades later, a mystic who also happened to be a professor was helping bring that invisible stream back to the surface, and with it, Judaism's ancient reverence for the Divine Feminine.

"When I started out writing about earth-based Judaism, I felt like I was on the fringes," Hammer told me in our last conversation.

Now, said her mentor Alicia Ostriker, she "joins the ranks of the creators of a tradition."

The Universe Is My Mirror

Swami Atmarupananda. Under the big tent.

"Truth is one, sages call it by many names."

Rig Veda

You might say Swami Atmarupananda is a clerk in the Walmart of spirituality. If you're looking for God, Atmarupananda will introduce you to Shiva, Kali and the many other deities of Hinduism. Not interested in the idea of a creator God? He will tell you all about the God that lies within you. On the fence? Atmarupananda has teachings that will help you understand both are equally true.

He's also quite happy to confirm the underlying validity of whatever religion happens to float your boat. Don't get the wrong impression; Atmarupananda isn't just out to tell spiritual supplicants whatever they want to hear. Rather, he represents a philosophy that takes the ultimate "big tent" approach to religion. Atlanta-born At-marupananda is a monk in the Ramakrishna tradition of Vedanta, a philosophy at the foundation of Hinduism.

In his worldview, all roads lead to enlightenment.

"We can think of Vedanta as a huge spiritual department store where you can find anything," Atmarupananda told me in one of our conversations. "In India, there was not this idea that when a new truth is discovered, old ideas have to be thrown out." Instead, they were absorbed into the spiritual culture. "The dominant view through Indian history has been that religion really is one thing, it's one impulse," he said with emphasis on "one," "and people do it in different ways."

As a result, he wrote in a 2010 primer, "Vedanta is more than just a religion and a philosophy, for it gives a place to all religions and philosophies in its encompassing vision."[1]

At the core of that vision is the belief that all beings are innately divine and the route to understanding is direct meditative experience of the "infinite reality out of which everything in the universe is made." His half century of study and practice has left Atmarupananda convinced that all religions offer valid paths to that goal, but that we shouldn't get hung up on the differences between what one person learns at church and another at the temple or mosque. As nineteenth century Vedanta philosopher Swami Vivekananda wrote, "Doctrines, or dogmas, or rituals, or books, or temples, or forms, are but secondary details."[2] It's all just *stuff*.

From the time he was twelve, Charles Ashmore was drawn to the idea of a spiritual life. He kept trying to read the Bible, but he couldn't quite get through it, even though he was inspired by the story of John the Baptist, who spent many years in the desert eating nothing but honey and locusts. That seemed pretty cool.

At one point, a girlfriend asked him what he wanted to be when he grew up. "I said, 'I want to be a hermit, living out in the forest thinking about the nature of life and death.' And she said, 'Well, I'll go to the forest with you.' And then I said, 'Well, I won't be a hermit then.' It wasn't a great pickup line," he added, rolling his eyes.

This would-be ascetic soon concluded that no religion had a monopoly on truth. That was long before he ever heard the word *Vedanta*. Growing up in South Carolina, both his parents were conservative Presbyterians—his brother would go on to become a minister—and he had been presented with a very no-questions-asked approach to religion. "It was basically, 'Just be good, believe, and after death you'll find out if it's true or not.' And that wasn't satisfying."

He recalls the sunny spring morning he stood outside church after Sunday school, waiting for Mass to start. The lesson had focused on the many Christian denominations and the fact that there were thirty-eight million Presbyterians in the world. For some reason, none of the other kids were around. So, with nothing else to do, he pondered what he had just learned. He *knew* that Christianity was the only true religion. And he *knew* that Protestantism was the only true form of Christianity. And he *knew* that Presbyterians were the best of the Protestants. "Then I thought, 'Well, how could it be that I was so lucky that I was one of just thirty-eight million people who was put by God into a family that belonged to the best denomination of the only true half of the only true religion?' And then I thought, 'What if the Catholics are right that *they're* the only true religion and Protestants are wrong?' And that gave a jolt to my surety. Then I thought, 'Well, I've got Jewish friends also. I don't know what they think about Christianity, but I know that they're different. And what if I'd been born in Saudi Arabia in a Muslim family? I might've thought Islam is the only true religion, and my form of Islam is the only true form of Islam. If I'd been born in a Chinese Buddhist family, I might have thought the same way about my form of Buddhism.' Then I thought, 'Well, it seems that what we take to be true religion depends on where we're born, but that can't be the standard of truth.'"

Nothing like this had ever happened to him before. "The thoughts came one right after another without any obvious reason. And so, I suddenly decided, 'Well, they can't all be true because they all teach different things. But then how do you know which is true?' And then I came to the conclusion: 'Probably *none* of them are true. They give impetus for moral action and that's all. But none of them are true.' And then the church bell rang, it was time to go into church and I was a newfound agnostic."

A year later, the seventeen-year-old headed to Sweden as an exchange student. The newfound agnostic felt right at home in a country where three-quarters of the population did not believe in God. At least until he wandered into a shop and picked up the book that changed everything. The red cover, on which the name of British writer Christopher Isherwood featured prominently, caught his eye. And the description on the back—which explained that Vedanta Hinduism viewed all religions as inherently true, with differences shaped by time, place, and culture—intrigued him.

The book was *Vedanta for the Western World*, a compilation of essays published in 1948. It was edited by Isherwood and included several chapters by Aldous Huxley, both of whom Ashmore already admired. With another British writer, Gerald Heard, they made up a trio dubbed the "mystical expatriates" for their role in bringing Eastern philosophy to the West.

"Reduced to its elements, Vedanta Philosophy consists of three propositions," Isherwood wrote in the introduction. "First, that Man's real nature is divine. Second, that the aim of human life is to realize this divine nature. Third, that all religions are essentially in agreement."[3]

As he immersed himself in the massive, 450-page tome, Ashmore was amazed. "I thought, 'Wow, these are my own ideas. But I never knew that I had them. I had no context for understanding what was going on. I had no idea of reincarnation or anything like that. It was unsettling in a very good and creative sense. It shook up all my ideas and I thought, 'Now I've found where I'm going; now I know what my life is about.' And the rest is, as they say, history."

Back in the U.S., a friend introduced him to a book by the influential Trappist monk and mystic Thomas Merton. "And that was the first I knew that there was such a thing as monks in the modern world."

Meanwhile, Ashmore tried college. He enrolled thinking he wanted to be a mathematician—"just to spin out pure mathematics, the less practical the better"—but then he had another disappointing discovery: His professors were not happy people. He dropped out and hit the road, sampling a few communes and reading widely about mysticism as he traveled, eventually landing in San Francisco.

In the famed Shambhala bookstore, he found a wall of books on Hinduism. He picked out seven. It turned out that all were published by the Sri Ramakrishna Society, the Vedanta organization to which he would later dedicate his life. But it took a near death experience to get him there. One night, as he hitchhiked back to South Carolina, the driver asked him to take a turn behind the wheel in the middle of a terrible rainstorm. Suddenly, at 75 miles-an-hour on a busy highway, the windshield wipers stopped working. "The rain was coming down in sheets. I'm in the middle of the highway, I couldn't see anything, just red blurs from the taillights. I couldn't tell distance or anything," he recalled later. "And I thought, 'This is gonna be the death of us.'" Like so many people in such situations, he tried to negotiate with God. "I just said to the powers that be, whoever they might be, that if I make it through this, then I'm going to dedicate my life to something good. I'm not just gonna go hitchhiking around and wasting my time."

Unlike most of us who have done that deal, he made good on his promise. "I didn't forget that thought." By the time he got back to South Carolina, he had decided he wanted to be a monk. He visited a Catholic monastery in Georgia, but it quickly became clear this was not the place for him. "The monks were rudderless," he told me. The reforms of Vatican II meant their centuries of silence had been broken, "and they couldn't stop talking," he recalled with a laugh.

He turned back to his books on Vedanta and soon decided, "Well, this is what I really love, so I'll go with that."

Ashmore eventually found his way to the Chicago outpost of the Ramakrishna Order of India, known in the U.S. as the Vedanta Society. The order is built around the teachings of Sri Ramakrishna, a Bengali saint and mystic who is credited with helping to revive Hinduism in the nineteenth century. "Many are the names of God, and infinite the forms that lead us to know Him," Ramakrishna told his followers. "As the same fish is dressed into soup, curry, or cutlet, so the Lord of the Universe, though one, manifests Himself differently according to the different likings of His worshippers." [4]

Ramakrishna is said to have achieved a high spiritual state through meditative absorption in the teachings of Hinduism, then practiced Islam, meditated on Christ, and immersed himself in Buddhism and Sikhism. "He came to the same ultimate realization through each path and was convinced too, thereby that all paths lead to the same goal," the future Atmarupananda told me in one of our early conversations.

It was a worldview that resonated with the young seeker. In 1969, he became a monk in the Ramakrishna Order of India. Vedanta, the heart of Ramakrishna's teachings, is one of the main schools of Hinduism. But its practitioners also see it as a universal philosophy that encompasses all spiritual knowledge. Vedanta means conclusion—*anta*—of the Vedas, ancient texts based on oral wisdom dating back as far as the fifth century BC, and *veda* means knowledge. Thus, Vedanta can be interpreted as *the end* or *essence* of knowledge. "This, then, is the ultimate meaning of Vedanta," according to Swami Tyagananda, the Hindu chaplain at Harvard and MIT and a monk in the Ramakrishna Order. "[I]t is the quest for spirituality. It is the Religion beyond all religions, or the Essence of Knowledge that frees us from ignorance, bondage and existential suffering."[5]

For Ashmore, that road to ending existential suffering involved a fair dose of real-world suffering. He was sent on a quick trip to India to be ordained by the head of the order, but when Ashmore, now known as Atmarupananda, returned to Chicago, he was assigned to the monastery's fruit farm in rural Michigan, ironically in the township of Ganges, named for the famed holy river of India. The accommodations were primitive, the food terrible, and the labor backbreaking. "We'd be out trimming pear trees twenty feet up in snowstorms with wind blowing." The monks lived in a three-room fruit picker's cabin with one heater. "It was a brutal five years, with no time for study. I joined to learn about the tradition and learn how to practice, and I was learning instead how to be a fruit farmer." He persevered, even as most of the other novice monks quit, because he knew that at the end, he would have the chance to go to India and study.

In 1974, he was sent to India for a two-year course. At the end of the course, he begged the order's leaders to let him stay. Against the Chicago swami's wishes, they agreed. Then, when Atmarupananda was recognized as a swami, or teacher, in the order two years later, his boss from Chicago flew to India to bring him back. The order's authorities took pity on Atmarupananda and refused to let him go. They sent him to an isolated monastery in a forested region high in the Himalayas. It was a place he had seen pictures of and always dreamed of visiting. "In the order, it's not that you can say, 'I want to go there and stay here.' You go where you're sent. And so, there was no hope of actually being sent there. And then suddenly at the end of training, they asked me if I wanted to go, and I said yes."

The center was dedicated to the contemplation of nondualism, the belief in the unity of all things at the heart of Vedantic teaching. "I've been in very silent places, but I've never experienced anything like the silence there. So, it was a wonderful place for meditation."

He spent his days studying, walking in the mountains in contemplation, and helping to edit the organization's journal, which involved
researching the teachings of Vedanta. "It was one of the best periods
of my life."

But after five years, he decided it was time to assimilate back into
the world. He was initially sent back to Chicago. Against the advice of others who worried it would anger the swami in charge, Atmarupananda asked to be allowed to go elsewhere. "Miraculously,
he said, 'Okay, go wherever you like.' He had never done that before. I felt like a door opened in front of me and all I had to do was
walk through."

Atmarupananda chose California, where he would eventually become the resident swami in the order's Hollywood center for the
next three decades.

The world is awash in gods. The Hindu pantheon of Ramakrishna's India alone is home to hundreds of deities, each of which at-
tracts legions of passionate devotees. Beyond that, every culture
on earth has its own figures of devotion. Ramakrishna taught that
while it is fine to worship those "personal deities," ultimate Truth
lies behind their guise.

The Bengali mystic used the analogy of ice to explain the relationship between the "personal god" recognized by practitioners of
various religions, and the "impersonal" all-encompassing Divinity
"that is like a vast shoreless ocean, without bounds and limits," of
which, Vedanta teaches, we are all a part. Like icebergs, the deities
are formed from that ocean and back into it they melt.

Atmarupananda described that concept another way in a primer
he wrote on Vedanta: "There is one reality with many faces, and
each face, each deity, each person, is the whole Reality, Divinity itself; God manifested to us in rich variety." Individuals may choose
to reject the very idea of God as a separate being, focusing on the
concept that we are all a manifestation of God, which Hindus call

"nondualism." But those who believe we are separate from a creator god—"dualism"—"they can have God or the Gods and Goddesses … because there are many ways to Truth and because there are many faces of Truth."[6]

In short, there's no wrong answer.

Atmarupananda was part of a small group of religious thinkers from eight traditions convened by Catholic contemplative Father Thomas Keating at the Snowmass monastery in Colorado for a series of dialogues that began in 1984. One of the group's core points of agreement was, "Ultimate Reality cannot be limited by any name or concept." At the time, it was a controversial declaration.

"In the West there's always this great fear of pantheism and of identifying God with the universe," Atmarupananda told me, his precise enunciation shaped by years immersed in the culture of India. "Vedanta says, 'Well, that's what we *should* do.' God *is* the universe; the totality of existence. Everything else is just a projection of God. And if my mind were sharpened enough through meditation and other disciplines, when I look at anything I should be able to see through the form, the outer covering, and see that luminous divine being shining through everything and manifesting as everything."

He recalled what Ramakrishna said: "One who has acquired supreme wisdom … sees the All-pervading Spirit both within and without; he lives, as it were, in a room with glass doors."[7] Religions, the Bengali mystic told his followers, were handed down by an array of prophets to fit the time and place. "[T]here are innumerable Ramas, Krishnas, Christs, etcetera; one or two of them come down into this world now and then and produce mighty changes and revolutions."[8] The particular rites and ceremonies of any given religion are "receptacles that contain the seeds of truth" and "the religious leaders of all climes and ages are but as many lamp-posts through which is emitted the light of the spirit flowing constantly from one source."[9]

None of this, Atmarupananda argues, is alien to the Abrahamic religions. "God is existence. The idea which Saint Thomas Aquinas and some other theologians took, and Sufi philosophers took, was that anything that exists, its existence is the borrowed existence of God. Nothing exists except for God, and so anything that seems to exist is borrowing its sense of existence from the divine being. That's very much similar to this Vedantic idea that whatever we see is a manifestation of that one reality."

But Atmarupananda takes it a very large step forward. *It's all an illusion.* None of it is *ultimately* real. A half century after the kid from South Carolina picked up a book on Vedanta in Sweden, that was the bottom line on his worldview: We're living in a dream.

"There's a cosmic dream of the heart of the universe, and within that dream, we are dreaming our own dreams and participating in that cosmic dream but creating our own dream within a dream." It was clear in his voice that he was still in awe of this concept. "The spark of cosmic consciousness within me is dreaming this life into being."

It's not something young Charles or his fellow thirty-three million Presbyterians ever heard in Sunday school: The world we experience exists because we *believe* it exists. The details are a little more complicated, but that's the essence. "Consciousness is reality itself," Atmarupananda explained in a commentary. "We never see an external world, but [instead see] the brain's reconstruction. … Matter is simply a hypothesis to explain our perceptions."[10] Or, as he put it in one of our conversations, "There are many different opinions within Vedanta about how this actually works, but my own point of view is that the world that I see is in a large measure the world that I have created, and others are dreaming their lives as well. And somehow, they're all interpenetrating and connecting. And so that's part of the mystery of the divine dance of life."

What prevents us from seeing through the illusion, Vedanta teaches, is the ego. That's not to be confused with the ultimate *Self*, which the tradition describes as the eternal ocean of consciousness of which the ancient sages taught we are all a part.

The *ego* is the *I* that temporarily rises from the waves and grasps at desire. "The ego gropes in darkness, while the Self lives in light," according to the Upanishads, a set of ancient Vedic texts.[11]

Descartes said, "I think, therefore I am." Atmarupananda begs to differ. He argues that the French philosopher was grasping at the ego. "The reason he fell short of the real truth was that he had nothing in his background and Western thinking to understand that there was a distinction between consciousness and existence," Atmarupananda told students in a 2018 teaching. "What he should have said was, 'I am, therefore I can either think or not think, but it's not my thinking that proves that I am.'"[12]

In Vedic terminology, another name for the Universal Self is *Atman*; God immanent. Brahman is the Vedic term for the sea of consciousness out of which the Self rises; God transcendent. The fundamental Vedic teaching is, "*Tat tvam asi*," or "Thou are That." Atman *is* Brahman; the individual *is* the whole. "The self in each person is not different from the Godhead."[13] Therefore, all things are contained in "I am." As Atmarupananda has written:

> The universe itself arises in the 'I am.' ... Samsara [the cycle of suffering] arises only with the arising of the ego, but I exist even without it. ... I am consciousness itself. ... [T]he body is within the mind, the universe itself is within my mind, and the whole universe together with the body and mind are within consciousness, within my Self.[14]

Even the term *self* can be misleading in this cosmology. "The self is a word that we use to describe something which is *not a thing*," Atmarupananda says, with a knowing smile. "It's beyond all description. It's neither subject nor object. It's described often as the ultimate subject because that's a handle by which to get to it, but ultimately there's no subject, no object. There's no definition. There's no '*thing*-ness.'"

As he explained in that 2018 teaching, "The *I am* within me is the *I am* within everyone, and *I am* within the universe itself. It cuts at the very root of egotism."[15] Or, one might say, it cuts off the ego at its root. It is the ego that creates the illusion that we are separate from what Atmarupananda calls "the all-pervading ocean of mind." As a learned sage proclaimed to the king in an ancient Vedic manuscript:

> How wonderful! In me, the shoreless ocean, the waves of individual selves rise, strike each other, play for a time and disappear, each according to its nature.[16]

"There's the all-pervading ocean of mind, out of which matter itself is appearing. And in that ocean of mind, my mind is a whirlpool as your mind is a whirlpool and we're all connected in the ocean of mind," Atmarupananda explained to me. But, he continued, it is the "I"—the ego—that creates the *illusion* of separation. "Because I identify with that whirlpool of *mine* rather than with the ocean of *mind* itself."

I pointed out that the universal ocean mind is a concept also found in Buddhism and other Eastern religions. "Yes, yes, yes. Exactly," he said excitedly. "One of the things I like about the ocean analogy is the idea of the wave. The wave rises and the wave sets, but there's nothing left after the wave sets. The wave was nothing but a form of water. And so, everything here is a form of that divine reality which is rising up and playing for a time and then stepping back into the infinite ocean. And so, from that standpoint, everything is made of that reality, is composed of that reality, even now in its present state of ignorance and sense of separation. I've never lost awareness of the fact that I am that same water, which is the water of the universe, the mystic part of the universe. And so, I to try to see that in myself and to see it in others."

Waking and dream states, therefore, are equally real—or equally an illusion: a play of the mind, which Hindus call *lila*. The realized soul experiences that play of the mind as an uninvolved witness, like a passenger watching the scenery pass by on a train. "The person who has realized that state makes no intention, and yet they do good naturally to others, not with the idea, 'I'm going to go do good to people,' or with the idea that, 'Oh, I see somebody suffering, I'm going to go help them out.' That kind of thinking has gone from within them. The illuminated soul is like the spring, from which water flows forth without intention."

The aspiration to see the whole world as a play is thus a core spiritual practice in Vedanta, as Atmarupananda wrote in a commentary.

> As we proceed with our practice, even long before illumination, we begin to feel that we are changeless, unlimited, beyond suffering, even when we can't avoid pain and limitation. That is, we begin to intuit something about us—something which we cannot yet perceive clearly—that is beyond limitation and changeless. We begin to feel something eternal, timeless, about our being. And we begin to feel that there is a depth to our being that is untouched by all suffering, even if we can't quite get there yet.[17]

The belief in reincarnation is fundamental to the Hindu worldview. So, too, the power of karma, as the sages wrote five millennia ago in the Upanishads, which have been described as "ecstatic slide shows of mystical experience."[18]

> *The Self takes on a body with desires,*
> *Attachments, and delusions, and is*

Born again and again in new bodies.
To work out the karma of former lives.

My conversations with Atmarupananda began during the Covid pandemic. The first time we spoke, via Zoom, he was locked down in India, unable to get back to Houston, where he was based at the time. Hospitals around the globe were struggling to cope with the deadly disease. Over the next two years, more than six million people would die, hundreds of millions more would be stricken by the disease. Atmarupananda worried about the fate of the people outside his locked monastery gates.

"If it spreads in India, as it has in some other countries like the U.S., it'll devastate the country," he told me, shaking his head with concern. "They don't have the infrastructure. And there are 1.3 billion people in a country one-third the size of the U.S.; crowding like you've never seen."

But if it's ultimately all an illusion, I asked, did it even matter? "Yes," he insisted. The answer lay in the nature of the illusion. Ultimately, we may be able to see through the veil, but until then, the suffering was real. Stick a knife in your leg, and it's going to hurt. Even those who had penetrated the illusion recognized that. "When we say that the universe is an illusion, it doesn't mean that it doesn't exist in a complete radical sense," he explained in another conversation. "What Vedanta means by 'illusion' is that it's not what we *think* it is. The reality is not *somewhere* else, it's not *something* else. It's what we're seeing; we're just not seeing it correctly."

An individual who is realized through practice and meditation can see through "the thin film of illusion" and recognize that the world around us just *appears* to exist. "We come to a state where we see that physical reality melts into higher reality and we see *that* is what was real all the time," he continued. The realized yogi understands that "everyone and everything within the universe is a manifestation of the state of enlightenment, but no one knows it, and so they suffer." He used the analogy of Buddhism, which teaches that we are all Buddha; most of us just don't see it, and until we do, dukkha—suffering—is very real.

"It's a necessity for us to have a view of the world which makes room for what actually happens in life," Atmarupananda said softly. "And through the experiences of good and bad, through the experiences of life and death, through the experiences of suffering and happiness, through joy and through tears, we're finding our way to that compassionate heart of the universe."

I pointed out that for those who had lost loved ones to Covid, seeing compassion as the nature of reality was a big ask. Ditto the idea that it was all an illusion.

"Yes, yes, yes. That's very true," he quickly agreed. "That's the ideal" for those on a spiritual path. For the rest, it was a matter of offering them support and empathy. After all, Vishnu, the second god of the Hindu triumvirate, repeatedly incarnated to relieve suffering and oppression in a Hindu version of the Christ story.

"To say, 'Well, everything's fine because everything's meant to be this way and all that,' no, that doesn't work," Atmarupananda insisted. Likewise, he continued, "When someone is suffering, you don't say, 'Well, that's your karma.' That's a completely heartless statement. Without context and without the other person already having understood the whole context of everything, that's an extremely cruel statement."

There is no shortage of metaphors in Hindu cosmology. In parallel with the "all-pervading ocean of the mind" is the concept of Indra's Net, an infinite fabric that encompasses the entirety of existence, with a jewel hanging at each knot. In the polished surface of each jewel "there are reflected all the other jewels in the net, infinite in number, a cosmos in which there is an infinitely repeated interrelationship among all the members of the cosmos."[19]

In this cosmology, *we* are the jewels. We are all interconnected, but we are also each unique. Atmarupananda believes the image speaks to the question of how we view the pandemic and other global crises. "Even if ten thousand of us died at the same time, each one of us died individually," he told me. "And *my* death was *my* death, *their* death was *their* death. It doesn't matter whether it's just me having a sickness or if there are a million people with the sickness. It's each one of us facing our reflection in the universe."

Was Covid, I asked, group karma for something mankind had done in the past? Atmarupananda hesitated. "There *is* a karmic component," he said carefully, then paused before resuming. "I experience the truth of karma on a daily basis. But that doesn't give me an understanding of why coronavirus is happening. What is the karmic reason for it? I don't know. Nobody knows. I can make up all sorts of things."

The problem, he said, was the degree to which people conflated karma with punishment from a vengeful god. Two decades before, he had taken time off from his Order and traveled the U.S. as a trucker to better understand the lives of ordinary people. It was during Hurricane Katrina and he recalled listening to a driver at a truck stop declaring that the hurricane was God punishing Americans for homosexuality and other "evils."

"No, that's completely foreign to my way," Atmarupananda told me. "Karma is often presented even in Hindu and Buddhist traditions as punitive: reward and punishment. That you do something good, you get something good, you do something bad, you get something bad. That's the least important part of karma. The most important part of karma is, it's educative. I do something, I get a response from the universe. And from that I learn. If I put my hand in a flame, I burn myself and I learn, 'Oh, living flesh and flame don't go together.'

"Karma is a way that the universe reflects back to us our behavior and from that we learn," he continued. "To me, karma is evidence that the universe is my mirror, that the face I make into the mirror, the universe makes back to me. And, so to see a pandemic or any human tragedy as punishment, I can't think in those terms. That just doesn't make sense to me. To see it as the universe rebalancing itself in some way, life rebalancing, that I can see. But to think that there is a deity who is intentionally punishing people for behavior, *no*," he said firmly.

Ultimately, no one can know Truth in its ultimate form, but Atmarupananda says that doesn't matter. He uses the analogy of clay. "You can't possibly know in your mind all of the forms of clay because there are an infinite variety. But if you know clay, you know the essence of all of them. And so, if you know the reality out of which this universe has come and in whom it rests and to whom it returns and which is its identity now, then you know what everything there is. You know the essence of everything.

"It doesn't do to have an idealized view of a heavenly life on earth where everything is supposed to happen nicely and benevolently. There are Hitlers, there are plagues. And so, in the midst of all of that, we have to find our way to reality, to a compassionate reality, and to know that the most important thing in life is to be a real person, which means a good person. Not goodie-goodie, not someone who's afraid to say "damn" or "hell" or "shit" or something like that, but a deep goodness, which is a goodness tied to the nature of reality itself and which learns to look on all beings with a compassionate heart, and with a joyful heart because it knows that at the heart of reality that there is goodness, there is love, there is compassion. That's the actual nature of reality."

After a half century of study and practice, for Atmarupananda, it all came down to a simple realization.

"If I can accept the experiences that come to me—birth and death, happiness and pain—then I've come to the mother heart of the universe."

Beyond Druid

Emma Restall Orr and the search for God-ness

"I am the wind that breathes upon the sea,
I am the wave on the ocean,
I am the murmur of leaves rustling...
I am the power of trees growing...
I am the thoughts of all people
Who praise my beauty and grace."
                        The Black Book of Camarthan

The gentle sounds of a harp draw us into the heart of the Neo-lithic circle like the flute of a Celtic Pied Piper.

The bard sits on the rock lip of what had once been a burial cairn; the base of the elegant triangular wooden frame of the *clàrsach*, as the Scots call the traditional harp, rests in the recess. He is bundled against the cold—even in late June the weather in Scotland's Outer Hebrides islands can be brutal—in a heavy, olive-green sweater woven with thick Celtic knots. His face, framed by a green beret pulled down low and a thick mustache and beard, is relaxed, resting in whatever world he has created with his hypnotic music. A travel-worn dragon doll pokes whimsically from the pocket of his vest. A raven-haired woman in a billowing cape and bare feet, oblivious to the cold, dances with abandon around the bard, silhouetted against the dark, threatening skies, becoming one with the music and the ancient energies.

This otherworldly scene plays out beyond time and space at the epicenter of the Callanish Stones, an ancient megalithic complex on Scotland's remote Isle of Lewis, erected two millennia before the Pyramids and centuries before the more famous circle at Stonehenge. The stones are associated with Cailleach, the one-eyed Celtic goddess of winter who sees beyond duality into the Oneness of all things.

> *I am old, older than you can imagine.*
> *Many have been my names and most are lost in the*
> *mists of time—even I cannot remember them all*
> *now.*
> *I am the Mother of this Land known to you as Alba*
> *or Scotland.*
> *I am the Mother of all the Gods and Spirits waking*
> *and sleeping in its mountains and valleys.*[1]

Resting against one of the rough-hewn monoliths, hunched against the raw winds that blew unhindered across two thousand miles of Atlantic Ocean, I could feel my own vibration rising as I absorbed the power of the moment. Falling into a light trance, my entire being began to respond to an ethereal hum that at some point had replaced the gentle Celtic music. Only later would I learn that it was the sound of nature herself playing the harp when the musician removed his fingers and the raging wind caressed the strings.

The bard was part of a band of Druids who had gathered from across the UK and as far away as the U.S. to mark the summer solstice, and the rare occurrence of an adjacent full moon, at this mystical site aligned to the solstice sunrises and sunsets. The scene was being played out at stone circles across the British Isles as Druids and fellow Pagans gathered to absorb the magic of Alban Hefin, the Light of Summer.

In previous decades, those celebrants would likely have included one of Britain's most renowned Druids, Emma Restall Orr, former joint chief of the British Druid Order and founder of The Druid Network. But on this solstice, Orr was at the other end of the British Isles, quietly ministering to the dead and dying. She had moved beyond Druidry. The rituals, the shapeshifting, the spells, and incantations—the framework of Druidcraft—were no longer of use to her. The goddesses and spirits who had been her companions for decades had dissolved back into nature.

Orr's mystic quest had taken her to a place where she realized that "the scaffolding" of the Druid tradition, of all traditions, "were just the clothes that the goddess was wearing" and that we are all but "the tiniest little twinkle in the sparkle of the mind of Darkness." That Darkness had become the heart of her spirituality.

Emma Restall was born in England, but growing up, she wandered through cultures and spiritual traditions on three continents. Her father, a noted British ornithologist, moved frequently: Denmark, Spain, South America, Japan, Hong Kong. Young Emma soaked in the traditions of her youth. Her first real exposure to religion was in Spain. There she became comfortable with death as she sat in the cool, dark cathedrals and watched, fascinated, as members of what she came to consider the Catholic "death cult" worshipped the "beautiful, exquisite human being" hanging dead above the altar. In the Amazon, she was entranced by the local tribesmen as they spoke to the jungle, the monkeys, the snakes, and the mist. And, in Japan, she embraced Shin Buddhism's respect for ancestors and love of the land. But ultimately, she did not feel a deep connection to these traditions. The spiritual lineages of the lands from which they had emerged did not run in her veins, and her own ancestors were far away. "I don't understand your God," she silently told them, "but I can feel a God-ness about it."

Coming back to England, she began to search for a tradition that allowed her to connect with the spirits and ancestors of her own land in a way the Amazonian tribesmen and Shin priests had done with theirs. The Church of England was soulless. The other Abrahamic religions left her cold. Eastern religions did not resonate with her connection to the energy of the British Isles. And then she found Druidry.

"I thought, no, I don't understand any of you, but there's something in there. So, I just kept on looking inside, underneath deeper and deeper until I realized, literally realized, that the source of Druidry is the spirits of *our* land. It's *our* ancient ancestors. It can be hard when it rains every day, but there's something exquisitely 'edge of the world' about this island. This island, which I love."

For some Druids, the tradition is about Celtic culture or the Anglo-Saxon and Viking influences. Orr looked far deeper into history, to the British Isles before the Romans. "The old English culture fascinates me, but it's not where my hero takes me," she told me, her voice wistful. Her connection reached back to what scholars today call the real Middle-earth, the civilization that inspired Tolkien; a time and place whose people "ascribed to the natural world a palpable energy called life-force [and] had a vision of life animated by beings beyond the material world."[2]

But Orr's connection was not found in the history books; it was entirely intuitive. "There are streams and strands of music and language and things that come through, but it's ancient animistic, pre-anthropomorphized. In Britain, it's just mist and rain, thunder and mud, darkness and sun and green and wood; those are my gods: how they laugh and dance through and fight through the breath of generations, through stories and song. So, I might hear the song in the land, hear the song in Celtic, in folk tradition, but I'm relating to the essence of it, not to the culture, which I think is what naturally took me to the underside rather than the surface."

The underside. The place beyond the view of most of us. The Darkness.

Orr's eventual piercing of the veil of illusion, Maya to the religions of the East, was the product of decades of intensive spiritual practice. It was precisely this journey into the mystic world beyond the Craft, as the Druids call their tradition, which had drawn me to the priestess.

When I asked Orr in our first conversation what it was about Druidry that she felt she no longer needed, she told me that to understand the answer, I needed to understand what being a Druid had meant to her. So, we will start there.

"It's an attitude, an understanding, an exquisitely simple and natural philosophy of living. For a great many it is a rich and ancient religion, a mystical spirituality. For others it's simply a guiding way of life," she wrote in her 1998 book *Spirits of the Sacred Grove*.[3]

At its core, according to Eimeer Burke, the Chosen Chief of the Order of Bards, Ovates and Druids (OBOD), the world's largest Druid organization, Druidry is "a nature based spiritual path, and we look to the seasons of the landscape as a metaphor for our lives." There is no Druid Bible, no holy book, no instruction manual. "If you ask ten Druids, you'll get at least eleven different answers to what Druidry is," Burke admitted to me with a laugh.

Druidry in the first millennia AD was an oral tradition. Poems, stories, music, all played a part in transmitting the teachings.

Nothing was written down. "We know *what* they did, but we don't know *how* they did it," Burke explained.

The descriptions of ancient Druidry are found in accounts penned by travelers and conquerors through the ages. The earliest references were those of the Greeks. In the first century BC, Diodorus Siculus wrote of the Druids' command of magic:

> [W]hen two armies approach each other in battle with swords drawn and spears thrust forward, these men step forth between them and cause them to cease, as though having cast a spell over certain kinds of wild beasts.[4]

Reincarnation was a recurring theme in these accounts. "Not only the Druids, but others [in the British Isles] as well, say that men's souls, and also the universe, are indestructible," Greek philosopher Strabo wrote in his famous late first century BC work, *Geographia*.[5] "The cardinal doctrine which [Druids] seek to teach is that souls do not die, but after death pass from one body to another," Roman Emperor Julius Caesar reported a half century later.[6] Many of these observers considered the Druids to be uncivilized heathen whose beliefs were based on superstitions. Their accounts included grisly tales of human sacrifice overseen by the Druid priests, in part as a tool of divination. "For it was their religion to drench their altars in the blood of prisoners and consult their gods by means of human entrails," wrote the Roman historian Tacitus in his famous *Annals*, as Rome's legions battled Welsh Celtic tribes in the first century AD:

> The enemy lined the shore in a dense armed mass. Among them were black-robed women with disheveled hair like furies, brandishing torches. Close by stood Druids, raising their hands to heaven and screaming dreadful curses.[7]

In the popular imagination, Druids are closely associated with stone circles, such as Stonehenge and the Callanish Stones. In fact,

scientists are divided on whether the Celtic tribes had even reached
the British Isles by the time the megaliths were built six millennia
ago. What *is* known is that by tenth century the Druids had been
consigned to history and myth, wiped out or driven underground
by the Romans and the Catholic Church. They were the snakes St.
Patrick so diligently banished.

Druidry reemerged in the eighteenth century as a fraternal cultural order akin to the Freemasons, called The Ancient Order of
Druids, with establishment figures such as Winston Churchill and
the Archbishop of Canterbury among its members and a rule against
discussion of religion. Esoteric Druidry was a fringe sub-culture in-
volving a handful of British occultists until it began to gain traction
in the 1980s.

With no guidebook to what the ancient Druids *actually* said, did,
or believed, modern Druids turned to accounts of medieval Celtic
Bards, considered inheritors of what has been called "the remnants
of pagan Druid tradition." But the clues were often swathed in poetic allusions, such as in the thirteenth century *Book of Taliesin*:

> *I am song to the last;*
> *I am clear and bright;*
> *I am hard; I am a Druid;*
> *I am a wright; I am well-wrought;*
> *I am a serpent; I am reverence, that is an open re-*
> *ceptacle.*[8]

To Orr and other modern Druid leaders, those dusty old texts
were irrelevant. "We make it up as we go along," Orr wrote in her
2004 book *Living Druidry*. The comment masked a deeply mystic process that tapped *awen*, the life force—the "flowing spirit essence"—that Druids say permeates all existence. It is a concept that

traces back to the pagan high kings of Ireland and features in the poetry of the Bards who followed:

> *The Awen I sing,*
> *From the deep I bring it,*
> *A river while it flows,*
> *I know its extent;*
> *I know when it disappears;*
> *I know when it fills;*
> *I know when it overflows;*
> *I know when it shrinks;*
> *I know what base*
> *There is beneath the sea.*[9]

It is from awen that Druids and other Celtic Pagans draw inspiration and knowledge, chanting the word in a low, guttural tone—like the Hindu mantra "*Om*"—to connect with spirit. As Orr once described it, the presence of awen at solemn Druid gatherings is almost tangible:

> The flow of energy, the exquisite awen that pours down, fills the whole Grove, spreading out from the centre, through each person, through every soul that stands within that spiritual kinship as a balance between the powers of earth and sky.[10]

According to Philip Shallcrass, founder of the British Druid Order, "Awen lies at the heart of the Druid tradition, for it is awen, the Holy Spirit of Druidry, that provides our true link, not only with the past, but with the deeper reality of the present, and with the infinite possibilities of the future, and which gives as its ultimate gift the recognition of our own divinity."[11]

To Celtic mystics, awen meant that written histories were superfluous. "Without words or doctrine, without rules that come from outside ourselves, we may instead access an inner knowing or sense of guidance that comes from both a wider, deeper source than any-thing we can comprehend, and at the same moment is something that dances in our veins and sits in our human bellies," Welsh sha-man Danu Forest explains. [12]

"The source of Druidry is our ancient ancestors of the land and how they interacted with the land," says Orr, who objects to what she calls "the myths" of Druidry found in libraries. "How nature was talking and communicating and working on those relationships and finding the priest, the medium, the shaman, the witch, whatever it was, the cunning person who knew, who could hear, who felt in the ephemeral liminal, and then could come back and say, 'It's okay. It's alright. We just need to go this way.'"

Perhaps it was awen that renowned occultist Rudolph Steiner tapped in the early twentieth century as he reached into his "imagi-nal consciousness" to bring back what he believed were the teach-ings of the ancient Druid sages:

> ... that plants are not just beautiful but are permeated by the
> weaving of the spirit; that the clouds do not just sail through
> the air but that divine spiritual elemental beings are active
> in them.[13]

But as Druidry gained traction in the latter part of the last cen-tury, there was a growing demand for something more tangible than whispers on the wind. Orr's books *Living Druidry* and *Ritual* were among a handful of texts that filled the void of written knowledge and instruction. Druids began to transform the practices she wrote about into a formal liturgy, and she asked herself, "What have I done?" It was the ultimate perfidy to one who was adamant that any dogma was "best respectfully ignored" and that "anything caged," whether an animal, human, or a living tradition trapped between covers, "lost its spirit, its life, its energy and validity."[14]

We had stepped through the Veil into Tolkien's Middle-earth. There was an otherworldly beauty to the barren, rocky hills that surrounded our isolated cabin on the East coast of Scotland's Isle of Harris, a visceral sense of the living energy of the land. Bubbling streams linked a network of ponds and lochs that ultimately spilled down into the Sea of the Hebrides, home to the mythic Blue Men of Minch, a race of mermen who lived in its treacherous waters.

My wife Indira and I felt ourselves enveloped in the almost tangible power of the place, as if the ghostly mists cloaking the hills had drawn us into their embrace. There are locations on earth where the veil between the dimensions is paper-thin. This was one of them. The ancestors, the Celts taught, believed that the earth spirits of a place shared a collective consciousness, which generated a special energy where they dwelled. I thought back to Emma's comment that Druidry was rooted in the spirits of the land. The Druid priest, she said, could hear the voices of nature and draw inspiration and direction from "the ephemeral liminal."

We knew intuitively that those icy ponds surrounding us were the fairy pools of ancient legend. It did not take much to imagine devas, elves, and nymphs emerging from the rocks and knolls to examine these interlopers from the physical world. We could feel the spirits of the ancestors of the land reaching out: a bagpiper silhouetted on the hilltop; a Viking warrior resting his horse in the vale; a shaman making offerings to the local goddess, whose name was known only to the initiate.

I thought of Ælfred the Great, the first king of a united England, whose very name embodied the ethereal wisdom whispered in the ears of the priests: "*Ælf*," Anglo-Saxon for elf; "*red*" meaning wisdom. *Ælf-red*, "Wisdom of the Elves." Perhaps we, too, would hear their wise words or catch a glimpse of the goddess of the local lands.

Druids would say it was no accident that Indira and I felt so powerfully connected with otherworldly energies in this remote landscape. "Earth spirits are more easily felt in places of natural beauty where the strength and health of the earth energy is flourishing," according to Danu Forest, the Celtic shaman.[15] We were tapping into the awen of the Druids, sensing the Otherworldly beings who inhabited the Druid pantheon.

"We behold and are not beheld," proclaimed Midir, Lord of the Sidhe, the race of elves, fairies and other fey who are said to dwell in a dimension parallel to our own.[16] But the Druids knew Midir's words were not entirely true. The fey were visible to the select few. As renowned anthropologist Walter Evans-Wentz wrote in his epic 1911 study of fairies, the Celtic seers

> say that Fairyland actually exists as an invisible world within which the visible world is immersed like an island in an unexplored ocean, and that it is peopled by more species of living beings than this world.
>
> [The seer] comes to feel instinctively the old Druidic Fires relit within his heart [and] is conscious that in Nature there are beings and inaudible voices which have no existence for the flippant pleasure-seeking crowds who come and go.[17]

Orr had listened to those 'inaudible' voices throughout her life. "As a child for whom spirit presences were not alarming or unusual, to slip through the framework of time and space into another landscape was not something strange," she wrote in her 1998 book, *Spirits of the Sacred Grove*.

"For me the attitude, the childish freedom of seeing all realities as equally valid was never constrained; the inner worlds I shared with spirits and faeries were as existent in their own right as the other world of agreed reality, itself filled with mystery and illusion." This hidden world is central to the Druid tradition. "It is understood in Druidry that many of our greatest teachers exist only within the inner planes. They are guides and *devic* energies, they are people now in spirit who bring wisdom from the past (or elsewhere), they are parts of our own soul. They are a source of our inspiration and the holders of the ancient's stories of the land and its people."[18]

And they are companions in the sacred circle, as Orr recounted:

> The grove begins to fill with the hidden company, spirits who are drawn to the high energy of peace and devotion. Many are devas, spirits of the wild, of nature, the trees. Beside one young Bard stands her father, a man with gentle eyes who passed on some five years ago. ... I can feel the little people dancing with me and I can hear the laughter of the elfish folk, the hum of the Earth.[19]

But those *elfish folk* were not always so welcoming. Orr described visiting remote stone circles that had seen few modern visitors "and found them to be guarded by the little people and devas, spirits who are far from willing to compromise or negotiate with a member of the human race."[20] Even the spirits who have been invited into a grove through offerings and prayer can shift from loving to wrathful if the priest holding the energy of the circle missteps. "A spirit of place will often take blood, a fire sprite the energy of pain, in response to insufficient devotions," Orr warned.[21]

Even so, it was with the spirits, not her fellow humans, that Orr felt most at home.

> I reach for acceptance from this sleepy great tree spirit, and I feel the same response: the subtle energy of the oak spreads out from the bark to embrace me, holding me.[22]

Mysticism is at the heart of Druidry: "[W]e learn to hear the wren's song with our fingertips ... We hear the earth pulsing with our feet. ... From within the vibration of our own notes, our own spirit tone, we hear another's vibration."[23] Yet Orr is adamant that there is nothing "supernatural" about Druidry. In other words, it is all completely natural. "My entire spiritual perspective is on nature

as it is," she told me. The issue is one of perception. Druids see nature through a very different lens than most other people: "Shifting
our point of perception to see the living energy of every creature,
of every aspect of creation, transforms our world and the way we
respond to it. The animistic view, which teaches us of the life force
and allows the life force to teach us, acknowledges everything as
being essentially of spirit."

There is no Druid *God*. An array of spiritual energies fills the
Druid pantheon, different for each person. Most Druids are *pan-
theistic*, they believe spirit exists in everything, but they may also
be *polytheistic*, recognizing an array gods and goddesses—modern
Druid compilations name more than four hundred deities—recognizing at the same time that these deities are spirit anthropomor-
phized for the benefit of human perception, and, like Cailleach, may
show different faces to different peoples.

The guardians of the sacred circles are many: devas, fairies, and
animal allies, who give a grove its unique color, smell and atmosphere, and deities who appear in their chosen form or disguised.
And then there are the elementals—the winds, rain, oceans, earth—
and spirits of place. All are aspects of the divine: "We crave a better understanding with nature and ask that these spirits appear in a
human or animal shape with which we can interact and converse
more clearly. Some do and some don't."[24]

Most Druids do not supplicate themselves to the gods or idealize
the deities with whom they interact, for as reflections of the arche-
types of our souls they "are potentially as cruel and as kind as humanity itself." Nor do the gods do the bidding of the Druids. "They
have better things to do," says Orr.[25]

In the forests and groves where the sacred ceremonies take place,
there is a constant conversation with the *dryads* of the trees and the
creatures, spirits, and ancestors drawn to the energy of the circle.

Working with animals as guides and "familiars" —spirits that are frequent companions—became second nature for Orr. "Learning to talk to other creatures, to learn the languages that exist across the web and the ways in which others will respond, what they are interested in, how they can help and how to motivate them to help, is an important part of Druidcraft."[26]

Central to it all is the *nemeton*, the protective bubble that the priestess creates to enclose a sacred circle. For Orr, this cocoon of energy also presented as a female deity, Nemetona, who she called "My Lady." It is a power that emerged from deep within her own heart. Orr discovered her nemeton when she was young. In the classroom, it shielded her from the teacher's view. On the train, it made her invisible to the ticket collector's gaze. In crowds, she would charge her nemeton with electricity to keep people at bay.

In her writings, there are frequent appeals to "My Lady, Nemetona," to whom she turns for inspiration. "As Nemetona said, and indeed she expresses it in many ways, I am ever within you and ever surrounding you. But as a polytheist I know she is not All. She is one colour of the spectrum, one note in the perfume of my experience of being."[27]

Other companions are also named, among them, her spirit guides Nathair the adder and Seabhac the hawk, who she believes was her teacher in a lifetime 1,500 years ago; her grove guardian Tyroshai; her lover, the Lord of the Hunt, a male god who goes by many names and is "too terrifying" to approach if she is not enveloped in Nemetona's energy; and Fearn, who taught her to fly:

> My robe is made of the fibres of the breeze, soft and swirling around me. As I touch the bodies of the trees, I rise up and seem to swim and stretch and dance in their canopies. Breathing deeply, as if refueled, prepared, I balance to land on a high oak branch. I am owl. I watch, invisible, the world shivering with its vitality. Then I lift off and fly through the trees without a sound.[28]

Shapeshifting is the stuff of Gothic horror stories and Hollywood fantasies. It is rarely part of a conversation about religious traditions. Yet Orr describes shapeshifting as one of the key elements of the Craft. Druidry "nurtures our ability to leave our bodies, to journey in our imagination into lands of fantasy, to dissolve into the eleventh percentile vision"—her term for second sight—"to travel up on the ether with the soul energy of our disincarnate mind" and "bridge the separation between species, between souls."[29]

In her books, Orr takes us on numerous journeys of her shapeshifting self.

> The air I breathe is sweet; it clears my throat and energizes me, enticing me to stretch my shoulder blades, poignantly aware of my wide, black raven wings opening out, taut with heavy anticipation to catch the wind.[30]

According to Orr, there are two primary methods of shapeshifting. "The first way is simply the releasing of the physical human form, letting the astral or the soul rise of out the body, and shifting into another form." In the second method, the person releases both human form and human perception, attuning to the frequency of the intended animal and then shifting their own energy to match. Some shifters, she explained, work with actual animals. Others "shift their mind set into another form and work on a soul level."

As Orr describes it, this is not just a meditative experience. "It's about easy transport most of the time, getting somewhere quickly, flying high or silent, swimming or running fast. It is also often used for freeing ourselves, living life a little more to the full." Shifters bring back with them memories and instincts from the animal whose form they took, impacting their perception when back in human form.

The shift, as Orr describes it, has both a mental and physical effect. "It is possible, at times, to be shifted for too long. The usual result is an incredibly sore human frame, with muscles and even bones pushed out of shape by the power of the mind. The longer one is out, the harder it can be to slide back into a normal human mentality."

Orr tells of taking many forms, but in Druid circles she is known as Bobcat for the feline characteristics she has absorbed in her many journeys on the pads of the wild cat, often with her companion Accolon, whose preferred form is that of the fox.

> So it is that the bobcat and the fox, stealing through the trees, stopping now and then to listen to the owls, make their way to a bank of pine, where, slipping between the spiky bare lower branches, they come out into the clearing that is the grove. Moving silently to the west, holding my staff firmly before me, I move my consciousness up from the cat's sight, centering myself once more in human form, rising up through the branches, the tall straight pine, the shining holly underneath the bare oak, out into the dark night and the shining stars, then slipping down through the staff and into the rich leafmould, the flint and clay beneath my feet.[31]

No matter how many times I read these accounts, I was never quite sure what was happening. In one of our conversations, I pressed Orr. Was this imagination, a form of astral projection, or was she saying she *physically* transformed into the creature of her choice?

"It sounds like I am shifting out of physicality and into astral projection, but I'm not. It's changing the shape of your coherence," she explained tentatively, her voice betraying her difficulty in putting the experience into words. "You're not starting with a strong sense of being physically bound, so physicality isn't solid anyway. The magic of change is not dramatic, it's ecstatic in that it is just breaking out of the human. Sometimes it's not breaking into animal form, it's becoming an ancestor, becoming a different human."

I still wasn't sure what I should be picturing. The Hulk's shirt tearing? Princess Fiona morphing into an ogre? Or some guy lost in meditation?

She struggled to explain. "It's not like I'm saying that their physical body changes shape. And it's not just about perception, it's about the *experience* of mindedness of how we are," she continued, carefully choosing her words. "You can come out of shape shifting with your body being really sore because you've been in a different shape. You're not changing this, but *something* is changing." She paused, then emphasized, "It's the *mindedness* that changes."

And yet, she continued, there *was* a physical impact. She paused again. I could hear the frustration in her voice at her inability to find the right words. "It's not because my body doesn't hurt when I get back in. There's just a part of me that's changed, and I can feel it when my whole body changes. It's embedded and it changes. I don't know how else to explain it."

In some ways, it seemed, the experience was beyond the bounds of ordinary concepts. If we shed the notion that the physical is ultimate reality, it opens the way for otherwise inexplicable experiences. "I'm just constantly trying to break apart this sense of, 'Is it that or that?' It's not. It's *everything*."

She told me of a friend who "had a Pine Martin in her." Whenever she shifted back after moving her consciousness into the bird, "the first moment of horror was always, 'I'm the wrong size.' Those sorts of experiences are very real." Or, as she put it in *Spirits of the Sacred Grove*, "The mind is certainly powerful enough for us, trained to shift, to get to a point where we are convinced that we have changed."[32]

In essence, it seemed, shapeshifting required us to transcend our sense of what is physical reality. And while an *ordinary* person would see no change in the shapeshifter, an intuitive would sense what was taking place on another level. "I've been with people — with the shaman, Druid, wild folk — who will disappear out of themselves, and I see them just tranced and I don't see anything except this tranced human body. And then they'll come back into this human body and their experiences of having been away in a different form, having lifted up on wings or pounced out, and I don't see any difference. But I've been with people where I *do* see a difference. Perception is about allowing what we see to be fluid, isn't it?" The mystic edges of many traditions had tales of students seeing the visage of ancient sages in the face of the teacher. Much the same, it seemed, was happening here, particularly if the witness was aware of the animal with which the shapeshifter had an affinity. "If I know what someone's becoming, then I can see it in them because I recognize the story that they're expressing in their soul, their being."

She was quick to acknowledge how all this must sound to the uninitiated. "The priest in deep trance can be seen as a mad woman, spluttering and swaying; the solemn gathering at an old stone circle might seem like costume theatre without a plot. We are the strange folk, the edge people."[33]

It was the success of the tradition she helped shape that drove Orr out of the sacred circle and into a place of solitude. She found herself surrounded by "cultural Druids," people there for the costumes and pageantry rather than "what can be the destructive inspiration" of the mystic path. "To truly practice Druidry, one needs to develop their psychic and their sentient abilities," said Orr. But too many of the people around her were just talking the talk or toying with New Age philosophies that she found "naive and irritating."

Orr is a vegetarian and committed environmentalist who says she will never again get on a plane. "It was hard being with people who were happily flying around the world and eating hamburgers and standing in ritual with people where the values were so different from my own," she told an Australian podcaster. "And I just got to a point where I would rather be with people that I shared values with—mystics of different traditions, naturalists, and eco activists—rather than people who work in big corporate companies and do Druid ritual at the weekend."[34]

As a high-profile Druid, she was also tired of being the center of attention and being forced into the shoebox of other people's expectations, "allowing people to trash your soul and change you and make you something you're not. It came to a point where it was obstructive to my spiritual journey. I had to slip away and be something different, be something that is softer, quieter, more invisible and closer to the gods and nature and the wholeness of it all in the process to be closer to my God, my goddess."[35]

"Mysticism in practice doesn't make socially functional people," she told me, with a sad laugh. "People who are hypersensitive, who feel the rhythm and the ground underneath their feet, who see the ancestors, all of these things, a lot of them are struggling to survive, and struggling to survive is not good because struggling to survive means you stop being good." Her face looked tired. It was clear she was talking about herself. "Mysticism requires that structure in order to allow us to function, while at the same time, the perception of the mystics is constantly deconstructing that structure. If we're functional, then we're lucky because we're not mad." Her smile conveyed the recognition that this was how some people saw her. "I think a lot of this feeling, the wild-inspired-me thing, the perception of energy in everything, the sensitivity to God, all of that doesn't necessarily make us functional human beings. It takes a lot to remain functional with that."

One of the jobs of a Druid priest is to energetically create and protect a safe space for others to let down their spiritual guard. Orr's spiritual evolution meant she was no longer interested in, or capable of, "holding space" for others. "I was so wild in my own insanity of spiritual exploration, I was losing so much of myself," she said, looking back. "I was finding so much wealth and richness in the Darkness, in the wholeness, in all the different elements, that I kept losing my ability to hold the space, which for me was irresponsible and I had to stop doing it."

She was inexorably slipping into the Darkness she had so long sought. "The mystic doesn't hold space for anybody, not even themselves. There's a madness about deep spiritual connection, which I've always wanted. A lot of people come into Druidry or Paganism to find a community and a sense of belonging. I never did. I came into Druidry to find the ecstatic connection with nature." The community of Druidry, the fellowship, "was just something I learned to cope with."[36]

She was also walking on the edge. The path on which she embarked had become too much for the more mainstream approach of the OBOD. "I just went a bit too far into the deep, old shamanic work. When you work with visions, in meditation and trance, and go through to the other side, exploring the subconscious and looking, as Jung did, at those edges between what is the subconscious and what is another reality, 'What is madness?' becomes a question," she told an interviewer. OBOD leadership tried giving her the job of looking after what she calls "the edge cases," those who were mentally or emotionally unstable. "I probably worked in a way that was a bit too dangerous for them. But I have always worked with the dying, with mad folk, with people in those edge places. I live in pain; I'm not frightened of the edge. I was comfortable in that place. But I was a liability in the end."[37]

Effectively expelled from OBOD, she became codirector of the British Druid Order. A decade later, she parted with her long-time friend and codirector, Philip Shallcrass, known in Druid circles as Greywolf, and formed The Druid Network, a loose online group of likeminded individuals with a mission to "Inform, Inspire and Facilitate Druidry as a Religion."[38] Not long after the group was granted nonprofit status, around the time the British census first included Druidry as a religion, Orr moved on again, plunging ever closer to "the edge."

Mystics of many traditions speak of layers of reality: teachings and secret teachings, outer and inner truths, the seen and the unseen. Orr had penetrated to a level that no longer needed the ritualistic framework of her chosen tradition. She now saw the gods, spirit guides, devas, and dyads with whom she had communed for so many years as dualistic constructs that conveyed the unknowable in a form her younger self could grasp. They were the "forces of minded nature" as humankind had shaped them.

This realization struck on a cold February afternoon. She was walking in the icy tall grass behind her home, struggling with the pain of her lifelong affliction and suddenly "the world around me, what I perceived to be the world, shattered." For decades, she had lived within the energy of the Druid gods, the spirits of the land, the power of place. In an instant, all that was gone. "When that shattered, all I was left with was a profoundly coherent wholeness of deity." It took her months to "rebalance [her] ability to understand shared reality." All the time, she was hearing music, reminiscent of Mozart, "as though every note is entirely within the fabric of the universe, just as it should be."

She had broken through to the Darkness.

"All my life feels like just calling into the Darkness, calling into the inside, the behind, the underneath, what's actually there; and suddenly I was looking at the fabric of the essence, and not just seeing what was through, but feeling myself within that Darkness. But there's no scaffolding. There's no language. It's not possible to explain it. It's not possible to remain functional in that space."

As she slowly readjusted to the physical world, she found herself irritated by the cultural structures, the frameworks, and the language of Druidry. "It just felt trivial, almost idolatrous."

Her journey as a Druid was over.

"There's no anthropomorphizing at all in my religion now," she told me. The way in which she interacted with the energies had fundamentally changed. "They don't speak English, even in my imagination," she said, with a laugh. She paused, then continued, slowly, carefully, stopping after each word for emphasis. "It's understanding the power of craving rage, ocean and where that is, where we are within that. *Those* are my gods."

Orr lives in an English village called Tysoe, named for the Norse god Tyr, whose presence there is strong. But her relationship with Tyr, like all gods, was transformed by her spiritual journey. She describes Tyr not as a discrete god, but as "a coherence of the ancestors of this land. It's their focus, their human craving for a father protector. Tyr is wrapped in every hoe, every plow, every ox tread, every sheep shorn. It's the butterflies. It's the hedgerows. It's everything that humanity has done to this valley where I live, for four thousand years. Reaching for what at some point of that history we called Tyr."

"Would it be fair to say," I asked, "that Tyr is a product of centuries of man focusing on that particular minded energy of that region?"

"A product, an eventuality," she quickly responded.

"And that because the peoples of that land have been focusing on that minded energy, they've given it a power as a finite, in relative terms, energy that drapes that land?" I prompted.

"Yes, yes. So it's not a *person*, it's a *power*. Just like the current in the stream is a power and the current in the stream is caused by the banks of the stream. It's the same thing. And it exists just like every other memory; it's recreated every time it's remembered, but it changes with each mindedness. Each minding event changes its shape, its nature."

It is difficult to overstate the degree to which Orr's mystic evolution meant decades of spiritual practice dissolved in the mists. She had written some of the most seminal works on Druidry. She painted vivid word portraits of almost unimaginable mystic experiences. Yet as we spoke and I made references to the books, her frequent response was, "Did I write that?"

"I can remember so many things happening in those early days in my twenties and thirties in things which seemed separate from the physical. I think my understanding of the fabric of nature was theoretical," she told me in one conversation. "I didn't experience how it was all connected. I think I still felt things to be separate and the relationship between those separate things to be somehow the essence of it all."

But then, in her garden, she had that realization: The dualism that had been a part of the Druid path was itself a construct. Nothing was separate. Nature itself was "minded."

"It's not seeing a spirit within the rock, in the sky, it's a rock that is filled with the mind of nature and in relationship with everything around it." Everything is mind; everything is the essence of creation.

The result was *The Wakeful World: Animism, Mind and the Self in Nature*, an exhaustively documented condemnation of the dominant narrative in Druid circles that the world "is colored and shaped and scented exactly as we perceive it to be." In the process, the mystic turned philosopher shattered stereotypes about the Emma she had described in her earlier books: a self-declared Pagan who danced naked in the sacred circle and bounded through the forest as a shapeshifting bobcat.

She built her case on the work of some of history's greatest philosophers. She wrote of the "wizardry" of Emmanuel Kant, who "removed humanity's certainty that what we are perceiving is what is actually before us" and effectively "made the universe disappear." She quoted British philosopher Bryan Magee, who concluded, "nothing you can ever do can make you experience anything other than the deliverances of your own consciousness." And she reached as far back as Enlightenment thinker John Locke, who posited that things exist only because we perceive them to exist. Built on this historic philosophical case, she then offered own theory of "reality."

The definition I propose then is this: what is real is that which
we need to believe exists in order that we might function.[39]

In short, our existence is simply an expedient construct. Echoing the Gnostics, she concluded that we were each just a "sparkle,"
and that the essence of existence lay in the Darkness between those
sparkles. There she found the true "*god-ness.*"

"In that Darkness is complete peace. The glorious everything. It's
the thing that makes me smile without being able to stop smiling,"
she told me, her longing to enter that place evident in her voice. For
her, this was the womb of creation, the god-ness. "And then through
that you get chaos, and things get formed out of that. The vibrancy
comes out of Darkness." She paused in thought. "That's what we
all crave. We might want the energy to live, but we all crave that
calm, that quiet."

When Orr was at school, she was voted least likely to live beyond
twenty-one-years-old. There was a reason for that. She had almost
died when she was about ten. Then again at fifteen. And again at
twenty-one. And a debilitating disease meant she had been in constant pain throughout her life. "So I am comfortable in that place,
on the edge of death," she told me, the lifetime of pain etched on
her face. She was also comfortable interacting with the dead, who
had been frequent companions on her mystic journey, as she wrote
in *Living Druidry*:

> I had throughout my [first] twenty years had visions … I had
> experienced the kicking power of deity, I'd seen the spirits of
> the dead and the fey, and I knew what it was like for my mind
> to be separate from my body. I had even had extraordinary
> experiences of what might be called religious revelation: the
> entirety of human experience in a tear rolling down the gaunt

cheek of a starving street child, the brilliance of universal
energy shining in a raindrop in sunlight ... all moments that
shattered the limitations of my adolescent mind.[40]

Cemeteries were one of her favorite places when she was a child.
A half century later, she had come full circle. In 2006, Emma and
her husband, Scotsman David Orr, purchased sixteen acres of land
in the countryside ninety miles north of London to create Sun Rising Natural Burial Ground and Nature Reserve. By 2024, more than
1,700 people had been buried in sustainable graves amid the wood-
lands and meadows. Orr helped many of them make their transition,
as she described in *Spirits of the Sacred Grove*:

> And when he had squeezed her hand and died, his soul rising
> into its freedom, she laid lilies on his chest and I held her as
> the tears flowed, sharing my strength as she let him go. ...
> Back in my temple room, my cat purrs against me. I light
> the candle in a white holder reserved for those who have
> journeyed on and called through my guides for news of the
> young man. ... suddenly the air is thick and dark and he is
> before me, no longer scarred by the violence of the cancer,
> but vibrant and glowing. "Tell her," he grins, a deep softness
> in his eyes.[41]

One might call Orr a death doula, or to use an old Anglo-Saxon
term, a *helrune*. She has found her spiritual calling in escorting the
dying to the other side.

> Firemen had cut through the metal to free drivers and pas-
> sengers. Ambulances were crawling away. As I passed I saw
> a women, wandering amongst the wreckage, dazed, trying to
> understand what was going on. She was looking for herself.
> ... She had died as her car was crushed beneath the truck, as
> had her child.[42]

Around her neck, she wears a bone scraper, the tool the ancients used to strip the flesh off the bodies of the dead. Working with death was the logical final step on her journey in the Darkness.

> Only a few choose or accept being chosen to work with the dark goddesses and grey gods of death and the underworlds. It most often takes a deeply disturbing, usually near fatal experience to shift the psyche sufficiently to be able to access these realms. And the tension brings with it the stench of its own substance, of decay and darkness, and the emptiness beyond, which cause most people to turn away with a chill of revulsion or fear.[43]

Orr saw her role as twofold: Prepare the individual for the transition and help their loved ones cope with the loss. "People are afraid of death and I'm here to explain. It's fine. It's a good thing. We need it. It's a happy thing." Once they reach a certain point, Orr finds, most people *want* to die, but they can't let go, particularly if unresolved relationships and issues keep them bound to the physical. Others just don't know how to let go. "Or they're taking too much morphine and they can't work out what to do next. They want to die, but in fact they're tripping. It's really hard to die when you're tripping because you don't know what to let go of."

It's also hard to die if others won't let go. "Families are holding his hand until the end. I don't say this, but he probably would have died a lot happier a couple of days before if you hadn't been there keeping him alive." So, she encourages people to leave the room. "Maybe he wants to die alone. It's okay."

To most of us, when the breathing stops, the person has departed. Orr sees something very different. "There is no black and white. It can look like, 'This is alive, this is dead.' But it doesn't really work like that. It's a much slower process. There's a disintegration, I think, which can happen over the course of minutes, days, weeks, hours, months. And people die in different ways. I think depending on what's holding them together." Those with a strong sense of self can move on quickly. For others, the process can be complicated.

"Some people, I feel them at the funeral. I can see them. I can hear them right there," particularly those with unresolved issues or young people who died unexpectedly. Such individuals are held back by what she calls "sticky attachments" or "sticky emotions" that keep them connected to the physical. Or at least some part of them.

"I very seldom feel that there is a person who is a whole person after death." In her experience, the individual begins to "disintegrate," to merge back into the god-ness. "My sense is that a good death leaves someone disintegrated. Just gone." In her worldview, the ongoing existence of an individual consciousness, what many religions call the soul, does not exist. "It's not like everyone survives after death in some form. My experience is that most people don't; the grave is empty, there's nothing there." Yet "there's a part of that person in a thousand people and a thousand places in memories and in actions and in stickiness of emotions."

Then there are graves where she can sense that the individual—the *stickiness*—is attached, leaving the energy of the grave unsettled. So, Orr gets to work. She speaks to the departed, sings, and recites poetry. She creates a calm atmosphere to "see if we can just bring it all into a sort of grounded, disintegrating, dissolving." Sometimes that will allow the person to complete her disintegration. But sometimes the work is undermined by a visit to the grave by the person upon whom the dead person is "stuck."

"My metaphysics says that this is part of the mindedness which creates a self. When we die, it eventually disintegrates, but parts of it can be held. If you're on an altar, if someone is remembering you and holding you in some point, some part of you will remain there."

Ultimately, however, it is into the god-ness that we merge. We are all just "component parts" of what she calls "minded nature." The "atomic mind." The "psychic universe."

Or, as she prefers, the Darkness. In that, there is ultimate peace.

"One of the wonderful things about life is that I arrived, but I'm going, I'm a blink. It's just everything I do is so important, I am so responsible for everything I do, but I am so insignificant. It's just the tiniest little twinkle in the sparkle of the mind of Darkness."

"When you go into an old forest, it's filled with death because the whole process of decay, of everything beneath you, is just disappearing to us or Darkness," Orr told me in one of our last conversations. "And that's that deep peace we long for as human beings. That's the heart of my spirituality. I think you said at some point that I talk about Darkness a lot, and I said, 'Yeah, absolutely. It's everything because …'"

"You want the full-on Darkness," I interjected.

"Completely. I've done my work."

The Traveling Nunk

Clear Grace Dayananda. Dharma on the road.

"Enlightenment is just intimacy with all things."
Thich Nhat Hahn

She calls herself a *nunk* and she is part of the next generation of Western mystics. For two years, her monastery was a beat-up 2003 Chevy van kitted out for life on the road. *Nunk* because Sister Clear Grace identifies as queer—hence the conjunction of nun and monk; a monastery on wheels because after life in Zen teacher Thich Nhat Hahn's mountaintop California monastery surrounded by upper-middle class, mostly elderly, mostly White people, this BIPOC forty-something monastic heard "the cries and suffering" and "needed to go down the mountain and walk in this world."

One of the first times I caught up with Sister Clear Grace she had gone back up a mountain—a very different mountain—and couldn't get off. She was deep in a national forest north of Boise, Idaho. Lost. The weather had knocked out her GPS. It was snowing hard, and she wasn't used to driving in such conditions. She was camped on the edge of a meadow in *The Great Aspiration*, as she had dubbed her two-wheel-drive van, which had no snow tires. "Camped," because she didn't dare to move. Earlier, she had spun out on the edge of a cliff as she was racing to find some semblance of refuge before it got dark. It was seventeen degrees outside, she was getting sick, there was no food left in the pantry, and she had run out of propane for the portable stove and heater.

She and her cat Pec—short for *Upekkha*, meaning non-discriminating mind in Pali—were clearly struggling. "I can probably get through the cold, but I'd like to have a warm cup of coffee," she said, her voice breaking up as the weather interfered with our Zoom call. "Food is nice, but it's more of a pleasing thing." She paused, reconsidering. "I don't wanna go the next twenty-four, forty-eight hours without food or something to drink."

Then her face lit up in a smile. "It's very pleasant, this journey. It's not about these moments. It can get difficult but I'm full of gratitude even in these moments. There's so much to be grateful for, you know?" She ticked off her blessings: enough money (barely) to refill the propane, buy a sandwich and a can of tuna for the cat when they eventually got off the mountain, and put gas in the van to get to her next stop, where a meditation center was going to let her park her van for a few days and plug into their electricity. She was hoping for enough *dana* (offerings) from the Buddhist community there to allow her to move on to wherever might call her next.

Sister Clear Grace's itinerate mission was firmly in the tradition of the *parivrajaka*, or homeless wanderers, of early Buddhism. "The most important practice is aimlessness, not running after things, not grasping," wrote Vietnamese monk Thich Nhat Hahn, whose students call him Thay.[1]

Clear Grace was ordained in Thay's Zen school. It is part of Buddhism's Mahayana tradition of Buddhism, which focuses on compassion for others. Its practitioners aspire to become bodhisattvas, spiritual masters who vow not to achieve individual enlightenment until they have helped all beings achieve enlightenment. Underlying this is the concept that we are all connected, all part of a whole. Thich Nhat Hahn called this Interbeing, "the understanding that nothing exists separately from anything else."

> By taking care of another person, you take care of yourself. By taking care of yourself, you take care of the other person. Happiness and safety are not individual matters. If you suffer, I suffer. If you are not safe, I am not safe."[2]

But in a contradiction worthy of a Zen koan, bodhisattvas are committed to that goal even though, as the Buddha told his disciple Subhuti in *The Diamond Sutra*, "there are no sentient beings to be liberated and no self to attain perfect wisdom." This is the essence of the teaching of emptiness: "All that is form is an illusory experience."[3] Even the Dalai Lama acknowledges that suffering in the world is very real to those forced to endure it. The bodhisattva meets that suffering with compassion and seeks to alleviate suffering of others wherever they find it, but he or she also perceives that, in the *ultimate* sense, there is no one to suffer, no one who needs compassion, and no one to offer compassion. "Form is empty of a separate self, but it is full of everything in the cosmos," Thich Nhat Hahn taught.[4]

It is this awareness to which Sister Grace aspired. In the meantime, she kept telling herself, it was all a teaching. "It's been a battle. It's suffering and it's unpleasant because it's like, 'Damn, calm this mind,' you know? There's a lot going on right now and it sucks," she arched her eyebrows and laughed again. "Yeah. The body is screaming, crying, and throwing a fit, you know? When it gets difficult, this is also the part of the practice. It keeps me grounded. It keeps me humble. I've just been sitting with it; just kind of exploring."

Sister Grace, whose birth name was Angela Estrada, grew up in an abusive household. Her mother, Yolanda, was seventeen-years-old when Angela was born; Yolanda was thrown out of her own parents' home because Angela's father was a drug addict who ended up in jail. Angela's mother brought home a parade of bad characters, some of whom sexually and physically abused them both. "I watched my mother get beaten for years, stabbed with knives and bled, choked, and beaten in the skull."

Running became a fixture of their lives. "When people ask, 'Where are you from?' I say, 'California,' because I lived all up and down the coast, sometimes in bus stops, sometimes in cars. My mom would often come in the middle of the night, pull me out of the bed, we'd grab the pillowcase off the bed I was sleeping in, and you stuff whatever in there, and we would run and flee from violence and fear, and we would start over again."

Yolanda eventually remarried, but Angela struggled with the fact that her mother had a new husband and two kids but still had not acknowledged the trauma her daughter had endured. At fourteen, after an argument with her brother's father, she decided she would be better off on her own and left. She came back briefly, but at sixteen, Angela moved in with a friend, graduated high school, then won a basketball scholarship to Long Beach State. However, she couldn't afford to live on campus and the two-hour bus ride home after late night games became too much. She dropped out but finally finished a business degree at a local community college and went to work in the restaurant industry, where she became a senior executive. It would be years before she and her mother reconnected. That nomadic childhood in many ways prepared her for her incarnation as the *Traveling Nunk*, as she came to call herself with intentional irony. "So now there's not a lot of fear to just say, 'Here we go.'"

As an adult working as a regional manager for Starbucks, she knew deep in her being there was something missing—and something wrong with the picture as she visited shops beyond the wealthy enclaves: "I would be driving in my company car, and I'd roll up to a stop sign and I'd do that California stop. I would kinda run the stop sign and look around, check my door and make sure it was locked. Then I realized, these are in my own communities that I grew up in, people that I work with."

In 2015, after two decades in the business world and one failed marriage, forty-three-year-old Angela packed it in and moved to New Orleans with the intention of working in a record store, riding a bike to work, and maybe getting a Mohawk. That lasted a few months until she got into a new relationship that involved a house and responsibilities. She ended up back in the corporate world, this time as a regional manager with the fast-food chain Wendy's.

Like many adults who were the product of a broken home, Angela Estrada desperately wanted to give a child a stable and loving environment. She and her new partner embarked on a seemingly endless round of IVF treatments. The repeated failures eventually led to the breakup of their relationship. But Angela kept trying on her own. When the report came back that the latest round of the expensive treatment had also failed, draining her bank account, Angela broke down in tears. She raged at God. "Why me?" she demanded. "Take everything I own, just give me a child."

And that's when she heard the voice. It told her that having her own child was not her path. She was to be a nun, the mother of not one but many. "I was like, WTF? What's a nun?" She pictured herself in a Catholic nun's habit. "So I was like, 'That's crazy talk.'" This was not the first time she had heard this voice. From the time she was a child, she had a "sense of knowing things other people did not." The voice itself had come to her at various critical points in her life. So as crazy as what she was hearing seemed, she had grown to trust its guidance. "When I receive word from that spirit, there's no question what I'm to do and where I'm to go. I just follow." It repeated three times: "'Because your path is to be a nun, to be a mother to many and not just one. Your path is to be a nun.' I'm like, 'Okay.'" She knew nothing about Buddhism at the time, but she had an inner sense the voice meant she was to be a Buddhist nun. She turned to Google. The website for Tibetan Buddhist teacher and nun Pema Chodron popped up. She read the requirements of ordination. "And I was like, yeah, I'm none of those things. I'm not celibate. I go to the bars. I'm hanging out in New Orleans. I was in the French Quarter last week throwing the beads, doing all this stuff. I'm like, 'This is not me. This is impossible. How can I be a nun?'" But she obeyed the voice and joined Thich Nhat Hahn's Mindfulness Community sangha in New Orleans. "The first time we did a walking meditation, when I put my foot on the ground in that way, it was like being a baby, taking the first step for the very first time. I was in connection with the Earth, with the ancestors, with the elder councils. I was hearing all things, and I had all insight and all wisdom in that step. I was born again." Not long after, she attended a three-month retreat at Thay's monastery in Mississippi. When it was over, she told the retreat leaders she wanted to become a nun. To do that, they said, she had to go to Thich Nhat Hanh's Deer Park Monastery in Escondido, California to study.

And so, she did. "I went cold turkey, like right away," she told me, sounding almost surprised at her old self. "I got rid of the cable, I got rid of the television, I cleaned out the house, and I took up the five precepts," the ethical commitments lay Buddhist practitioners at Deer Park were expected to live by, the heart of which was compassion for others.

Thich Nhat Hahn, who passed away in 2022 at the age of ninety-five, was one of the leading peace activists during the war in his native Vietnam. He taught a form of Engaged Buddhism steeped in social justice and centered on the principal that we are all one, encapsulated in the Bodhisattva Vow: "All beings, one body, I vow to liberate." He once wrote, "The bodhisattva is a flower that can only spring up in places where there is a great deal of garbage or suffering."⁵ It is there that Sister Grace would eventually sow her seeds of compassion.

After being exposed to his teachings, Angela, who would take the name Sister True Moon of Clear Grace when she was ordained in Thay's Plum Village Zen tradition, found she could "be that monk who goes into the gang ridden neighborhood, or into the drug ridden neighborhood, or the racist neighborhood and look at people with eye contact and wouldn't look over my shoulder and be afraid I was gonna be mugged or robbed. I was able to see again and to look into the eyes of beings with compassion, which is now my practice."

In 2001, long before Sister Grace entered the dharma, I wrote a piece for a Buddhist magazine asking why there were so few Black Buddhists. "It's about class," Wesleyan University religion professor Jan Willis, a Black practicing Buddhist, told me. "Buddhism is a commodity like everything else in the States. You can choose among hundreds of different traditions and lineages in the spiritual supermarket, and then you pay."

"One of the most common phrases I hear from young Black Buddhists when they do step out into the White Buddhist *sangha* is that they feel uncomfortable," observed Insight Meditation teacher Ralph Steele.⁶

Two decades later, Sister True Moon of Clear Grace looked at the predominantly White, middle-aged Buddhists walking the lush paths of Deer Park Monastery, high above the working-class neighborhoods of her youth, and looked at her own brown skin. She heard them make vows of compassion for all living beings, then watched as they returned to their comfortable suburban lives.

"Did they hear the same teaching I just heard?" she wondered. And she decided that after four years of teachings and meditation, it was time for the Buddhist rubber to meet samsara's road. "I could hear the cries and the suffering of not just the land, but of what was happening on the border, the shootings, the hate crimes. I was sitting in meditation, and I had this visual experience come up, and it was the ancestors of the land of California. It was the Kumeyaay nation," she said, referring to the indigenous peoples of what is now southern California and Baja, Mexico. "It was the beings in the earth. It was the trees. The earthworms. And I could see all things of the past in that land. And what they asked of me was to get up; that I was at my ceiling in my practice, and I could no longer help them by staying here."

She came out of the meditation and felt a teardrop rolling down her cheek. "I looked over at my elder dharma sister, who was one of those ones that I always emulated. I wanted to be like her. I love her. I love the sangha. But I knew that our relationship was over at that point."

She gathered her three robes and a bowl and walked back down the mountain. She had no plan. She just knew that she wasn't going to give up being ordained "just because the sangha couldn't embody a Black queer woman." That first night was spent on the street among the homeless. It was exactly where she wanted to be.

Her goal was "not to be a *savior*" or change how people lived, but "to remain in love, remain in nondiscrimination, and to be fully present." This would be her practice. "When I'm in community and I see their struggles and their sufferings, it allows my heart to just be expansive in my giving and my loving and in my understanding. So, this is the call that I'm answering." She took to heart Thich Nhat Hahn's teaching on the ultimate nature of our interconnectedness: "The objective reality we think exists independently of our sense perceptions is itself a creation of collective consciousness. Our ideas of happiness and suffering, beauty and ugliness are reflections of the ideas of many people. Collective consciousness is not just the consciousness of three or four people but of hundreds or thousands of people."[7]

As she came down off the mountain into her community, Sister Clear Grace was walking in the footsteps of the monks and nuns of Asia who wandered the villages and towns with a begging bowl. Dana, the tradition of providing food and financial support to monastics, meant those who they encountered would share what little they had. Most Americans don't understand dana, and Clear Grace's ordination vow of poverty precluded her from asking. That made life on the road for an ordained monk or nun who is living outside the retreat center in twenty-first century America particularly challenging. Especially for those, like Clear Grace, who didn't have an organization or cadre of students supporting them. "When one takes up homelessness, we rely on the refuge of the community and *what* comes *when* it comes and when it's *not* there, that is also a part of the practice," she told me that day she was trapped in the snow with only a few dollars in her pocket. "Being a monastic makes it really difficult, not being able to ask, 'Hey, I can really use some help right now.'"

It's not that the people she crossed paths with weren't generous, it was that they simply didn't know they needed to be. "Not too many people hear about the hard parts, the struggles and the suffering. You know," she smiled ironically at the thought of their perception of her journey, "it's all good times and beautiful van life travels."

Waiting for others to be moved to generosity was "within [her] vows and those feel really good," she told me another day when funds were again running short, on the side of another road, with her hungry cat again purring insistently at her side. "But I've been wondering, at what point, you know, up to what point do I suffer? I've just been sitting with it, just kind of exploring that." She saw other ordained Buddhists adapting those ancient vows to twenty-first century America—charging for talks and soliciting donations—and wondered about her own path. "So I've just been kind of working with that and wondering at what point will I have to, um," she hesitated, "request support on the path. Because there will be a point that I need to." She went silent for a moment, contemplating those words. "I'm not there yet. I feel," she briefly paused, then nodded in confirmation, as she often did after considering a thought, "umhmm, I feel really good with withholding the space of letting this experience strengthen my practice."

When we spoke a few weeks later, she had made it to Portland, Oregon, where she had been able to recover from her mountaintop ordeal in a welcoming sangha of Buddhist practitioners. "You were really in a pickle back there on the mountain," I told her. "It was a pickle," she replied with a laugh. "But since then, there's been recovery, and I met some wonderful people, and it just continues. And it reminds me, this is what it's all about. This pickle, that's the *offering*. This is the offering of this life, this body," she nodded, as much to herself as to me, "*that* is the offering."

On the way to Portland, picking up a few essentials at a Dollar Store in Bend, Oregon, a homeless man who lived in his car with his dog had seen her van and invited her to stay at a homeless camp on the outskirts of town. "Fires at night and arguments and, you know, all the things that street life brings. So many stories. So much suffering," she recalled.

In fact, she was taken aback by the level of suffering. By 2023, the population of unhoused people in the greater Portland area had soared to more than six thousand. Streets were full of tents and cars or vans that had become permanent homes. Sister Clear Grace interacted with those in need wherever she went, making it a point to look them deep in the eyes, call them by name, and share whatever she had. Parked in a homeless encampment behind city hall in one town on the outskirts of Portland, she let Pec out for a wander one morning and began offering coffee to her neighbors. "It's not much, but there's something about being in the cold when you're waking up in the morning about being able to put a hot cup of fresh coffee in someone's hands." She paused, acknowledging the memory. "That interaction, the gratitude shows up and the connection is there. I say good morning out of respect before I come up to their place or their space. And it's just the greatest thing. And we sit and we talk, and we start connecting. So, I've met so many people since being back in civilization." There was that laugh again.

"It's the humanity piece that has really slipped our minds." Sister Clear Grace knew this from experience. When she was a regional manager for Wendy's and workers tried to accommodate the un-housed when they wanted to buy food or use the toilet, other customers would complain and they had to turn them away. "This has been such a different journey of really seeing people and meeting them where they are."

But sadly, she said, it sometimes reminded her of India, where she spent a few months mindfully walking the crowded slums with fellow initiates from Deer Park. The practice involved being present to the suffering but not interacting with the crowds of children begging for money. One day, a little girl who was following them broke through that concentration. Sister Grace saw it as a teaching. The child was trying to mimic Sister Grace's mindful walking, which involved, as Thay had taught, "walking as if you are kissing the earth with your feet."[8]

"I grabbed her hand and then kind of exaggerated my footsteps to show her how we were doing it. And then we got on this pace, and we started walking together. And I remember looking in her eyes, and they were these beautiful yellow eyes. She was filthy. Her hair was dirty. So, I put my hand in her head to caress her hair like this," she mimicked the motion on her own bald head. "And I remember it being matted, hard as a rock. And I always remembered my teacher talking about defilement and impurities and how we remain with what our mind thinks is defiled. And at that point I was able to let all things go and love her as if she were my own child, as a mother loves a child, and embrace what I think is defiled and let go of ideas that she needs help, or we need to wash her hair, or 'this poor child,'" she paused. "Really to let go of all that thinking and just love and be present."

It would become a seminal moment in Sister Grace's spiritual evolution. "That's what the practice for me is about: embodying it and sharing it with others who may not know, but that they can catch it, they can catch a piece of that moment."

After she left Deer Park, Sister Clear Grace slowly made her way across the country to North Carolina, where she sought out the Venerable Pannavati Karuna, a Black former Christian pastor and social activist ordained in both the Theravada and Vajrayana Buddhist traditions. She would spend the better part of the next two years at the Heartwood Refuge, studying under both Venerable Pannavati and the late Venerable Pannadipa, a White former Taoist monk, receiving initiations and teachings in the Theravada and Vajrayana traditions.

But at Heartwood, she encountered a new form of discrimination: Sect. She was effectively shunned by the Theravada monks at the retreat center. Clear Grace's Zen ordination somehow made her an outcast. "There was just a lot of boundaries and lots of discomfort around just existing in the world." When it came time for Clear Grace to take her own Theravada bhiksuni ordination, the monks wanted her to abandon her Mahayana Zen robes and effectively renounce her earlier teachings. For Clear Grace, that was "definitely not okay." It would take a year and require Clear Grace to go to another monastery in New Jersey to complete the ordination, taking the additional name Dayananda, which means One Who Delights in Mercy.

She had grown in her time at Heartwood Refuge. When she arrived, she was still burning hot with social outrage. Through her own fifty years of activism, Venerable Pannavati knew firsthand that Buddhism offered an alternative to confrontation. "You have to have a certain quality by which you can disarm, break down, and shift the view of the enemy; you make the enemy your friend," the abbess told me. "There is an arising of being, a kind of surrender to the principles and qualities of the dharma you say you embrace, and living that out. There are not many people who can do that. Grace is one of them."

Venerable Pannavati, who was in her early seventies when we spoke, had hoped Grace would be her successor. But the majority of the center's members were White, and Grace had other ideas. "She had a great thirst to be with her people," Pannavati recalled. "She'd be like, 'Who's gonna be with *them*? I will be that one.' So even while she was here, I'd have to look around for her. 'Where's Grace?' 'Grace is over there on the railroad tracks with the homeless people.'"

There was a bittersweet note in Clear Grace's voice when she spoke of leaving Heartwood. "She was basically handing me the keys of a great monastery," she said of Venerable Pannavati. "They saw me as a continuation, which was a great honor, but I heard the call of the Hungry Ghosts." It was a reference to the Buddhist concept of beings reborn into realms where they are consumed by unquenched desire. It was an apt analogy for marginalized communities trapped in need and suffering. For her, there was no question of staying in the relative luxury of the monastery. The Hungry Ghosts needed her. "For me, the practice of Interbeing means we are one with those in need, not taking on their sufferings, but we will have understood fully the joy and the suffering of another."

She packed her few belongings and once more headed down the proverbial mountain to nearby Hendersonville. Again, with no clear plan. That night, she sat in meditation against the brick wall of a grocery store, huddled in her robes against the cold. In the middle of the night, in the pitch black, she was jostled awake. A homeless man asked if she was hungry. She said she had eaten, but he handed her a granola bar and told her to keep it for later. "His worldly belongings are in his backpack. That's his whole world. He has so much less than I do, and he's willing to give that to me and say, 'Hang on to this for when you need it.' And I knew that I was right where I was supposed to be. So, there was no thinking, 'How am I gonna get off the street? How am I gonna survive this? What is next? Do I need to turn in my robe?'"

The next morning, as she sat contemplating the sunrise, two heavily tattooed White guys came along, said "Hi," and asked how long she was going to be there. One of them, who was holding some wilted flowers, asked her name. She said Grace, "and he goes, 'What? I got your name tattooed on my arm.' And he's got these big old block letters, G-R-A-C-E, really big on his arm!" She asked his name. "James." She would later discover his street name was Juice. He gave her the flowers, then walked off. Grace spent the next week in a filthy basement nearby. "That was not the place for a nun, you know?" she said pragmatically. "We have these ideas of how we should practice and how we should be, and I really feel that we can transcend all of those, we should be able to be anywhere." Her smile said, "Anywhere other than a filthy basement."

Eventually, she went to stay with a dharma friend and soon stumbled upon a derelict 2003 Chevy van that no one wanted. Her friend's husband rebuilt vans for a living, so he helped it gain rebirth as The Great Aspiration.

By the time the rebuild was complete, this was no ordinary van. Immediately inside the double doors was a beautifully finished stained bookcase with a small Shakyamuni Buddha statue; a crystal pyramid; a lavender crystal; and a tightly packed line of dharma books, including six volumes of the *Discourses of the Buddha*, Thich Nhat Hahn's biography of the Buddha; *Old Path, White Clouds*; and the *Path of Purification*, a seminal Theravada text. Above that was her altar with an intricately carved wooden statue of Guanyin, the female manifestation of the Bodhisattva of Compassion; her ordination certificate from Deer Park; a photo of Thich Nhat Hahn; and a plant. The floor was bamboo, and a Vietnamese hat hung on the wall above the narrow bench she slept on. Up front behind the driver's seat was a two-burner stove, a small refrigerator, and a compost toilet.

In September 2021, six months before the Covid pandemic shook the world, Sister Clear Grace hit the road.

Five foot four inches tall, with a bald head, a cherubic round face, a smile that alternated between impish and beatific, and flowing brown robes, Sister Grace does not exactly blend in anywhere, yet there is a certain fearlessness that characterizes her approach to walking amid suffering. That's true whether among marginalized communities of color and the homeless with whom she feels at peace, or places where someone who looks like her is not normally welcome.

She rarely has more than a few dollars to her name, but she relishes sharing what little she has: toilet paper, toothpaste, socks. Her favorite offering to the destitute whose paths she crossed on her travels in The Great Aspiration were "hot hands." At Walmart or Sam's Club, where she often camped in the parking lot, she would buy a box of the pocket-sized hand warmers and keep them on the dash to give out when stopped at a red light. "It's really just meeting people where they are and being present with love. You don't have to have a lot to give a lot, you know? And I think sometimes when we do have a lot, and we do give, we miss the opportunity to meet people where they are and to see that the joy and the sufferings are the same."

Sister Clear Grace isn't naive about the political divisions of America, but she chooses to see beyond them. "In our divided world, we need to lean into love, resist with love, and not be afraid to go where nobody wants to go. Or where the world is saying, 'Don't go there because that looks like this.' There are still human beings who are on a long journey and are hungry and need water and love."

In places like Santa Fe, Nashville, and Oklahoma City, Sister Grace spent her waking hours among the unhoused and marginalized, but as a child of homelessness, she was street smart enough to spend her nights in places where she was not likely to hear gunshots and fights or have people banging on her van door. She was also savvy enough to know that not all safer environs welcome a brown woman living in a van.

As she pulled into a new town, she consulted an app that offered a guide to safe—and legal—places folks in vans or RVs could spend the night. One evening, she followed the app's suggestion and drove to a camping spot at a trailhead outside the Oregon town she was visiting. But the travelers who posted the review were White. In the middle of the night, there was a knock on the van door. When Sister Grace put on her robes, grabbed the cat, and opened the door, she was met by a police officer. The department had received a complaint, and they wanted to know why she was there. The female officer was friendly and relaxed, but beneath the small talk Sister Grace could hear the century of racism that had shaped Oregon.

"So, I'm looking down the lights of the body cam, just, you know, really being present, really knowing that we are here navigating our collective seeds, our individual seeds, the seeds of the land, through a system of deep-rooted racist history." Eventually, the policewoman told Sister Grace that even though, technically, overnight parking was not allowed in that location, she could stay, adding that she was on duty overnight and would watch out for her. "I can tell you she was very aware of the deep-rooted history of these kinds of interactions, and she didn't bring that to the situation. I was very grateful. So, it was really just a wonderful moment of practice. I was happy to be part of that and reflect on that."

Not all encounters were quite so positive. "Where there is danger, sometimes psychotic outbreaks, mental health issues, people with needles and drugs and Covid, the mind wants to be like, 'Ooh,' you know, 'Don't spit on me.' Or, 'What if I get stabbed by a needle?' When I'm working in those kinds of places, or I'm met with adversities or challenges, right away I remind myself, there's no self. I'm really in that place of, 'Here's the breath.' I'm with the breath. I'm aware of every movement. My discernment is *so sharp*, my awareness is *so sharp*. But then I'm like," she laughed, "these things are not real. These are the stories, these are the sense impression, impressions on the consciousness, these are the media impressions, all of these things. The question is, 'How do I remain in love and awareness and presence?'"

That was certainly the question on her mind the morning she opened the door to her van in a remote campsite to find a dozen tough-looking White men clad in black tactical gear sitting in a circle with an American flag in the center. Her mind raced to the January 6th assault on the U.S. Capitol a few months before.

"If they were to harm me, I don't know that I would've been able to remain out of fear," she said softly. "But I feel confident that I can remain in love." Another long pause. "I mean *I*, and this *body* is not *me*." In the end, they barely took notice of her and eventually left. But that was not the point. "When the mind starts to create mental formations of aversion or difference or othering, or I'm experiencing a potentially dangerous situation or discrimination or racism or hatred, I'm always in both worlds, you know? In the relative and in the ultimate. It allows me to navigate those places.

"It's the same when I walk into a rebel trailer park with crosses and confederate flags or if I walk down a dark alley with drugs and prostitutes. It's so powerful. These moments for me are dharma experiences. I could compare it to a meditative experience on the cushion when the mental states are just clear and vast all-knowing and all seen." Again, the reflective pause and internal acknowledgement. "Yeah."

On the road, freed from the restrictions of the monastery, Grace found a new way of encountering the dharma by "uprooting those things within the self that the monasteries actually teach us to hold onto," such as separation and judgement. "I would like to have a vastness in my heart that all is okay and that cannot always be expressed when we are following certain ways of being."

Those "ways of being," she pointed out, were often the result of how "White-bodied monastics" and monastics from the Asian immigrant community interpreted the structures that contained the teachings, oblivious to the suffering of "those in black and brown bodies" or immigrant families being torn apart at the border.

"Some of these core concepts like emptiness, or non-self, are said through a colonial lens or dominant lens" without clearly differentiating between the relative and ultimate truths, Sister Grace explained. "As a BIPOC body, often we have to fill the self. We have to free the self, to liberate, to come to our fullness, to come to the wholeness of the measure before we can have a non-self. Then, once we experience non-self, we can come back to stand up for the ways that we are in the relative world. It's kind of walking in that middle way between the two realms."

In the dharma talks of many White teachers, that blurring of the two truths—ultimate truth of non-existence and relative truth of embodied experience—could seem to devalue or negate the suffering of practitioners from marginalized communities. "For somebody who has grown up in California as a queer, multiracial person, we always look for others to know what our suffering is. We want to matter. We want to be seen. We want to be heard. The relative world tells us differently."

Just as she saw sectarian discrimination at Heartwood Refuge, she found discrimination embedded in the fabric of American Buddhism. "It's very harmful, for example, when you move to a monastery to become a monk if you are queer, if you are BIPOC, and you have a passion about queer justice, trans justice, racial justice, earth justice. It's like, 'Let go of that; we're taking vows to renunciate,'" she arched her eyebrows, "but there is no line to sign up to let go of our Whiteness when we enter that place, right?"

Her face telegraphed outrage. "This freedom and liberation that the Buddha talks about. I *want* that. Where do *we* get that?"

Yet Sister Grace firmly believed that Buddhists of color and Buddhists from other marginalized communities shared in the blame. In a 2021 teaching, she warned her students that focusing on the history of discrimination created "a web of knots that bind us. 'I was a victim of this.' 'I experienced this.' 'This has happened to me.' 'This has happened to my people.' We condition it and we cultivate it. And we're sort of enslaved to these traumas." The antidote to their suffering, she said, could be found on the meditation cushion: "To enter in and to shatter these internal formations and these knots and these seeds, to see the reality, the direct perception." Yet she identified with the students from marginalized communities in whom the fires of outrage burned. Without the dharma, she told me, she, too, would want change, and that would have left her trapped in "a mind of suffering."

Sister Grace also had little time for identity politics. I asked her one day about the inherent contradiction between "Sister" Clear Grace and the Traveling Nunk.

"I am she, her, hers, they, them," she quickly replied, her voice telegraphing her lack of interest in the differentiation. "Sometimes I feel Clear Grace, sometimes I'm Sister Clear Grace. But I'm all of those things and none of those things at the same time. And nothing is required from anybody for me to love them, to accept, acknowledge any of those things, because I am way more than those things. 'I,' 'they' don't even exist, they're only for the world. They're only for this kind of interaction. And for me, they hold no weight."

A few weeks before we had that conversation, she had given a talk to a group of BIPOC Buddhists, which included several from Native American tribes. She admonished them for their focus on labels:

> We heard 'hers,' 'they,' 'them.' 'I'm this descendant.' We have the Squamish and the Duwamish land, and dah, dah,

dah, dah. And we're all BIPOC folks. I'm all for our pro-
nouns and for the ways that we embody, but if we cultivate
that and we grasp and we cling, and I'm 'they,' 'them,' we
make this box for ourselves. We're so much bigger and so
much more vast than that.

As long as we cling, she told the group, suffering will continue,
no matter what Buddhas come a thousand years from now. The goal
should be to transcend identity politics and identity itself.

In America, we have BIPOC sanghas, we have LGBTQ
sanghas, we have recovery sanghas, we have trauma informed sanghas. So, we break up into all these little groups
and we take the dharma and we make it smaller and we dumb
it down.

For this BIPOC, queer "nunk," ultimate reality lay far beyond
labels. "I no longer remain bound in this world. I have found a
liberation that is so beautiful and so powerful that the ways that I
show up in this world don't even hold weight to the vastness that I
experienced through the dharma."

But her bodhisattva vows meant that for her alone to embody
that perspective was not enough. Her path involved everyone. "And
when I look back on that path, I want to see who's on the path with
me. They don't have to look like me, but is that path all encompassing? Is it inclusive?" She paused, echoing the military mantra: "No
being left behind."

Woven through our conversations were comments that one
would not normally hear from a homeless, middle-aged, American
woman in a van—or anyone. "For one who has seen and understood

oneness, there aren't any words that really need to be shared, you know, 'cause all has already been understood. All has already been seen."

Or, on another day, "I'm no longer attached to this self, but this self is me in this relative world."

To those unfamiliar with bodhisattva teachings, such talk might be jarring. But as the Dalai Lama and Venerable Thubten Chodron wrote,

> Self-confidence is essential to begin, continue, and complete the path to awakening, and our buddha nature is a valid basis on which to generate it. Reflecting on emptiness helps us to recognize our buddha nature, for we see that the defilements are adventitious and can be removed.[9]

From the beginning, Clear Grace's disarming smile and self-deprecation stripped away even my journalist's cynicism of such seemingly self-aggrandizing comments. "Here comes this big, Brown, bald Buddhist nun living in her van with a cat," she would often say with a laugh, describing how some people react when she rolls into town.

"There's roadkill all over the place. And accidents." She exclaimed another day. Sister Grace meant this as a *good* thing. She was talking about life on the road as a meditation. It was all a reminder of impermanence, the most fundamental of Buddhist teachings. I told her she seemed to be in a permanent state of meditation.

"For me that is the goal. In order to be *in* the world, but also not *of* the world, I have to remain connected, 'cause suffering will sway and it will tear us right off the path very quickly. I have found peace in this. I have found a true happiness that doesn't require conditions of the external world. I have found a joy that, even in suffering, I know is there and can touch."

"It's not that I don't suffer," she told me quietly another day, "suffering is in every moment, but there's a joy that remains at all times."

Her enthusiasm could also be disarming: "I spent last night at the Walmart for the very first time in the snow." She was in New Mexico, feeding people out of her van. "And boy was that a beautiful experience because there's a community in Walmart parking lots, you know, of folks that live together." Some people would have seen her as a missionary, pushing the dharma alongside the dealers pushing drugs. She vehemently rejected such a notion.

A famous Buddhist text says, "The Buddha has no doctrine to convey. The truth is ungraspable and inexpressible."[10] She took that to heart, literally. "This is more about my practice and my heart expanding than proselytizing the dharma. It's about what the dharma has done for me and how I can take that into the world and share that with others who might not have an opportunity to see something different."

When speaking of herself, Clear Grace often used the term "this body." It was a perspective that reflected her aspiration to be *in* the world, but not *of* the world. "I have been fortunate to take up the lineage of the Buddhas and the higher beings," she told me. "However, in this relative world and the way that I have been embodied—being a queer person and a multiracial person and seeing that suffering and coming through the intersectionality of those sufferings—I am seen a certain way, but *I* am *not* this body. I am *all* of those things and *none* of those things at the same exact time."

Sister Clear Grace is not the first to say that in the modern world we have lost our connection with our fellow human beings. Unlike most of us, she manifests a burning passion to heal those divides. Buddhism, she believes, has taught many to talk the talk, but few have learned to walk the walk. "We use the spirituality as self-healing. It's all there, and it all has been touched, suffering has been penetrated, suffering has been understood. But we think the cessation of suffering is that we should remain in this pleasant feeling, this present moment, happiness. But at the same time, we're stepping over that person that's laying on the ground in seven-degree weather in front of the grocery store. The world is on fire in every direction, and we turn away in denial."

Interbeing, she told me, involves seeing all beings as ourselves. She brought up the video of Memphis police beating to death Tyre Nichols, a twenty-nine-year-old Black man, just a few months before our conversation. "Can you watch that video and look deeply into how we play a part in that beating of that selfless human being? Am I the mother? Am I the father? And I the police officers who raised that baton? Have I understood that suffering? Have I understood its roots in the slave patrol and how the slave catchers weren't all White-bodied folks? And how this internalized hatred and anti-blackness doesn't just stay on the White bodies, you know, and the world that's capsizing on all of us: Asian shootings in California, mass shootings, political terror, domestic terror, racial terror. The Buddhadharma should give us the capacity to look into that, to touch that, to penetrate that, and then to abandon it."

She paused for a moment, reflecting, then continued with even more passion in her voice: "Do we say, 'I abandon hatred, I abandon violence, I vow to take up the life that abandons clinging?' 'That I take refuge?'" she asked, using the term for becoming a Buddhist. "'That I touch the earth to the Buddha, the dharma, and the sangha?' 'That I want to be the one who uproots hatred and violence in my very being and the way that I am, and the way that I want to walk in the world?'"

I told her that her Buddhism sounded a lot different than the Buddhism often found on the shelves of bookstores.

"Yeah," she said with a smile. "Those kinds of books are sometimes the traps I'm talking about. When we're not on the path, and we're in the samsara world, all we have is a book on mindfulness."

She stopped, and interjected in her own monologue, "There are some really good books and there's an opportunity to awaken through those books." Then she returned to her point. "But they can be a trap, trap us in self-care."

The corollary to self-care, she believes, is self-indulgence. During one of the stops on her journey, Clear Grace was invited to take part in a teaching on breath meditation at a local Buddhist center. She was shocked when, after the meditation, participants were asked to share their experiences. "Everybody was so stuck on the body and they were like, 'Oh, I get anxious, and my heart was pounding, and I was sweating, and I couldn't breathe.' Or, 'The fear started coming and I had to rock because it was so traumatic.' And I was like, 'What kind of Buddhadharma is this?' I mean everybody had something to share and they were so stuck in the *self* of the body. Where's the dharma? It's almost like we need trigger warnings!"

Buddhism, she warned, is going to be stripped of its essence. "If we're too busy cultivating safe spaces. Dharma as medication, not meditation to awaken self and liberate all beings," she added dismissively.

Clear Grace sat in equipoise. Framing her on the wall behind were two of Thay's teachings rendered in calligraphy: "Breathe" and "Listen to yourself." On a shelf above her head was a photo of two of her teachers. She wore her brown robes with a simple brown bodhi seed mala draped around her neck. "Each cell of our body contains all our ancestors and all future generations," she told the dozen students attending this Zoom teaching, reading from Thich Nhat Hahn's book *Understanding the Mind*. "Each seed, mental formation, and consciousness in us contains the whole cosmos, the whole of time and space."

She allowed that to sink in, then expanded on those words of her teacher. "So, we have those seeds that are transmitted from our spiritual ancestors," she explained. "We also have the consciousness of the individual and of the collective, consciousness of the land. Only when they manifest in your mind consciousness do we become aware of them." The book was still in her hands. She put it aside and continued. "There's that *koan* where you look at your hand and you say, whose hand is this?" She held up her right hand. "Is this my hand? My grandmother's hand? My great-grandmother's hand? The hand of the earth? The four elements?" She paused, then nodded toward her outstretched palm. "This is not my hand."

The ancestors are a dominant presence in Sister Grace's spiritual worldview. Her family's ancestral roots wove a complex path. On her mother's side, they stretched in one direction to Ireland, Scotland, and Norway, and in the other, south to indigenous Mexican culture and on to Nicaragua. The ancestors on her father's side traced back to Africa through the plantations of Virginia and Louisiana. They included Freemen—freed slaves who intermarried with Native Americans—and Creek, the Native American tribe whose lands stretched from Georgia to the Gulf of Mexico.

For Grace, the ancestors were not only those who lived in her DNA. "My core spiritual teachers are the ancestors, it's elders, it's wise ones who have been here before. Those are the ones I can tap into; I can have access to. If I am confused about something and I go to meditate, I can tap into that stream of wisdom and knowledge of wise ones who have walked here before. They don't always have a name. They're not some book that I read, but I can go to that stream and get answers and clarity and wisdom from them. There's an all knowing that will never lead me wrong."

The first time she visited Louisiana, it was with Teena Marie, a White R&B singer with whom she was close from her mid-teens until Marie died in 2010. It was Marie, who Sister Grace described as a Black woman in a White body, who first acknowledged young Angela's ability to see with what she called her "dharma eye."

They landed at a tiny rural airport in the bayou. As they walked across the tarmac, Sister Grace recalled, "I could feel the ancestors.

And I started hearing the *voices* of the ancestors, and I was like, 'What is that?'" Her voice rose emphasizing each word. "It was like a Catholic church when they have those organs playing."

For Sister Grace, those ancestors were as real as the teachers at Deer Park or Heartwood. "When I speak of the ancestors, I'm really talking about the powers that come with the dharma. When one gets still and one can hear voices from across the land, or one can see that which is in the past, present, and the future of the three times," she said, using the Buddhist concept that the nature of the mind is timeless. "And then there's the ancestors of the land who speak very loudly through Mother Earth and all of its beings."

"With the dharma comes power," she said in a matter-of-fact tone. "There is a dharma eye and there is a hearing and a seeing that is beyond this realm of worldly seeing. We don't always speak of these because they say we shouldn't, right?" she asked rhetorically. "Only to another dharma practitioner steeped in these mundane powers that the wisdom, insight, and meditation practice can give you."

But she quickly added, "Not that I have attained awakening or that I see myself in that way, but to have a great aspiration to allow others to go forth where I might remain back, to be where there is suffering, this is the great freedom and liberation that I have found."

It had been almost a year since Sister Grace and I had begun our conversations. We had learned much about each other over those many months and an easygoing relationship had evolved. Like the Buddhist teachings themselves, layer upon layer of this unique individual had been revealed. One day, I returned to her comment many months before about hearing the *Hungry Ghosts* calling. At the time, I saw that as an apt analogy for the homeless and disenfranchised. It turned out Grace meant it literally. As she saw it, her work among the poor and hungry of the physical world was "baby practice" for what "I am called to do in the *bardo* by the ancestors, the spirits, and the teachers."

The cosmology of Buddhism includes six realms of existence, each as real as the next. Individuals can be reborn in any of those realms depending on their karma from previous lives. These include the realms of the gods, the demigods, humans, and animals, the bardo of the Hungry Ghosts, and the hell realms. In Vajrayana Buddhism, there are many esoteric practices that involve efforts to ease the suffering of beings in the bardo and hell realms. For example, practitioners of Chod envision themselves being cut to pieces and offering their bodies as food for the Hungry Ghosts.

"I'm actually able to leave this physical body and to walk through those sufferings without the phenomena of the mind saying, 'This is me,'" she told me one day. "When I'm in those spaces of the underworld, I'm not trying to heal them. I'm offering something: my presence, my ability to be there, to understand their suffering, to *really* see them, just stare them down to a point where they are able to have a moment of pausing the karmic actions that cause their suffering, and remembering that there's a true self that's always constantly changing, and that they can return to that. And that second I found to be so valuable and so important, even if it relieves them from suffering for that one little second. It's like a wounded healer, a wounded practice."

By early 2024, The Great Aspiration was the worse for wear. So was the Travelling Nunk. Bad roads, limited upkeep, and a meager diet meant that by the time Clear Grace reached New Orleans, they had both given in to relative truth; broken shocks and an ailing body. It was time for the Travelling Nunk to put down roots. NOLA was a place, she had told me the previous year, where her ancestors still walked, and she heard "the voices of wisdom," and could become one with the music of the ancient rituals.

"Something guides me here," Clear Grace said when we connected a few weeks after she arrived in the city. "Anytime that I'm here on this soil, the many planes of consciousness are active in all ways. I am fed spiritually, emotionally. I have access to all the elders, to all the ancestors, to all the spirits, to all the divine wisdom."

For her, Louisiana and other parts of the deep South, where so much Black and Native American blood had been shed, were sacred. "You're walking on the banks of the Mississippi, on soil which is drenched in the blood of the ancestors that were thrown into this river, into this abyss, and to the genocide, into enslavement, into the capitalistic notions of tobacco and alcohol. It's all there, you know?"

A local sangha under Clear Grace's leadership was already taking shape. For Venerable Pannavati, Grace's pause was no surprise. She had predicted as much. "This is her wilderness experience," she had said of The Great Aspiration pilgrimage. "I think that Grace's emphasis will shift and that she will be more useful not in the independent individual journey she's on, but it will provide her with the experience on what it means to give up self for the sake of others," the abbess told me six months before the Great Aspiration broke down. "There are not that many people who have what it takes to lead others. And I think she does."

Grace's vision was not confined to the parishes of NOLA or the blue highways that she had traced. She longed to help create an "African Buddhism" that would resonate with little boys in the bayou and little girls in the inner city. But first, there was the prosaic work of paying the rent on her new Sangha House NOLA, attracting a following, and continuing to tend to those who were suffering. She even wondered if she might have to set aside her robes—and vow of poverty—to keep the vision alive.

But whatever happened, she was also accepting of that. She and The Great Aspiration had taken the dharma to more than a dozen states, she had provided comfort where she could, and she had grown in her own practice.

"When we take our last breath, what's important is this: 'Have we been true to ourselves?' That's what I aspire to be. Free, free of self, free of differentiated mind, to be loved and to see all beings. If this is the last breath, already more than enough has been done."

Lessons

> *"We meet at the depths where the great traditions embrace each other."*
>
> Cynthia Bourgeault

U ltimate Truth may lie beyond the grasp of mere mortals, but, as we have seen in these pages, truths with a small *t* are accessible to those who look.

The mystics who were generous enough to share their experiences with us do not return from their internal journeys bearing a tablet filled with laws, but rather a set of insights that are striking in their similarities, no matter the path they took to the mountaintop. Here are some of those shared understandings.

We are all part of a universal consciousness.

"God is an energy field," Michael Holleran told us, "and Christ is just another word for everything." Hindus know this truth as Satcitananda the ultimate, unchanging Ground of Being, a term shared with Buddhists, Jewish mystics, and even Christian contemplatives. For the Sufis, God is the fundamental energy that has existed before time. "Allah said, 'I was a hidden treasure, and I wished to be known. So I created man in order to be known,'" Shems Friedlander wrote, quoting a Hadith.

Jewish mystics call it *Ein-Sof*, the infinite Godhead. "No existence has existence other than the self-existence of God," according to the Rabbi Bal Shem Tov, the seventeenth century founder of Hasidic Judaism, who had a powerful influence on Jill Hammer. Anandamayee Ma told Ram Alexander and Atmananda much the same: "There is nothing save He alone; everyone and everything is but a form of God," an energy inseparable from the very atoms of our being. *Tat tvam asi*, translated as Thou are *That*; the universal energy permeating all things. Atmananda experienced this as a sixteen-year old in her first mystic encounter, when she perceived everything around her—rocks, trees, the sky—as filled with divine light and understood there was no separation between the seer and the seen. Hazrat Inayat Khan, founder of the Sufi lineage into which Shems Friedlander was first initiated, said the Sufi "bows before the air, fire, water, and earth, recognizing the immanence of God in his manifestation."[1] That vision is also the touchstone of Emma Restall Orr's post-Druid mystic reality.

For all these traditions, existence is an eternal dance. We emerge from the cosmic stream of life and then dissolve back again. Mystics may differ on whether some aspect of our consciousness then reemerges as a new ego, lives on in the energy of the world, or reunites with the Godhead, but they all agree that we came from primordial energy, we contain that primordial energy, and to that cloud of primordial energy we return.

God experiencing Himself; Shekhinah giving birth.

"Everything here is a form of that divine reality which is rising up and playing for a time and then stepping back into the infinite ocean," Swami Atmarupananda told us. That ocean analogy can be found across traditions. "I am the wave on the ocean," an ancient Celtic bard wrote in the *Book of Camarthan*. "Once the wave realizes that it is only water, that it is nothing but water, it realizes that birth and death cannot do it harm," Sister Clear Grace's teacher Thich Nhat Hahn explained seven centuries later. Emma Restall Orr says she has seen that firsthand as the consciousness of those she has helped transition to the afterlife disintegrates into "minded nature." "We are all just component parts of the atomic mind," she told us.

We are all connected.

"There's just Mind. Therefore, we are all very intricately interconnected with each other," Tenzin Palmo explained. "Interbeing" is what Thich Nhat Hahn calls that connection; the term is found in the pre-Kabbalah text Sefer Yedzirah as well. Sufis refer to *Waḥdat al-Wujūd*, the Unity of Existence. To Christian Mystics, it is the Body of Christ. In Vajrayana Buddhism, it is represented by the Cosmic Mandala, symbolizing the interconnectedness of the cosmos; Hindus look to Indra's Net, each of us a jewel on the net in which all other beings are reflected. And then there are the sefirot of the kabbalists, a network of channels by which divine creative energy becomes created beings. "Sparks," Jill Hammer called this embodied energy, a term that echoes Emma Restall Orr's perception of us as "sparkles," with "god-ness" found in the space between us.

All roads lead to the mountaintop.

No religion holds a monopoly on Truth. "I think that there is ultimate reality within us. And if it's the ultimate reality, it cannot be different for different religions," Tenzin Palmo told us. To Swami Atmarupananda, all religion is "one impulse." Michael Holleran thinks it is time for religious leaders to stop arguing about whose finger points more directly at the moon and acknowledge that we can all see the moon, no matter how we worship.

The doctrine of religion, these mystics tell us, is just a framework designed to convey religious concepts in a way that fits a particular time and place. Sufis believe that through the ages, God has sent more than two hundred thousand prophets. "Allah said, 'There are various paths and people that I've created so that you can understand one another,'" Shems Friedlander recounted, reminding us that Rumi wrote, "The roads are different, the goal is one."

The many religious traditions of the world, said Jill Hammer's teacher Rabbi Zalman Schachter-Shalomi, "is God making certain that every nation has access to the Divine in the forms that fit the ethnic and environmental ways of that people."[2]

The gods of the world's religions show many faces, but ultimately they are all like ice, forming from the infinite ocean of mind then melting back into the pure formlessness of water. "He is infinite, there is an infinite variety of conceptions of Him, an infinite variety of paths to Him," Anandamayee Ma taught. Ramakrishna, for whom Swami Atmarupananda's tradition is named, taught that, "Whenever there is any waning of religion in any part of the world, God sends His Avatara there. It is one and the same Avatara that, having plunged into the ocean of life, rises up in one place and is known as Krishna, and diving again rises in another place and is known as Christ."[3]

Swami Atmarupananda once heard Father Thomas Keating, co-founder of the Centering Prayer movement, say of the Creator, "You can call him Butch if you want. The name doesn't matter."[4]

Buddhists use the term *kaya* to describe these varieties: nirmanakaya for the physical form of Buddhas in this realm, such as Shakyamuni Buddha in the sixth century BC; sambhogakaya, the realm of the Buddhas; and *dharmakaya*, the body of ultimate reality or primordial wisdom from which all else emerges. For the Hindus, it is Atman, God immanent, and Brahman, the vast sea of consciousness out of which Atman rises. For the Druids, we are awen, the flowing spirit essence of the lifeforce encompassing all things.

"You're the whole thing," Holleran told his Zen students. "You're Christ, the universe, Samantabhadra and Samantabhadri. You're the Ramakrishna and the dakinis. All of you are One; everything at the same time."

Sacred teachings are a metaphor.

Just as religions themselves are shaped to fit the capacity of the intended audience, so, too, are doctrines within those religions. Religious texts, whether the Bible, the Buddhist sutras and tantras, or the Upanishads, use metaphor and simile to convey concepts that resonate with the intended audience.

The most fundamental truths are written in white fire between the words of the Torah, in the deepest layers of knowledge in the Qur'an, and in the awen of the Druids. The only way to reach this level of understanding, the mystics tell us, is to listen to the voices inside ourselves. "There is a hearing and a seeing that is beyond this realm of worldly seeing," Sister Grace explained.

And the mystics warn that a literal reading of the texts can be a barrier to realization. "God does not inscribe tablets with lightning bolts on Mt. Sinai; these are all metaphors for the presence and action of God in our lives," insists Michael Holleran. Ramakrishna counseled: "Waste not your energies in useless scriptural discussions and arguments. The little brain will otherwise be muddled."[5]

The mystics we met all agree that even after the many layers are peeled back, what's left is still just a version of Truth. Ultimate Reality lies beyond even their grasp. And that's probably a good thing. According to Bernadette Roberts, the Christian contemplative whom Holleran frequently quotes, "An authentic unmediated glimpse of ultimate Truth and man would go out like a light."

Our world is a construct.

"We are dreaming our own dream within the cosmic dream that encompasses all reality," Swami Atmarupanda told us. Tenzin Palmo put it another way: "We are all projecting our own movie." For Jewish mystics, this illusion is created by *tzimtzum*, the concealment and contraction of the light of Ein-Sof, the infinite Godhead.

The idea is not that the table in front of us is not solid or the pain we feel is not real; rather, it is real because we *believe* it to be real. "A Sufi is one who knows this world and is not fooled by it," Shems Friedlander's teacher, Sufi Sheikh Muzaffer Efendi, once told his students.[6]

A screen of mental obscurations blocks our view of reality. The mystic can get glimpses of what lies behind that. "We come to a state where we see that physical reality melts into higher reality and we see *that* is what was real all the time," says Swami Atmarupananda. "The reality is not some*where* else, it's not some*thing* else. It's what we're seeing; we're just not seeing it correctly." Thich Nhat Hanh taught Clear Grace much the same: "The objective reality we think exists independently of our sense perceptions is itself a creation of collective consciousness."

With her shapeshifting, Emma Restall Orr offers perhaps the most tangible manifestation of this idea of perception as malleable. "I'm just constantly trying to break apart this sense of, 'Is it that or that?'" she said of physical reality. "It's not. It's everything."

At some level, we can shape this construct by listening to our inner voice, trusting our intuition, and being open to synchronicity. The mystics are living proof of that. Nick Ribush, Tenzin Palmo, Swami Atmarupananda, and Ram Alexander each picked up one book from among thousands of others that changed their lives. Right place, right time, right action. And then there is trust. "The dharma will provide," someone told Ribush shortly after he met his lamas, in a Buddhist version of the biblical injunction, "God provides" (Genesis 14:21-24). In the half-century since, he has never been without a (progressively beautiful) roof over his head. Tenzin Palmo, with no money or support structure, was tasked with the seemingly impossible job of reviving an entire Buddhist lineage; as this book was going to print, her nunnery was celebrating its twenty-fifth anniversary. "Whenever I'm about to go under financially, I'll get a phone call," Ram Alexander told us from his farmhouse in Italy. And even as Sister Clear Grace sat snowbound on an Idaho mountaintop with her provisions running out and her wallet empty, she trusted that, somehow, enough money would manifest for food, fuel, and a can of fish for her cat. Eighteen months and a few thousand miles later, she was celebrating the opening of her new sangha house in New Orleans.

We are more than our tiny ego.

The ego prevents most of us from seeing through the illusion. Thus, "No Self" is the mantra of mystics across traditions. "In the end, every self, even the true self, is a false self because it's a self," says Holleran. That self, our ego, prevents us from reaching what mystics call the nondual state; recognizing that the true self—the universal Self—is buried beneath the *false* self of *I*. "God eats the ego," Ma told her followers. "This ego death entails abandoning all of one's beliefs and concepts that make up one's passionately held idea of who one is," Ram Alexander explains.

Through their *turn*, the Whirling Dervishes try to escape the earthly cage of the Self and reach the state of fana, the annihilation of the self. Hindus and Buddhists aspire to the same by sacrificing their ego on the altar of the guru. "The transformative presence of a living Guru is by definition a great threat to the status quo of the ego," says Alexander. Submission to the guru undermines the ego, even as exposure to the darshan of the teacher raises the student's vibration, loosening the ties that bind us to the *I*.

Overcoming our attachment to ego is vital to achieving a level of realization. Hammer says we must realize that we are just the "empty space that God is filling with God's imagination." The conundrum, mystics tell us, is that while the ego ultimately does not exist, it fights a powerful battle to convince us otherwise. "I revolt and revolt. My ego doesn't want to be killed," Atmananda wrote in despair. That death of ego, Holleran reminded us, was vividly described by Bernadette Roberts, who said the falling away of self is the true nature of Jesus's death on the cross, followed by a descent into Hell. "From this void," she wrote, "Christ rises to reveal the divine nature of the body, the Eternal form or mystical body of God."

"*Ana'l-Haqq*," chant the Sufis. "I am the Absolute Truth."

The sad fact is that the more layers of reality we penetrate, the more meditative experiences we have, the more ammunition we are giving the ego. Each time there is a realization or vision in meditation, Alexander says, "The ego grabs a hold of it and says, 'Oh, this happened to me. It didn't happen to anybody else. I must be special.'" Thus Ma, like many gurus, counseled, "If you have any experiences in your meditation, don't bother about them." Hammer's beloved Sefir Yetzirah instructs meditators to instead shift their focus from the experience grasped at by the ego to a recognition that we are all channels for divine energy. Swami Atmarupananda says much the same thing: "The *I am* within me is the *I am* within everyone, and *I am* within the universe itself. It cuts at the very root of egotism." Christian contemplatives call it the crucifixion of the false self.

We experience many lives.

The idea that we are reborn again and again is at the foundation of Eastern traditions but also present in esoteric Judaism, as well as Druidry and other Pagan traditions. It is even accepted by some Christian mystics and Sufis. "Whenever you get to the esoteric edge of any tradition, even the esoteric dimension of the Catholic tradition, it's taken as a given," says Michael Holleran, pointing to Valentin Tomberg, the influential Catholic Hermetic author of *Meditations on the Tarot*, who writes of rebirth as a "fact," and the process of redemption occurring "by way of repeated incarnations."[7]

The question is: What is being reborn? This links back to the issue of the self, the soul, and ways of knowing. Orthodox Hindu teachings tell us that the Atman, the soul, is born in the physical, dies, returns to Brahman, the supreme self, and then takes a new body in the physical. Most Tibetan Buddhists will tell you that the Dalai Lama is reborn again and again as the Dalai Lama *ad infinitum* until he decides his work is done. Christianity teaches that our individual soul leaves our body and, after purification in Purgatory, ends up in Heaven. But here is where many of these mystics penetrate the outer layers of knowing and provide a more nuanced understanding. They tell us that this is not the *reincarnation* of a discrete self, but rather the *rebirth* of some element of the energetic continuum of which that individual is a part. The wave has settled back into the ocean and when a new wave rises it contains only some portion of the previous wave.

The idea is that the unique individual has not returned. Rather, the new being is a composite of the previous person and aspects of many others. Nick Ribush saw that firsthand when a fifteen-month-old Spanish boy was recognized as the incarnation of his beloved teacher. "You sort of have this idea that the incarnation is going to have the same personality or be basically the same person in a small body again, but it doesn't seem to work like that at all," he told us.

"Each time a body and soul leave this planet, someone else, so to speak, dons the hat which has been left behind," Friedlander's teacher Sheikh Muzaffer explained. "The attributes are carried over and the function is filled; but it is not the same person."[8]

In this worldview, the cycle of rebirth continues until all the drops in the ocean have been purified. At the esoteric level, each tradition has its own description of what is happening. For the Hindus and Buddhists, karma has been shed. For practitioners of esoteric Judaism, the repairs—*tikkun*—to the world are complete. For Christian

mystics, this process of purification represents the universal transformation of the energies of God that had taken on a physical mantle
and then reintegrate into the resurrected body of Christ, completing
the cosmic drama of the fall from grace to reunion with the One:
Alpha and Omega.

Words are powerful.

"In the beginning was the Word, and the Word was with God,
and the Word was God," the first line of the Bible tells us. It's easy
to overlook the true meaning of that sentence. "And the Word *was*
God."

The power of the word—the *Divine Logos*—is written through
the texts of the world's religious traditions. The Sefir Yedzirah tells
us that God fashioned all existence from sacred letters. It was the
vibration of those letters that created the Temple—the sacred architecture of the universe—in the Void.

Sound is primordial; thus, mantras are the essence of meditative
practices across traditions. *Om. Marantha. Awen. La ila 'il Allah.*
To Jewish mystics, the wordless *niggunim* chants are keys that open
the windows of the soul to the Infinite Light. Druids and other Celtic
mystics speak of *Oran Mór*, the Great Melody that sang creation
into existence. For Vedic seers, each syllable embodies sacred creative powers. That power is heard in the Muslim Call to Prayer,
which, as Friedlander describes it, "reverberates from *minaret* to
minaret, creating a harmonic rope that fastens the night to prayer."[9]

Quantum physics tells us that sound moves energy. The essence
of meditation is to shift to a higher vibration in order to reach samadhi, accessing higher layers of the self. This was why sanyasis
in Anandamayee Ma's ashram didn't want Ram Alexander or Atmananda anywhere near them; they dragged down the vibration.

But, the mystics tell us, there is also a power beyond words. "Which is the best word?" a student once asked Hazrat Inayat Khan. The Murshid replied: "Silence."[10]

We are not alone.

To our mystics, the world we ordinary folk live in is just one reality among many, and we are just one among countless other intelligences that fill existence. Michael Holleran begins each day communing with angels and other celestial beings. Emma Restall Orr has spent her life talking to goddesses and dancing with the fey. Denizens of other dimensions are Sister Clear Grace's constant companions on her Buddhist journey: the spirits of the land that told her to leave the monastery, the voices of the ancestors who welcomed her the first time she landed in the Louisiana bayou where she would establish her sangha house, and the Hungry Ghosts whose suffering she seeks to ease on her forays into the bardo realms.

Devas, a term for angels, and *mahadevas*, great angels, are an intrinsic part of the complex Hindu pantheon, sometimes referred to as gods or demigods. Buddhists also recognize these and a variety of other nonhuman entities living in dozens of other realms. Some are malevolent, such as the *rakshasas* and *yakshas* who Tibetan Buddhists believe were subdued by an eighth century vajra master; others are guardians, such as the half-serpent *nagas* and the dakinis, female beings said to be the embodiment of enlightened wisdom. "We used to see them much more often in the hills around the nunnery," Tenzin Palmo told me matter-of-factly one day when we were discussing these ethereal "sky-dancers."

Angels and otherworldly beings are also part of the cosmology of the world's Muslims and are a particular focus for Sufis. Shems Friedlander's sheikh was a *sakalayn*, one who taught both humans and jinns and other beings of the subtle realms. Jill Hammer, meanwhile, bemoans the fact that the historic Jewish belief in spirits and the power of ancestors was "swept under the rug" in the modern age. But she and the priestesses who walk the mystic path with her "experience the energies of the world as multiple and alive."

We are here to do good.

"May all beings have happiness and the causes of happiness." The prayer is Buddhist, but its sentiment can be found in the conversations with each of our mystics. The Kabbalah tells us that each act of kindness creates an angel. The ancient Hindu Bhagavad Gita calls on the meditator to see the self in all beings and all beings in the self. Rumi wrote, "Listen with the ears of tolerance! See through the eyes of compassion! Speak with the language of love." Druids aspire to "the love of all existences," knowing awen flows through all things.

The first step to developing that love is shattering the illusion of self and other. "The principal cause of happiness and suffering lies within, in our own minds, not externally, in the material world or other people," said Nick Ribush, quoting his teacher.

Across traditions, there is one common measure of mystic experience, Michael Holleran told us: "Is it making us compassionate, joyful, and peaceful? Is it energizing us? Is it affirming us? Is it making us affirm others? Is it making us affirm the universe? Is it the fruits of the spirit, love, joy, peace?"

After all, recognizing that we are all one is ultimately what the journey to the mountaintop is all about.

So that's my take on what these modern mystics are saying. Of course, if you were paying attention, you know that none of this is Absolute Truth. This book is a far cry from Ultimate Reality. And our mystic guides can't necessarily convey their deepest experiences. Sefer Yedzirah tells us there are levels of understanding that "the mouth cannot say and the ear cannot hear."[11]

Bottom line: This is a set of insights filtered through the experiences of these ten mystics and those who influence them, conveyed within the limitations of words and human concepts, then interpreted by this writer for those of us who Dionysius the Areopagite called "foolish people who live by their senses."

Sure, even we can detect the striking commonalities of the insights each of our mystics brought back from their very personal mountaintops—what has been called the "perennial wisdom" at the heart of the world's religions—but in the end, it's all relative.

Sufi teacher Hazrat Inayat Khan once wrote: "Things appear different from every different plane from which you look at them, and when a person standing on flat earth asks a person standing on top of a mountain, 'Do you also believe something?' the person cannot tell much. The questioner must come to the top of the mountain and see."[12]

Few of us will make it there. Until then, we foolish people will continue to struggle on the lower slopes, grateful for the perspectives of those who have scaled the heights and hoping to glimpse a few insights of our own.

Author's Note

For an author, there is often a sense of relief and accomplishment when we come to the end of a book. But writing the last pages of this particular work is bittersweet. Over the past four years, I have developed a special relationship with each of the individuals I profiled. *Spiritual friends*: It's a term used across the traditions. I would like to think that perfectly encapsulates our relationship. They may think otherwise.

In graciously sharing their time and wisdom, these extraordinary men and women have peeled back the layers of understanding of their respective traditions, taking me deep into their mysteries and teaching me so much, even about religions I thought I knew well.

I will be sad for these lessons to end.

Usually when I write a book, I spend years doing the research, then sit down for a month or two and bang out the manuscript. Not this time. In my conversations with our mystics, I wasn't just looking for a few pithy quotes. I needed to do a deep dive into each tradition. And my little mind could not possibly wrap itself around the complexities of all of them at the same time. So, my approach was to research and write one chapter at a time. That allowed me to immerse myself in the texts and, for a time, adopt as my own the meditation practices of that particular tradition: the zhkir of the Sufis, the Christian Centering Prayer, the Vedic mantras, and mindfulness meditation as taught by Thich Nhat Hahn. I plunged into the awen of the Druids and entered the celestial temple described in the Sefer Yedzirah. Only then could my conversations—not interviews—have the depth needed to truly probe the complexities of their mystic worldviews. And then I wrote, while it was all still alive in my mind. When that chapter draft was finished, I moved on to the next.

As I trust is clear in the text, I have known some of these individuals for decades. I got to know others while researching the book. Several spiritual friends of a different sort helped make that possible. I would like to thank Buddhist teacher Lama Surya Das; author Perle Epstein, who has written about both esoteric Judaism and Sufism; Rabbi Rami Shapiro, himself a prolific author; Jennifer Sartori of the Jewish Women's Archive; and the staff of the Center for Spiritual Imagination; all of whom played a role in helping me to connect with an array of fascinating individuals, some of whom you have read about in these pages.

One of the lessons of the book is to trust synchronicity, and it was synchronicity that led me to Ram Alexander. At breakfast at Kathmandu's Hotel Tibet back in 2015, I was introduced to two American sanyasis, Royal Lillge and Bob Wallace. At the time, I was a dean at Washington State University (WSU), on the border between Washington and Idaho. It turned out that Lillge had taken the first step on his spiritual journey when he attended a Transcendental Meditation workshop at WSU in the 1970s while he was a student at the nearby University of Idaho. I knew better than to ignore such a "coincidence." We stayed in touch and during a conversation a few years later Lillge and Wallace suggested that Ram Alexander might be an ideal candidate for the book. And so he was.

I also want to thank the mystics who did not make it into this book, in most cases because they ultimately were not comfortable with the idea: a granddaughter of Black Elk, the famous Oglala Lakota holy man, who was herself a healer; a Black American academic and mystic seen by many as a spiritual guide in the style of Howard Thurman; an Iranian-American socialite who had a profound spiritual experience that led her to walk away from her jet-setting life and devote herself to the children of India's slums; and a German textile merchant who inherited the mantle of the late teacher of a branch of Kejawen, Java's tradition of syncretic mysticism.

And a huge thanks to the spiritual heavyweights who graciously agreed to read an early, incomplete version of the manuscript and offer a few words of support, which were invaluable as I sought a publisher: Sharon Salzberg and Joseph Goldstein, pioneers in bringing Buddhism to America; renowned Sufi teacher Kabir Helminski; and Simran Jeet Singh, author of a powerful book on the relevance of Sikh tradition to everyday life for those walking any spiritual path. Thanks also to Steven Harrison, the cofounder of Sentient Publications, for seeing the merit of this book. It ended up at exactly the right house.

My wife and muse, Indira, kept me on track when I veered; our daughter, Shantara, tried to keep me culturally sensitive; and my long-time friends Running Deer and Nukananda provided guidance along the way. I am deeply grateful.

There are many unseen energies at work on a project like this. I acknowledge them all.

And finally, I want to apologize to the individuals I have profiled for the shared karma we created with this book. It may take a few lifetimes to get rid of me.

Bibliography

Abram, David. *The Spell of the Sensuous: Perception and Language in a More-Than-Human World.* 20th anniversary edition ed. New York: Vintage Books, 2017.

Ashtavakra Samhita. Translated by Swami Nityaswarupananda. Mayavati, Almora, Himalayas: Advaita Ashrama, 1940.

Atmananda. *As the Flower Sheds Its Fragrance.* 3rd; Kindle ed. Varanasi, India: Shree Shree Anandamayee Sangha, June 15, 2020.

Atmananda and Ram Alexander, Death Must Die, Kindle ed. Ram (Lee) Alexander in conjunction with New Delhi: Shree Shree Anandamayee Archive Trust, 4th edition, 2018.

Atmarupananda, Swami. *Advaita Makaranda (the Nectar of Non-Duality).* Kolkata: Advaita Ashrama, 2018.

— — —. *Brahma in Everyday Experience.* Podcast audio 2018. YouTube.

— — —. *Vedanta: A Religion, a Philosophy, a Way of Life.* Kindle ed. Hollywood: Vedanta Press, 2010.

Bates, Brian. *The Real Middle-Earth: Exploring the Magic and Mystery of the Middle Ages, J.R.R. Tolkien and "the Lord of the Rings".* 1st ed. New York: Palgrave Macmillan, 2003.

Berzin, Alexander. *Wise Teacher, Wise Student: Tibetan Approaches to a Healthy Relationship.* Ithaca, N.Y.: Snow Lion Publications, 2010.

Blann, Gregory. *Lifting the Boundaries: Muzaffer Efendi and the Transmission of Sufism to the West.* Kindle ed. Nashville, Tenn.: Four Worlds Pub., 2005.

Blann, Gregory, and Netanel Miles-Yepez. *When Oceans Merge: The Contemporary Sufi and Hasidic Teachings of Pir Vilayat Khan and Rabbi Zalman Schachter-Shalomi.* Rhinebeck, New York: Adam Kadmon Books; Monkfish Book Publishing Company, 2019.

Bourgeault, Cynthia. *The Holy Trinity and the Law of Three: Discovering the Radical Truth at the Heart of Christianity.* 1st ed. Boston: Shambhala, 2013.

Brett, Julie. *Forest Spirituality.* Podcast audio 2020.

Bruteau, Beatrice. *Radical Optimism: Practical Spirituality in an Uncertain World*. 1st ed. Boulder, CO: Sentient Publications, 2002.

Carmel, Reba. "Midrash: The Stories We Tell." Jewish Currents. Accessed Feb. 2, 2024.

Cook, Francis Harold. *Hua-Yen Buddhism: The Jewel Net of Indra*. University Park: Pennsylvania State University Press, 1977.

"Dalai Lama on Consort Practice and Crazy Wisdom." YouTube, Updated Jan. 26, 2020.

Delio, Ilia. *The Hours of the Universe*. Maryknoll, NY: Orbis Books, 2021.

Dennis, Geoffrey W. *The Encyclopedia of Jewish Myth, Magic & Mysticism*. Kindle ed. Woodbury, Minnesota: Llewellyn Publications, 2016.

— — —. *The Encyclopedia of Jewish Myth, Magic & Mysticism*. Second edition. ed. Woodbury, MN: Llewellyn Publications, 2016.

"The Druids and Druidism." Roman Britain. roman-britain.co.uk.

Eckhart, and David O'Neal. *Meister Eckhart, from Whom God Hid Nothing*. 1st ed. Boston: Shambhala, 1996.

Eknath, Easwaran. *The Bhagavad Gita*. *The Classics of Indian Spirituality*. 2nd ed. Tomales, CA: Nilgiri Press, 2007.

Eknath, Easwaran, and Michael N. Nagler. *The Upanishads*. *The Classics of Indian Spirituality*. 2nd ed. Tomales, CA: Nilgiri Press, 2007.

Eliade, Mircea. *A History of Religious Ideas*. 3 vols. Chicago: University of Chicago Press, 1978.

Evans-Wentz, W. Y. *The Fairy-Faith in Celtic Countries*. Kindle ed. London and N.Y.: Evinity, 2009.

Forest, Danu. *Nature Spirits: Wyrd Lore & Wild Fey Magic*. Glastonbury, Somerset, UK: Wooden Books, 2024.

— — —. *Wild Magic: Celtic Folk Traditions for the Solitary Practitioner*. First edition. ed. Woodbury, Minnesota: Llewellyn Publications, 2020.

Friedlander, Shems. *Mevlana Jalaluddin Rumi's Forgotten Message*. 1st ed. Istanbul: Sufi Kitap, 2018.

— — —. *When You Hear Hoofbeats, Think of a Zebra*. 1st ed. New York: Perennial Library, 1987.

— — —. *The Whirling Dervishes: Being an Account of the Sufi Order, Known as the Mevlevis, and Its Founder, the Poet and Mystic, Mevlana Jalalu'ddin Rumi*. New York: Macmillan, 1975.

— — —. *Winter Harvest: Bob Dylan to Jalaluddin Rumi*. 1st ed. Istanbul: Timas Publishing, 2015.

Garb, Jonathan. *Shamanic Trance in Modern Kabbalah.* Chicago; London: The University of Chicago Press, 2011.

Greywolf. "Awen – the Holy Spirit of Druidry." (1991). druidry.co.uk.

Griffiths, Bede, and Thomas Matus. *Bede Griffiths: Essential Writings. Modern Spiritual Masters.* Maryknoll, N.Y.: Orbis Books, 2004.

Gupta, Mahendranath. *The Gospel of Ramakrishna.* Kindle ed. New York: Ramakrishna-Vivekananda Center, 1942.

Haberman, Bonna. "The Yom Kippur Avodah within the Female Enclosure." In *Beginning Anew: A Woman's Companion to the High Holy Days,* edited by Gail Twersky Reimer and Judith A. Kates, 243-57. New York: Touchstone, 1997.

Hahn, Thicht Nhat. *How to Fight.* Berkeley, California: Parallax Press, 2017.

Hahn, Thicht Nhat, Annabel Laity, and Anh Huong Nguyen. *The Diamond That Cuts through Illusion: Commentaries on the PrajñAparamita Diamond Sutra.* Rev. ed. Berkeley, Calif.: Parallax Press, 2010.

Hahn, Thicht Nhat, and Peter Levitt. *The Heart of Understanding: Commentaries on the PrajñAparamita Heart Sutra.* 20th anniversary ed. Berkeley, Calif.: Parallax Press, 2009.

Hahn, Thicht Nhat, and Rachel Neumann. *Understanding Our Mind.* Revised paperback edition ed. Berkeley, Calif: Parallax Press: Distributed by Publishers Group West, 2006.

Hammer, Jill. *The Book of Earth & Other Mysteries.* Cinncinati: Dimus Parrhesia Press, 2016.

———. *Return to the Place: The Magic, Meditation and Mystery of Sefer Yetzirah.* New Jersey: Ben Yehuda Press, 2020.

———. *Sisters at Sinai: New Tales of Biblical Women.* 1st ed. Philadelphia, PA: Jewish Publication Society, 2001.

———. *Undertorah: An Earth-Based Kabbalah of Dreams.* Ancient, Medieval, and Chasidic Texts. 1st ed. Brooklyn, New York: Ayin Press, 2022.

Hammer, Jill, and Taya Shere. *The Hebrew Priestess: Ancient and New Visions of Jewish Women's Spiritual Leadership.* Teaneck, New Jersey: Ben Yehuda Press, 2015.

Hammer, Rabbi Jill. "Wedding the Dragon: The Powerful Feminine as Seen in Jewish Women's Dreams." Journal of Lesbian Studies 23, no. 1 (2019): 105-18.

Harvey, Andrew. *The Essential Mystics: The Soul's Journey into Truth.* 1st ed. San Francisco: HarperSanFrancisco, 1996.

Hastrup, Kirsten, and Frida Hastrup. *Waterworlds: Anthropology in Fluid Environments*. Ethnography, Theory, Experiment. First paperback edition. ed. New York: Berghahn Books, 2017.

Hita, Tenzin Osel "One Big Love/Warriors of Clear Light." (May 17 2020). one-big-love.com.

———. "Tenzin Osel Hita." (2022).

Holleran, Fr. Michael K. "The Banquet Where Science Dines with Religion." Discovery Magazine. (Fall 2006).

———. "Hermeneutics of the Bible." In How the Bible Was Written Engaged Media, 2016.

———. "The Way up Is the Way Down." National Catholic Reporter. (Feb. 28-March 13, 2014).

———. *The Wound of Love*. St. Hugh's Charterhouse: Gracewing Publishing, 2006.

Humphreys, Christmas. *Buddhism*. Pelican Books. Harmondsworth, Middlesex,: Penguin Books, 1951.

Hutton, Ronald. *Blood and Mistletoe: The History of the Druids in Britain*. New Haven: Yale University Press, 2009.

"The Infinite Library." Sri Ramakrishna. theinfinitelibrary.net.

"Introduction to Sri Ma's Life." (2007). anandamayi.org.

Isherwood, Christopher. *Vedanta for the Western World*. London: George Allen & Unwin, 1948. microform.

Jenkins, Jolyon. "Osel Hita Torres - the Reluctant Lama." BBC.com. (Sept. 28 2012).

Johnson, Kurt, and David Robert Ord. *The Coming Interspiritual Age*. Vancouver, BC: Namaste Publishing, 2012.

Karmapa, 9th Gyalwa, and Alexander Berzin. *The MahāMudrā: Eliminating the Darkness of Ignorance*. 1st ed. Dharamsala: Library of Tibetan Works and Archives, 1978.

"Khamtrul Lineage." Gyalwa Doghampa, 2017, 2022, gyalwadokhampa. org.

Khan, Hazrat Inayat. *Biography of Pir-O-Murshid Inayat Khan*. Suresnes, France: Pantarehi Uitgeverij/Nekbakh Foundation, 2020.

———. *The Teaching of Hazrat Inayat Khan*. hazrat-inayat-khan.org.

Klaushofer, Alex. *The New British Druids: Connecting with Nature in the 21st Century*. Kindle ed.: Hermes Books, 2016.

Knitter, Paul F. *Without Buddha I Could Not Be a Christian*. Kindle ed. London: Oneworld, 2013.

Lama, Dalai, and Ven. Pema Chodron. "The Self-Confidence of a Bodhisattva." Tricycle. (Spring 2015).

Leahy, Arthur Herbert. *Heroic Romances of Ireland*. Irish Saga Library,. 2 vols. London,: D. Nutt, 1905.

Matt, Daniel Chanan. *The Essential Kabbalah: The Heart of Jewish Mysticism*. 1st ed. San Francisco, CA: HarperSanFrancisco, 1995.

Meditations on the Tarot: A Journey into Christian Hermeticism. Translated by Robert Powell. New York: J.P. Tarcher/Putnam, 2002.

Merton, Thomas, and William Henry Shannon. *The Inner Experience: Notes on Contemplation*. San Francisco: HarperSanFrancisco, 2003.

Merton, Thomas, and Jon M. Sweeney. *A Course in Christian Mysticism*. Collegeville, Minnesota: Liturgical Press, 2017.

Michaelson, Jay. *God in Your Body: Kabbalah, Mindfulness and Embodied Spiritual Practice*. Kindle ed. Woodstock, Vt.: Jewish Lights Pub., 2007.

Miles-Yepez, Netanel. *The Common Heart: An Experience of Interreligious Dialogue*. New York: Lantern Books, 2006.

"Mission Statement." druidnetwork.org.

Moore, Thomas. *Care of the Soul*. 1st ed. New York, NY: HarperCollins, 1992.

Morrison, Chanan, and Abraham Isaac Kook. *Gold from the Land of Israel*. Jerusalem; New York: Urim Publications, 2006.

Mu, Soeng. Diamond Sutra: *Transforming the Way We Perceive the World*. Boston, Mass.: Wisdom Publications, 2000.

Muller, F. Max. *Ramakrishna*. Ohio: Pinnacle Press, 2017. Public domain.

Nhât Hạnh, Thích. *The Heart of the Buddha's Teaching*. 1st Broadway Books trade pbk. ed. New York: Broadway Books, 1999.

Nhât Hạnh, Thích, and Arnold Kotler. *Peace Is Every Step: The Path of Mindfulness in Everyday Life*. New York, N.Y: Bantam Books, 1991.

Orr, Emma Restall. *Living Druidry*. London: Piatkus, 2014.

———. *Principles of Druidry*. London Thorson's, HarperCollins Publishers, 1998.

———. *The Wakeful World: Animism, Mind and the Self in Nature*. Kindle ed. Alresford, Hants, UK: Moon Books, John Hunt Publishing, 2011.

Padmasambhava. *Advice from the Lotus-Born*. Translated by Erik Pema Kunsang. 8th ed. Edited by Marcia Binder Schmidt. Boulder, CO: Rangjung Yeshe Publications, 2004.

Palmo, Tenzin. *Buddhism and Ageing: In Praise of Aging*. Dongyu Gatsal Ling Nunnery (India: 2013).

———. *Discovering Our True Buddha Nature*. Dongyu Gatso Ling (India: June 1 1997).

———. "Gyatsal Teaching: 37 Practices of a Bodhisattva, Part Vi." *Newsletter of the Dongyu Gatsal Nunnery 26*. (Spring 2019).

———. "Gyatsal Teaching: 37 Practices of a Bodhisattva, Part Vii." *Newsletter of the Dongyu Gatsal Nunnery 36*. (Spring 2020).

———. "Gyatsal Teaching: 37 Practices of a Bodhisattva, Part Viii." *Newsletter of the Dongyu Gatsal Nunnery 37*. (Fall 2020).

———. "Gyatsal Teaching: Thoughts and the Environment." *Newsletter of the Dongyu Gatsal Nunnery 23*. (October 2009).

———. *Into the Heart of Life*. Boulder: Snow Lion, 2011.

"Jetsunma Tenzin Palmo on Chogyam Trungpa Rinpoche." YouTube, Updated Jan. 11, 2012.

Palmo, Tenzin. *Reflections on a Mountain Lake*. Boulder: Snow Lion, 2002.

———. *Three Teachings*. Buddha Dharma Education Association, Inc., 1999.

———. *Time to Change*. Dongyu Gatsal Ling Nunnery. tenzinpalmo. com.

Philips, Noah. "Who Will Lead the Priestesses?" *Moment*, no. Winter. (Jan. 23 2024).

Pintak, Lawrence. "Something Has to Change: Blacks in American Buddhism." *Shambhala Sun*, Sept. 1, 2001.

Potia. "Voice of the Cailleach." (October 2006). druidnetwork.org.

"Publishing the Fpmt Lineage: An Interview with Lama Yeshe Wisdom Archive Director Nicholas Ribush." *Mandala* October. (2012).

Reininger, Gustave. *Centering Prayer in Daily Life and Ministry*. New York: Continuum, 1998.

Restall Orr, Emma. *Spirits of the Sacred Grove: The World of a Druid Priestess*. Collective Ink. Kindle Edition ed. Winchester UK and Washington, D.C.: Moon Books, John Hunt Publishing, 2014.

Ribush, Nick. "Birth of a Buddhist Publishing Company." In *The Path of the Buddha: Writings on Contemporary Buddhism*, edited by Renuka Singh, xxi, 221 p. New Delhi; New York, NY: Penguin Books, 2004.

"How to Meditate with Dr Nick Ribush 5/5." Kurukulla Center, You Tube. Updated Jan. 4, 2021,

"More Than a Spiritual Friend." Karma Lekshey Ling Institute, 1987.

"How FPMT and the Centers Benefit Others." Foundation for the Preservation of Mahayana Teachings. Lama Yeshe Wisdom Archive. Updated June 21, 2006,

"Lama Zopa Rinpoche's Story of Meeting Lama Yeshe." Foundation for the Preservation of Mahayana Teachings, 1982, 2022, fpmt.org.

Roberts, Bernadette. *What Is Self?: A Study of the Spiritual Journey in Terms of Consciousness*. 1st ed. Boulder, CO: Sentient Publications, 2005.

Rohr, Richard. *The Universal Christ: How a Forgotten Reality Can Change Everything We See, Hope for, and Believe*. 1st ed. New York: Convergent, 2019.

Schachter-Shalomi, Zalman. "Reb Zalman on Conversion and Renewal." *Jewish Renewal Hasidus*.

Schachter-Shalomi, Zalman, and Netanel Miles-Yepez. *A Heart Afire: Stories and Teachings of the Early Hasidic Masters*. Revised edition. ed. Rhinebeck, NY: Adam Kadmon Books, 2017.

Scholem, Gershom. *Major Trends in Jewish Mysticism*. New York: Schocken Books, 1995.

Sefer Yetzirah.

Siculus, Diodorus *Bibliotheca Historica, Book V*. Chicago: University of Chicago Press, 1839.

Snibbe, Scott. *A Skeptic's Path to Enlightenment*. Podcast audio. Women, Buddhism, and Equality with Jetsunma Tenzin Palmo 2021. skepticspath.org.

Steiner, Rudolf. *The Druids: Esoteric Wisdom of the Ancient Celtic Priests*. The Pocket Library of Spiritual Wisdom. Edited by Andrew Welburn. East Sussex, UK: Sophia Books, 2012.

Steinsaltz, Adin. *The Thirteen Petalled Rose: A Discourse on the Essence of Jewish Existence and Belief*. Rev. ed. New York: Basic Books, 2006.

Tacitus, Cornelius, Alfred John Church, William Jackson Brodribb, and Cornelius Tacitus. *The Annals and the Histories. The Great Histories*. New ed. New York: Barnes & Noble Books, 2005.

Teasdale, Wayne. *The Mystic Heart: Discovering a Universal Spirituality in the World's Religions*. Novato, Calif: New World Library, 1999.

Teilhard de Chardin, Pierre. *The Phenomenon of Man*. New York,: Harper, 1959.

Tillis, Malcolm. *New Lives: 50 Westerners Search for Themselves in Sacred India*. Varanasi: Indica, 2004.

Tov, Baal Shem. *Tzava'at Harivash*. Kehot Publication Society. chabad. org.

Travers, Andrew. "How Thomas Keating Launched a Global Interfaith Movement from a Snowmass Monastery." *The Aspen Times*. (Oct. 31 2019). Accessed Sept. 6, 2024.

Tyagananda, Swami. "Vivekananda's Vision of Vedanta." (Sept. 21 2002). vendanta.org.

"What People Are Saying About Big Love." Lama Yeshe Wisdom Archive, 2022,

Wolters, Clifton. *The Cloud of Unknowing, and Other Works*. Penguin Classics. Harmondsworth; New York: Penguin, 1978.

Yeshe, Lama Thubten. "Practicing Dharma in the West: Q&a with Lama Yeshe." (1983). Lama Yeshe Wisdom Archive.

Yogananda, Paramahansa. *Autobiography of a Yogi*. Los Angeles, Calif.: Self-Realization Fellowship, 1997.

Endnotes

A Rumi Life

1   Shems Friedlander, *The Whirling Dervishes: Being an account of the Sufi order, known as the Mevlevis, and its founder, the poet and mystic, Mevlana Jalalu'ddin Rumi* (New York: Macmillan, 1975). The book's title was later shortened to *Rumi and the Whirling Dervishes*. It has gone through numerous reprints through the decades. A new revised edition was released in 2019 as *Mevlana Jalauddin Rumi's Forgotten Message*.

2   Unless another citation is provided, all quotations in this book are from interviews with the author.

3   Shems Friedlander, *Winter Harvest: Bob Dylan to Jalaluddin Rumi*, 1st ed. (Istanbul: Timas Publishing, 2015). 175.

4   Friedlander, *Winter Harvest*. 134.

5   Friedlander, *Winter Harvest*. 83.

6   Friedlander, *Whirling Dervishes*. 73.

7   Friedlander, *Winter Harvest*. 107.

8   Friedlander, *Winter Harvest*. 133.

9   Friedlander, *Winter Harvest*. 159.

10   Shems Friedlander, *Mevlana Jalaluddin Rumi's Forgotten Message*, 1st ed. (Istanbul: Sufi Kitap, 2018).

11   Shems Friedlander, *When You Hear Hoofbeats, Think of a Zebra*, 1st ed. (New York: Perennial Library, 1987).

12   Gregory Blann, *Lifting the Boundaries: Muzaffer Efendi and the Transmission of Sufism to the West*, Kindle ed. (Nashville, Tenn.: Four Worlds Pub., 2005). Loc. 4713.

13   Friedlander, *Mevlana Jalaluddin Rumi's Forgotten Message*. 3.

14   Friedlander, *Winter Harvest*. 164.

15   Friedlander, *When You Hear Hoofbeats, Think of a Zebra*.

16   Friedlander, *Rumi's Forgotten Message.*

Double Belonging

1   Clifton Wolters, *The Cloud of Unknowing, and Other Works*, Penguin classics, (Harmondsworth; New York: Penguin, 1978). 12.

2   Thomas Merton and William Henry Shannon, *The Inner Experience: Notes on Contemplation* (San Francisco: HarperSanFrancisco, 2003). 59

3   Beatrice Bruteau, *Radical Optimism: Practical Spirituality in an Uncertain World*, 1st ed. (Boulder, CO: Sentient Publications, 2002). 55.

4   Fr. Michael K. Holleran, *The Wound of Love* (St. Hugh's Charterhouse: Gracewing Publishing, 2006). 1.

5   Richard Rohr, *The Universal Christ: How a forgotten reality can change everything we see, hope for, and believe*, 1st ed. (New York: Convergent, 2019). 137.

6   Cynthia Bourgeault, *The Holy Trinity and the Law of Three: Discovering the radical truth at the heart of Christianity*, 1st ed. (Boston: Shambhala, 2013). 208 and 84.

7   Bourgeault, *Holy Trinity.* 20.

8   Pierre Teilhard de Chardin, *The Phenomenon of Man* (New York,: Harper, 1959). 169.

9   Ilia Delio, *The Hours of the Universe* (Maryknoll, NY: Orbis Books, 2021). 240.

10   Wolters, *Cloud of Unknowing.* 89.

11   Bourgeault, *Holy Trinity.* 7-8.

12   Teilhard de Chardin, *The Phenomenon of Man.* 169.

13   Bernadette Roberts, *What is Self?: A study of the spiritual journey in terms of consciousness*, 1st ed. (Boulder, CO: Sentient Publications, 2005). 146.

14   Gustave Reininger, *Centering Prayer in Daily Life and Ministry* (New York: Continuum, 1998). 41.

15   Merton and Shannon, *Inner Experience.* 6-7.

16   Roberts, *What is Self?* 20, 63.

17   Roberts, *What is Self?* 187.

18   Kurt Johnson and David Robert Ord, *The Coming Interspiritual Age* (Vancouver, BC: Namaste Publishing, 2012). 347.

19   Fr. Michael K. Holleran, "The way up is the way down," *National Catholic Reporter* (Feb. 28-March 13, 2014). .

20   Thomas Moore, *Care of the Soul*, 1st ed. (New York, NY: HarperCollins, 1992). 35.

21   Fr. Michael K. Holleran, "Hermeneutics of the Bible," *How the Bible Was Written* (Engaged Media, 2016).

22   Fr. Michael K. Holleran, "The Banquet Where Science Dines with Religion," *Discovery Magazine* Online (Fall 2006).

23   Holleran, "Hermeneutics of the Bible."

24   Andrew Harvey, *The Essential Mystics: The Soul's Journey Into Truth*, 1st ed. (San Francisco: HarperSanFrancisco, 1996). xii.

25   *Meditations On the Tarot: A Journey Into Christian Hermeticism*, trans. Robert Powell (New York: J.P. Tarcher/Putnam, 2002). 659-661.

26   Paul F. Knitter, *Without Buddha I Could Not Be a Christian*, Kindle ed. (London: Oneworld, 2013). 23:21.

27   Knitter, *Without Buddha*. 140.

28   Thomas Merton and Jon M. Sweeney, *A Course in Christian Mysticism* (Collegeville, Minnesota: Liturgical Press, 2017). 3.

29   Netanel Miles-Yepez, *The Common Heart: An Experience of Interreligious Dialogue* (New York: Lantern Books, 2006).

30   Wayne Teasdale, *The Mystic Heart: Discovering a universal spirituality in the world's religions* (Novato, Calif: New World Library, 1999).

31   Bede Griffiths and Thomas Matus, *Bede Griffiths: Essential writings*, Modern Spiritual Masters, (Maryknoll, N.Y.: Orbis Books, 2004). 98.

32   Griffiths and Matus, *Bede Griffiths*. 98.

33   Roberts, *What is Self?* 141.

At the Feet of the Mother

1   "Introduction to Sri Ma's Life," (2007). anandamayi.org.

2   Paramahansa Yogananda, *Autobiography of a Yogi* (Los Angeles, Calif.: Self-Realization Fellowship, 1997). 587.

3   Malcolm Tillis, *New Lives: 50 Westerners search for themselves in sacred India* (Varanasi: Indica, 2004). 29.

4   Atmananda and Ram Alexander, *Death Must Die*, Kindle ed. (Ram "Lee" Alexander in conjunction with New Delhi: Shree Shree Anandamayee Archive Trust, 2018). Loc. 226.

5   Atmananda, *As the Flower Sheds its Fragrance*, 3rd; Kindle ed. (Varanasi, India: Shree Shree Anandamayee Sangha, June 15, 2020). 316

6   Atmananda and Alexander, *Death Must Die*. Loc. 135.

7   Atmananda and Alexander, *Death Must Die*. Loc. 318, 703, 233.

8   Atmananda and Alexander, *Death Must Die*. Loc. 637.

9   Atmananda and Alexander, *Death Must Die*. Loc. 18, 605.

10   Atmananda and Alexander, *Death Must Die*. Loc. 579.

11   Atmananda and Alexander, *Death Must Die*. Loc. 579, 656.

12   Tillis, *New Lives*. 37.

13   Atmananda and Alexander, *Death Must Die*. Loc. 663, 39-40.

14   Atmananda and Alexander, *Death Must Die*. Loc. 45.

15   Tillis, *New Lives*. 58-59.

16   Atmananda and Alexander, *Death Must Die*. Loc. 383.

17   Atmananda and Alexander, *Death Must Die*. Loc. 601, 537.

18   Atmananda and Alexander, *Death Must Die*. Loc. 704.

19   Atmananda and Alexander, *Death Must Die*. 191, Loc. 284, 305, 307, 342.

20   Atmananda and Alexander, *Death Must Die*. 608, Loc. 134.

21   Atmananda, *As the Flower Sheds its Fragrance*. Loc. 663.

22   Atmananda and Alexander, *Death Must Die*. Loc. 703.

The Yogini and the Scribe

1   Milarepa, *Songs of Milarepa*. Dover Thrift Editions (Mineola, New York: Dover Publications 2003).

2   Tenzin Palmo, *Into the Heart of Life* (Boulder: Snow Lion, 2011). 150.

3   Tenzin Palmo, *Reflections on a Mountain Lake* (Boulder: Snow Lion, 2002). 10, 12.

4   Palmo, *Reflections*. 13.

5   Alexander Berzin, *Wise Teacher, Wise Student: Tibetan approaches to a healthy relationship* (Ithaca, N.Y.: Snow Lion Publications, 2010).

6   Palmo, *Reflections*. 210.

7   "More Than a Spiritual Friend," Karma Lekshey Ling Institute, 1987.

8   Palmo, *Reflections*. 13.

9   Palmo, *Reflections*. 14.

10   Palmo, *Reflections*. 14.

11   Christmas Humphreys, *Buddhism*, Pelican books, (Harmondsworth, Middlesex,: Penguin Books, 1951). 189-190.

12   Palmo, *Reflections*. 24-25.

13   Palmo, *Reflections*. 20.

14   Tenzin Palmo, *Three Teachings* (Buddha Dharma Education Association, Inc., 1999).. 34-35.

15   Palmo, *Reflections*. 244

16   "Publishing the FPMT Lineage: An Interview with Lama Yeshe Wisdom Archive Director Nicholas Ribush," Mandala October (2012).

17   "Publishing the FPMT Lineage."

18   "Lama Zopa Rinpoche's Story of Meeting Lama Yeshe," Foundation for the Preservation of Mahayana Teachings, 1982, 2022.

19   Lama Thubten Yeshe, "Practicing Dharma in the West: Q&A with Lama Yeshe," (1983). Lama Yeshe Wisdom Archive.

20   Padmasambhava, *Advice from the Lotus-Born*, trans. Erik Pema Kunsang, 8th ed., ed. Marcia Binder Schmidt (Boulder, CO: Rangjung Yeshe Publications, 2004). 20.

21   Scott Snibbe, *A Skeptic's Path to Enlightenment*, podcast audio, Women, Buddhism, and Equality with Jetsunma Tenzin Palmo 2021, Skepticspath.org.

22   Snibbe, *Skeptic*.

23   Snibbe, *Skeptic*.

24   Palmo, *Heart of Life*.

25   Palmo, *Three Teachings*. 30.

26   Palmo, *Reflections*. 152, 144.

27   Tenzin Palmo, "Gyatsal Teaching: 37 Practices of a Bodhisattva, Part VII," *Newsletter of the Dongyu Gatsal Nunnery* 36 (Spring 2020).

28   Palmo, *Three Teachings*. 44.

29   Palmo, *Reflections*. 210.

30   Tenzin Palmo, Time to Change, "Dharma talk in Tasmania," June 2008, Dongyu Gatsal Ling, India, tenzinpalmo.com. 3.

31   Tenzin Palmo, "Gyatsal Teaching: 37 Practices of a Bodhisattva, Part VIII," *Newsletter of the Dongyu Gatsal Nunnery* 37 (Fall 2020). 1.

32   Palmo, "Gyatsal Teaching: Part VIII." 2.

33   Palmo, *Reflections.*

34   Tenzin Palmo, *Discovering our True Buddha Nature*, Dongyu Gatso Ling (India, June 1 1997), tenzinpalmo.com.

35   Palmo, "Gyatsal Teaching: Part VIII." 3.

36   Tenzin Palmo, "Gyatsal Teaching: Thoughts and the Environment," *Newsletter of the Dongyu Gatsal Nunnery* 23 (October 2009).

37   Palmo, *Three Teachings.* 43-44.

38   Palmo, *Time to Change.* 6.

39   Palmo, *Buddha Nature.*

40   9th Gyalwa Karmapa and Alexander Berzin, *The Mahāmudrā: Eliminating the darkness of ignorance*, 1st ed. (Dharamsala: Library of Tibetan Works and Archives, 1978).

41   Palmo, *Buddha Nature.*

42   Palmo, *Buddha Nature.*

43   Palmo, *Heart of Life.* 13.

44   Palmo, "Gyatsal Teaching: Part VII." 3.

45   Palmo, *Reflections.* 19.

46   Palmo, *Reflections.* 45.

47   Palmo, *Reflections.* 244.

48   Jolyon Jenkins, "Osel Hita Torres - The Reluctant Lama," BBC.com (Sept. 28 2012).

49   Tenzin Osel Hita, "One Big Love/Warriors of Clear Light," (May 17 2020). one-big-love.com.

50   Tenzin Osel Hita, "Tenzin Osel Hita," (2022). https://one-big-love.com/osel-hita-bio/.

51   "Khamtrul Lineage," Gyalwa Doghampa, 2017, 2022, gyalwadokhampa.org.

52   Palmo, *Reflections.* 209.

53   Palmo, *Reflections.*

54   "Jetsunma Tenzin Palmo on Chogyam Trungpa Rinpoche," YouTube, updated Jan. 11, 2012.

55   "Dalai Lama on consort practice and crazy wisdom," YouTube, updated Jan. 26, 2020.

56 "How to Meditate with Dr Nick Ribush 5/5," (Video), Kurukulla Center, updated Jan. 4, 2021.

57 "What People Are Saying About Big Love," Lama Yeshe Wisdom Archive, 2022.

58 Nick Ribush, "Birth of a Buddhist Publishing Company," in The Path of the Buddha: Writings on contemporary Buddhism, ed. Renuka Singh (New Delhi; New York, NY: Penguin Books, 2004).

59 "How FPMT and the Centers Benefit Others," Foundation for the Preservation of Mahayana Teachings. Lama Yeshe Wisdom Archive. updated June 21, 2006.

60 Tenzin Palmo, "Gyatsal Teaching: 37 Practices of a Bodhisattva, Part VI," *Newsletter of the Dongyu Gatsal Nunnery* 26 (Spring 2019). 1-2.

61 Palmo, *Three Teachings*. 36.

62 Ribush, "Birth."

63 Ribush, "Birth."

64 Tenzin Palmo, Buddhism and Ageing: In Praise of Aging, Dongyu Gatsal Ling Nunnery (India, 2013).

65 Palmo, *Heart of Life*. 61-62.

66 Palmo, *Reflections*. 25.

The Jewish Bard

1 Noah Philips, "Who Will Lead the Priestesses?," *Moment*, Winter (Jan. 23 2024).

2 Zalman Schachter-Shalomi and Netanel Miles-Yepez, *A Heart Afire: Stories and Teachings of the Early Hasidic Masters*, Revised edition. ed. (Rhinebeck, NY: Adam Kadmon Books, 2017). Loc 3594.

3 Jill Hammer, *Sisters at Sinai: New Tales of Biblical Women*, 1st ed. (Philadelphia, PA: Jewish Publication Society, 2001). Loc 91-92.

4 Chanan Morrison and Abraham Isaac Kook, *Gold From the Land of Israel* (Jerusalem; New York: Urim Publications, 2006). 179-181.

5 Reba Carmel, "Midrash: The Stories We Tell," *Jewish Currents*. Online archive. Undated.

6 Hammer, *Sisters at Sinai*. Loc 64.

7 Hammer, *Sisters at Sinai*. Loc 93.

8 Rav is a transliteration of "rabbi" often used in Orthodox Judaism.

9   Jill Hammer, *The Book of Earth & Other Mysteries* (Cinncinati: Dimus Parrhesia Press, 2016). xv.

10   Hammer, *Sisters at Sinai*. Loc 168.

11   Jill Hammer and Taya Shere, *The Hebrew Priestess: Ancient and New Visions of Jewish Women's Spiritual Leadership* (Teaneck, New Jersey: Ben Yehuda Press, 2015). 5.

12   Hammer and Shere, *Hebrew Priestess*. 7.

13   Hammer and Shere, *Hebrew Priestess*. 33, 39.

14   Zohar I, 148.

15   Geoffrey W. Dennis, *The Encyclopedia of Jewish Myth, Magic & Mysticism*, Kindle ed. (Woodbury, Minnesota: Llewellyn Publications, 2016). 388-389.

16   Baal Shem Tov, *Tzava'at Harivash*, Online (Kehot Publication Society/Chabad).

17   Hammer and Shere, *Hebrew Priestess*. 41.

18   Hammer and Shere, *Hebrew Priestess*. 10.

19   Philips, "Who Will Lead the Priestesses?."

20   Hammer and Shere, *Hebrew Priestess*. 12.

21   Jill Hammer, *Undertorah: An Earth-Based Kabbalah of Dreams*, 1st ed., Ancient, Medieval, and Chasidic Texts, (Brooklyn, New York: Ayin Press, 2022). 17, 29, 18.

22   Hammer, *Undertorah*. 18.

23   Bonna Haberman, "The Yom Kippur Avodah Within the Female Enclosure," in *Beginning Anew: A Woman's Companion to the High Holy Days*, ed. Gail Twersky Reimer and Judith A. Kates (New York: Touchstone, 1997).

24   Dana Gioai, Heuresis, in Interrogations at Noon. Graywolf Press. St. Paul, Minn. 2001.

25   Hammer and Shere, *Hebrew Priestess*.

26   Schachter-Shalomi and Miles-Yepez, *Heart Afire*. Loc. 1029.

27   Dennis, *The Encyclopedia of Jewish Myth, Magic & Mysticism*. Kindle edition. Loc. 122.

28   Schachter-Shalomi and Miles-Yepez, *Heart Afire*. Kindle edition. Loc. 980.

29   Schachter-Shalomi and Miles-Yepez, *Heart Afire*. 985.

30   Daniel Chanan Matt, *The Essential Kabbalah: The Heart of Jewish Mysticism*, 1st ed. (San Francisco, CA: HarperSanFrancisco, 1995). 12 and 15.

31 Schachter-Shalomi and Miles-Yepez, *Heart Afire*. Loc 1029.

32 Jill Hammer, *Return to the Place: The Magic, Meditation and Mystery of Sefer Yetzirah* (New Jersey: Ben Yehuda Press, 2020). 7, 13, 38, and 13-15.

33 Hammer, *Return*. 6.

34 Mircea Eliade, *A History of Religious Ideas*, 3 vols. (Chicago: University of Chicago Press, 1978). Full text https://shorturl.at/aFHIQ. 402.

35 Jay Michaelson, *God In Your Body: Kabbalah, Mindfulness and Embodied Spiritual Practice*, Kindle ed. (Woodstock, Vt.: Jewish Lights Pub., 2007). Loc. 1536.

36 Hammer, *Return*. 4.

37 Jonathan Garb, *Shamanic Trance in Modern Kabbalah* (Chicago; London: The University of Chicago Press, 2011).

38 David Abram, *The Spell of the Sensuous: Perception and Language in a More-Than-Human World*, 20th anniversary edition ed. (New York: Vintage Books, 2017). Kindle edition. Loc. 68.

39 Adin Steinsaltz, *The Thirteen Petalled Rose: A Discourse on the Essence of Jewish Existence and Belief*, Rev. ed. (New York: Basic Books, 2006). 7-8, 20-21, 47.

40 Zalman Schachter-Shalomi, "Reb Zalman On Conversion And Renewal," *Jewish Renewal Hasidus*.

41 Schachter-Shalomi and Miles-Yepez, *Heart Afire*. Loc. 757.

42 Rabbi Jill Hammer, "Wedding the Dragon: The powerful feminine as seen in Jewish women's dreams," *Journal of Lesbian Studies* 23, no. 1 (2019). 105.

43 Gershom Scholem, *Major Trends in Jewish Mysticism* (New York: Schocken Books, 1995).

The Universe Is My Mirror

1 Swami Atmarupananda, *Vedanta: A Religion, A Philosophy, A Way of Life*, Kindle ed. (Hollywood: Vedanta Press, 2010). Loc 127, 168.

2 Atmarupananda, *Vedanta*. Loc. 212.

3 Christopher Isherwood, *Vedanta for the Western World* (London: George Allen & Unwin, 1948), microform. 1.

4 Mahendranath Gupta, *The Gospel of Ramakrishna*, Kindle ed. (New York: Ramakrishna-Vivekananda Center, 1942). 94.

5   Swami Tyagananda, "Vivekananda's Vision of Vedanta," (Sept. 21 2002). vedanta.org.

6   Atmarupananda, *Vedanta*. Loc 639.

7   "The Infinite Library." Sri Ramakrishna. InfiniteLibrary.net. 779.

8   F. Max Muller, *Ramakrishna* (Ohio: Pinnacle Press, 2017), Public domain. 106.

9   Muller, *Ramakrishna*. 158, 100.

10   Swami Atmarupananda, *Advaita Makaranda (The Nectar of Non-Duality)* (Kolkata: Advaita Ashrama, 2018). 42, 56.

11   Easwaran Eknath and Michael N. Nagler, *The Upanishads*, 2nd ed., The classics of Indian spirituality, (Tomales, CA: Nilgiri Press, 2007). 80.

12   Swami Atmarupananda, *Brahma in Everyday Experience*, You Tube, podcast audio 2018.

13   Easwaran Eknath, *The Bhagavad Gita*, 2nd ed., The classics of Indian spirituality, (Tomales, CA: Nilgiri Press, 2007). 26.

14   Atmarupananda, *Advaita Makaranda (The Nectar of Non-Duality)*. 63, 25.

15   Atmarupananda, *Brahma in Everyday Experience*.

16   *Ashtavakra Samhita*, trans. Swami Nityaswarupananda (Mayavati, Almora, Himalayas: Advaita Ashrama, 1940). 32.

17   Atmarupananda, *Advaita Makaranda (The Nectar of Non-Duality)*. 49.

18   Eknath, *The Bhagavad Gita*. 23.

19   Francis Harold Cook, *Hua-yen Buddhism: The Jewel Net of Indra* (University Park: Pennsylvania State University Press, 1977). 19.

Beyond Druid

1   Potia, "Voice of the Cailleach," (October 2006). https://druidnetwork. org/the-druid-heritage/seeking-deity/voice-of-the-cailleach/.

2   Brian Bates, *The Real Middle-earth: Exploring the Magic and Mystery of the Middle Ages, J.R.R. Tolkien and "The Lord of the Rings"*, 1st ed. (New York: Palgrave Macmillan, 2003). 4.

3   Emma Restall Orr, *Spirits of the Sacred Grove: The World of a Druid Priestess*, Collective Ink. Kindle Edition ed. (Winchester UK and

Washington, D.C.: Moon Books, John Hunt Publishing, 2014). Loc 132.

4 Diodorus Siculus, *Bibliotheca Historica, Book V* (Chicago: University of Chicago Press, 1839)..

5 "The Druids and Druidism," Roman Britain.co.uk.

6 Ronald Hutton, *Blood and Mistletoe: The History of the Druids in Britain* (New Haven: Yale University Press, 2009).

7 Cornelius Tacitus et al., *The Annals and The histories*, New ed., The Great histories, (New York: Barnes & Noble Books, 2005).

8 Greywolf, "Awen – The Holy Spirit of Druidry," (1991). druidry. co.uk.

9 Greywolf, "Awen – The Holy Spirit of Druidry."

10 Restall Orr, *Spirits of the Sacred Grove*. 132.

11 Greywolf, "Awen – The Holy Spirit of Druidry."

12 Danu Forest, *Wild Magic: Celtic folk traditions for the solitary practitioner*, First edition. ed. (Woodbury, Minnesota: Llewellyn Publications, 2020). 2.

13 Rudolf Steiner, *The Druids: Esoteric Wisdom of the Ancient Celtic Priests*, ed. Andrew Welburn, The Pocket Library of Spiritual Wisdom, (East Sussex, UK: Sophia Books, 2012). 58.

14 Emma Restall Orr, *Living Druidry* (London: Piatkus, 2014). 43. And Restall Orr, *Spirits of the Sacred Grove*. 167.

15 Danu Forest, *Nature Spirits: Wyrd Lore & Wild Fey Magic* (Glastonbury, Somerset, UK: Wooden Books, 2024). 22.

16 Arthur Herbert Leahy, *Heroic Romances of Ireland*, 2 vols., Irish saga library, (London,: D. Nutt, 1905).

17 W. Y. Evans-Wentz, *The Fairy-Faith in Celtic Countries*, Kindle ed. (London and N.Y.: Evinity, 2009). 29-30, 21.

18 Restall Orr, *Spirits of the Sacred Grove*. 33, 38-39.

19 Restall Orr, *Spirits of the Sacred Grove*. 60-61.

20 Restall Orr, *Spirits of the Sacred Grove*. 87.

21 Restall Orr, *Spirits of the Sacred Grove*. 122.

22 Orr, *Living Druidry*. 44.

23 Orr, *Living Druidry*. 58.

24 Restall Orr, *Spirits of the Sacred Grove*. 90.

25 Restall Orr, *Spirits of the Sacred Grove*. 119.

26 Restall Orr, *Spirits of the Sacred Grove*. 57.

27   Restall Orr, *Spirits of the Sacred Grove*. 89.

28   Restall Orr, *Spirits of the Sacred Grove*. 124.

29   Orr, *Living Druidry*. 57. Emma Restall Orr, *Principles of Druidry* (London Thorson's, HarperCollins Publishers, 1998). 118.

30   Orr, *Living Druidry*. 105.

31   Restall Orr, *Spirits of the Sacred Grove*. 59.

32   Restall Orr, *Spirits of the Sacred Grove*. 154.

33   Orr, *Living Druidry*. 12, 7.

34   Julie Brett, *Forest Spirituality*, podcast audio2020, orestspirituality. com.

35   Brett, *Forest Spirituality*.

36   Brett, *Forest Spirituality*.

37   Alex Klaushofer, *The New British Druids: Connecting with Nature in the 21st Century*, Kindle ed. (Hermes Books, 2016). 129-130.

38   "Mission Statement." Druidnetwork.org.

39   Emma Restall Orr, *The Wakeful World: Animism, Mind and the Self in Nature*, Kindle ed. (Alresford, Hants, UK: Moon Books, John Hunt Publishing, 2011). 27.

40   Orr, *Living Druidry*. 26-27.

41   Restall Orr, *Spirits of the Sacred Grove*. 44-45.

42   Restall Orr, *Spirits of the Sacred Grove*. 42.

43   Restall Orr, *Spirits of the Sacred Grove*. 132.

The Traveling Nunk

1   Thicht Nhat Hahn, *The Heart of the Buddha's Teaching*, 1st Broadway Books trade pbk. ed. (New York: Broadway Books, 1999).

2   Thicht Nhat Hahn, *How to Fight* (Berkeley, California: Parallax Press, 2017).

3   Soeng Mu, *Diamond Sutra: Transforming the way we perceive the world* (Boston, Mass.: Wisdom Publications, 2000). 89.

4   Thicht Nhat Hahn and Peter Levitt, *The Heart of Understanding: Commentaries on the Prajñaparamita Heart Sutra*, 20th anniversary ed. (Berkeley, Calif.: Parallax Press, 2009). 8.

5   Thicht Nhat Hahn, Annabel Laity, and Anh Huong Nguyen, *The Diamond That Cuts Through Illusion: Commentaries on the*

Prajñaparamita Diamond Sutra, Rev. ed. (Berkeley, Calif.: Parallax Press, 2010).

6   Lawrence Pintak, "Something Has to Change: Blacks in American Buddhism," Shambhala Sun, Sept. 1, 2001.

7   Thicht Nhat Hahn and Rachel Neumann, *Understanding Our Mind*, Revised paperback edition ed. (Berkeley, Calif: Parallax Press: Distributed by Publishers Group West, 2006).

8   Thicht Nhat Hahn and Arnold Kotler, *Peace is Every Step: The Path of Mindfulness in Everyday Life* (New York, N.Y: Bantam Books, 1991).

9   Dalai Lama and Ven. Pema Chodron, "The Self-Confidence of a Bodhisattva," Tricycle (Spring 2015).

10   The Diamond Sutra.

Lessons

1   Gregory Blann and Netanel Miles-Yepez, *When oceans merge: the contemporary Sufi and Hasidic teachings of Pir Vilayat Khan and Rabbi Zalman Schachter-Shalomi* (Rhinebeck, New York: Adam Kadmon Books; Monkfish Book Publishing Company, 2019). 65.

2   Schachter-Shalomi and Miles-Yepez, *Heart Afire*.

3   Muller, *Ramakrishna*. 106-107

4   Andrew Travers, "How Thomas Keating launched a global interfaith movement from a Snowmass monastery," *The Aspen Times* (Oct. 31 2019).

5   Muller, *Ramakrishna*. 159.

6   Blann, *Lifting the Boundaries*. Loc. 2590.

7   *Meditations On the Tarot*. 253

8   Blann, *Lifting the Boundaries*. 84.

9   Friedlander, *Winter Harvest*. 152.

10   Hazrat Inayat Khan, *Biography of Pir-o-Murshid Inayat Khan* (Suresnes, France: Pantarehi Uitgeverij/Nekbakh Foundation, 2020). 243.

11   *Sefer Yetzirah*, sefaria.org. 4:4.

12   Hazrat Inayat Khan, *The Teaching of Hazrat Inayat Khan*, hazrat-inayat-khan.org.